DarkBASIC Programming for the Absolute Beginner

Jerry Lee Ford, Jr.

Course Technology PTR
A part of Cengage Learning

COURSE TECHNOLOGY
CENGAGE Learning™

Australia • Brazil • Japan • Korea • Mexico • Singapore • Spain • United Kingdom • United States

)LOGY

Publisher and General Manager, Course Technology PTR: Stacy L. Hiquet

Associate Director of Marketing: Sarah Panella

Manager of Editorial Services: Heather Talbot

Marketing Manager: Mark Hughes

Acquisitions Editor: Mitzi Koontz

Project Editor: Jenny Davidson

Technical Reviewer: Keith Davenport

PTR Editorial Services Coordinator: Erin Johnson

Interior Layout Tech: Value Chain

Cover Designer: Mike Tanamachi

Indexer: Sharon Shock

Proofreader: Sara Gullion

For product information and technology assistance, contact us at
Cengage Learning Academic Resource Center, 1-800-354-9706

For permission to use material from this text or product, submit all requests online at **cengage.com/permissions**
Further permissions questions can be emailed to
permissionrequest@cengage.com

DarkBASIC is a copyright of The Game Creators Ltd, all rights reserved.

All other trademarks are the property of their respective owners.

Library of Congress Catalog Card Number: 2007923317
ISBN-13: 978-1-59863-385-6
ISBN-10: 1-59863-385-6

Course Technology
25 Thomson Place
Boston, MA 02210
USA

Cengage Learning is a leading provider of customized learning solutions with office locations around the globe, including Singapore, the United Kingdom, Australia, Mexico, Brazil, and Japan. Locate your local office at:
international.cengage.com/region

Cengage Learning products are represented in Canada by Nelson Education, Ltd.

For your lifelong learning solutions, visit **courseptr.com**

Purchase any of our products at your local college store or at our preferred online store **www.ichapters.com**

Printed in the United States of America
1 2 3 4 5 6 7 11 10 09 08

To my mother and father for always being there, and to my wonderful children, Alexander, William, and Molly, and my beautiful wife, Mary.

ACKNOWLEDGMENTS

There are a number of individuals who deserve credit for their work on this book. I would like to thank Mitzi Koontz who served as the book's acquisitions editor. Special thanks also go to Jenny Davidson and Keith Davenport for serving as the book's project and technical editors. In addition, I would like to thank everyone else at Course Technology for all their hard work.

ABOUT THE AUTHOR

Jerry Lee Ford, Jr. is an author, educator, and an IT professional with over 18 years' experience in information technology, including roles as an automation analyst, technical manager, technical support analyst, automation engineer, and security analyst. He is the author of 24 other books and co-author of two additional books. His published works include *AppleScript Studio Programming for the Absolute Beginner, Microsoft Windows PowerShell Programming for the Absolute Beginner, Microsoft Visual Basic 2005 Express Edition Programming for the Absolute Beginner, VBScript Professional Projects, Microsoft Windows Shell Scripting and WSH Administrator's Guide, Microsoft Windows Shell Script Programming for the Absolute Beginner, Learn JavaScript in a Weekend,* and *Microsoft Windows XP Professional Administrator's Guide.* Jerry has a master's degree in business administration from Virginia Commonwealth University in Richmond, Virginia, and has more than five years' experience as an adjunct instructor teaching networking courses in information technology.

TABLE OF CONTENTS

Chapter 2 **GETTING COMFORTABLE WITH THE DARKBASIC PROFESSIONAL INTEGRATED DEVELOPMENT ENVIRONMENT**... **45**

Part II **LEARNING HOW TO WRITE DARKBASIC APPLICATIONS**.. **95**

Chapter 3 **WORKING WITH DATA TYPES, VARIABLES, AND ARRAYS**... **97**

INTRODUCTION

Welcome to *DarkBASIC Programming for the Absolute Beginner!* DarkBASIC is a programming language built from the ground up with one primary purpose in mind, supporting the development of computer games. This book's goal is to teach you everything that you need to know to learn how to program using DarkBASIC Professional. This goal is accomplished through a step-by-step approach that emphasizes hands-on learning through the creation of computer games.

DarkBASIC Professional runs on computers that use Microsoft Windows. Although most programmers use DarkBASIC Professional to develop computer games, the language can be used to develop many different types of applications, such as the development of custom MP3 and DVD players and even business applications, making it an excellent first programming language for anyone to learn.

DarkBASIC is based on the extremely popular and easy to learn BASIC programming language. As such, the language itself is easily learned. In addition, the creators of DarkBASIC have added over 1,000 commands to the language, each of which is specifically targeted at simplifying and removing the complexity from game development. The result is a simple and straightforward programming language optimized for game development that is a perfect first step for anyone interested in learning how to create computer games.

DarkBASIC Professional provides you with everything you need to begin the development of professional-quality software and games, which you can share with your friends or even market and sell royalty-free. Therefore, whether you are just interested in having a little fun or are interested in creating the next great 2D or 3D arcade-styled computer game or first-person shooter, you will find that DarkBASIC will suit your needs quite well.

WHY DARKBASIC PROFESSIONAL?

DarkBASIC Professional is one of two programming languages sold under the DarkBASIC brand. The other language is named DarkBASIC. DarkBASIC Professional is derived from DarkBASIC. DarkBASIC Professional is far more powerful than its predecessor and it provides a number of features not found in DarkBASIC. These features include built-in support for multiplayer gaming (over networks and the Internet) and Windows registry access as well as support for music and DVD playback, just to name a few key differences.

DarkBASIC Professional provides everything you need to create computer games, supporting both 2D and 3D graphics. Like other modern programming languages, DarkBASIC provides everything needed to test, debug, and run Windows applications and games. It is easier to learn than other programming languages such as Microsoft Visual Basic .Net or Microsoft C++ .NET. By leveraging DarkBASIC Professional's built-in library of commands, you can easily develop professional-quality computer games that you can distribute as stand-alone .EXE executable files.

If you want to develop Windows applications, especially computer games, DarkBASIC Professional will serve you well. Once you have gotten the hang of DarkBASIC programming, you will be well positioned to make the jump to other programming languages, leveraging the programming knowledge and skills that you will have developed.

WHO SHOULD READ THIS BOOK?

DarkBASIC Programming for the Absolute Beginner is designed to teach you the fundamental steps involved in the development of Windows applications and games using DarkBASIC Professional. Although helpful, previous programming experience is not required. This book makes no assumptions regarding your computer background other than that you have a good understanding of how to work with Microsoft Windows.

Whether you are an experienced programmer interested in learning DarkBASIC or you are completely new to programming, this book will provide you with everything you need in order to get started. In addition to providing you with a solid overview of programming in general and DarkBASIC Professional in particular, I think that you will find this book's games-based approach to teaching DarkBASIC programming both instructional and entertaining.

WHAT YOU NEED TO BEGIN

All of the instructions and examples presented in this book apply to DarkBASIC Professional, though much of what is covered can also be applied to the original DarkBASIC programming language. All of the figures and examples that are presented will be shown using DarkBASIC Professional running on a computer using Microsoft Vista. If you are using a different Windows operating system, you may notice small differences in the way things look, but all of the features and functionality provided by DarkBASIC Professional should be the same. Therefore, you should not have any problem following along with the examples presented in this book.

The first thing that you will need is a computer running one of the following versions of Microsoft Windows.

- Windows Vista
- Windows XP
- Windows ME
- Windows 2000
- Windows 98

Of course, you will also need a copy of DarkBASIC Professional, which you can purchase directly from the company that creates it at www.thegamecreators.com, which at the time this book was written cost $69.99. Alternatively, you can purchase DarkBASIC Professional from online stores such as amazon.com and compusa.com. As of the writing of the book, these two stores were selling DarkBASIC Professional for $83.99.

 If you want to try out DarkBASIC Professional before purchasing it, you may do so by downloading a 30-day full-featured trial version available at http://darkbasicpro.thegamecreators.com/?fltrial.

Before purchasing DarkBASIC Professional, you should make sure that your computer has the necessary hardware requirements to run it. DarkBASIC Professional's minimum hardware requirements are listed in Table I.1. While a computer that just meets these minimum requirements can certainly be used to run DarkBASIC Professional, it may not run fast. In order to really take advantage of DarkBASIC Professional, you will be a lot happier if your computer meets the language's recommended requirements, which are also listed in Table I.1.

TABLE I.1 MINIMUM REQUIREMENT FOR RUNNING DarkBASIC PROFESSIONAL		
Requirement	**Minimum**	**Recommended**
Processor	300 MHz Pentium II	733 GHz Pentium III
Memory	64 MB	128 MB
Hard Disk	400 MB	400 MB
DirectX	Version 9.0C	Version 9.0C
Direct Graphics Card	16 MB memory	64 MB memory
Sound Card	Direct X-compatible	Direct X-compatible

DirectX is a Microsoft technology designed to facilitate the development of high performing audio and graphics programs and is essential to the operation of DarkBASIC applications. DarkBASIC Professional requires the availability of DirectX version 9.0C or higher on any computer you use to develop your applications as well as on any computer where your applications may ultimately be run.

That's it. All you need is a computer that meets the specifications outlined in Table I.1, a copy of DarkBASIC Professional, and this book. Everything that you will need to write, test, and compile DarkBASIC applications is provided as part of DarkBASIC Professional.

How This Book Is Organized

DarkBASIC Programming for the Absolute Beginner is organized into four parts. This book was written with the assumption that you would read it sequentially from beginning to end. However, if you have prior programming experience with another programming language, you might instead jump around a bit focusing only on those topics that are of the most interest to you.

Part I of this book consists of two chapters that provide you with an overview of DarkBASIC Professional and its integrated development environment. Part II is made up of four chapters that teach you the fundamentals of the DarkBASIC professional programming language. This includes learning how to work with and store different types of data and learning how to use conditional logic to develop applications that can make decisions and take different courses of action based on the data that they are presented with. You will also learn how to repeatedly execute groups of program statements, which is an essential element in the development of computer games, allowing you to replay animated sequences or to continue to repeatedly prompt the player to keep making moves. You will also learn how to improve the organization of your applications with subroutines, allowing you to group related statements together in a manner that helps make your application code easier to understand and maintain.

Part III of this book is made up of four chapters that focus on advanced topics, covering the use of graphics, sound, and animation. You will also learn how to work with different types of interface devices such as the keyboard and mouse. The last of these four chapters will teach you how to locate and fix errors that inevitably occur during application development. Part IV is made up of two appendices and a glossary. The appendices provide a review of the application code files located on this book's companion website and provide you with additional information to learn more about DarkBASIC Professional and game programming.

The basic outline of the book is as follows.

- **Chapter 1, "Introducing DarkBASIC Professional."** This opening chapter is designed to provide you with an overall understanding of DarkBASIC Professional and its capabilities. You will learn about the different components that make up DarkBASIC Professional, including a brief overview of the roles played by the DarkBASIC game engines and Microsoft DirectX. You will learn how to install and update DarkBASIC Professional.

- **Chapter 2, "Getting Comfortable with the DarkBASIC Integrated Development Environment."** This chapter provides an overview of the DarkBASIC Professional application development environment. In addition, it also examines several alternative development environments that many in the DarkBASIC community prefer to use. You will learn how to work with different menus and toolbar buttons and to work with different editor features.

- **Chapter 3, "Working with Data Types, Variables, and Arrays."** In this chapter, you will learn different ways in which you can store and manipulate the data collected and used by your applications. This includes learning how to store individual pieces as well as related collections of data.

- **Chapter 4, "Implementing Conditional Logic."** In this chapter, you will learn how to implement conditional logic to provide your application with the ability to analyze the value of the data that it collects and manages. Based on the result of this analysis, you will then be able to selectively execute different sets of programming statements, resulting in applications that can react in an intelligent manner to different scenarios based on the data they are presented with.

- **Chapter 5, "Repeating Statement Execution Using Loops."** This chapter teaches you how to set up the repeated execution of code statements. An understanding of loops is critical to developing applications that need to continuously replay graphic animation sequences or repeatedly interact with players during game play.

- **Chapter 6, "Organizing Code Logic Using Functions."** This chapter teaches you how to improve the overall organization of your application code using subroutines. You will learn how to create subroutines that process data passed to them as arguments. In addition, you will learn how to develop a special type of subroutine, referred to as a function, which can not only process input but also return output back to calling statements.

- **Chapter 7, "Working with Graphics and Sound."** This chapter will introduce you to how to work with graphics and sound within your DarkBASIC applications. This includes an overview of 2D graphics as well as an overview of DarkBASIC Professional's 3D capabilities.

- **Chapter 8, "Generating Animation Using Sprites."** In this chapter, you will learn how to generate and control graphic animation using sprites. This includes learning how to control the movement of sprites and to control their interaction with other game elements using techniques like collision detection.

- **Chapter 9, "Working with Input Devices."** This chapter covers the basics of controlling interaction with the user through different input devices such as mouse, keyboard, and joystick control.

- **Chapter 10, "Finding and Fixing Application Errors."** This chapter reviews the differences between different types of errors. It will provide you with instruction on how to deal with errors that inevitably occur in any programming project. You will learn how to use the DarkBASIC Professional debugger program to trace logic flow within your applications as well as how to keep an eye on the assignment of values to variables and arrays.

- **Appendix A, "What's on the Companion Website?"** This appendix provides a review of the DarkBASIC Professional applications that are developed in this book and made available as downloads on this book's companion website (www.courseptr.com/downloads).

- **Appendix B, "What Next?"** In this appendix, I will provide you with additional advice on how you might continue to further your DarkBASIC Professional programming education.

- **Glossary.** This unit provides a glossary of terms used throughout the book.

CONVENTIONS USED IN THIS BOOK

This book uses a number of conventions to make it easier for you to read and work with the information that is provided. These conventions are as follows.

Hints are things that you can do to become a more proficient DarkBASIC programmer.

Traps are areas where problems are likely to occur so I provide you with advice on how to stay away from or deal with those problems, hopefully saving you the pain of learning about them on your own the hard way.

Tricks are programming shortcuts designed to help make you a better and more efficient programmer.

CHALLENGES.

Each chapter in this book ends with a series of challenges intended to provide you with ideas that you can apply to improve chapter game projects and further your programming skills.

Part

I

Introducing DarkBASIC Professional

CHAPTER 1

INTRODUCING DARKBASIC PROFESSIONAL

DarkBASIC Professional is a computer programming language designed specifically to support the creation of computer games. A computer game is a video game played on a personal computer in which one or more players interact and compete in a make-believe world. DarkBASIC Professional provides you with everything you need to create professional quality computer games. In this chapter, you will learn more about DarkBASIC Professional and what makes it tick. This chapter will explain how to install DarkBASIC Professional and how to download and install the latest updates, ensuring that your copy of DarkBASIC Professional is the most current release. On top of all this, you will also learn how to create your first application, the Dark Jokes game.

Specifically, you will learn:

- About DarkBASIC Professional, its capabilities, and underlying architecture
- How to install and update DarkBASIC Professional
- How to create your first DarkBASIC professional game
- How to compile and execute DarkBASIC Professional applications
- How to supplement DarkBASIC Professional with add-on products

PROJECT PREVIEW: THE DARK JOKES GAME

In this chapter and in every chapter that follows, you will learn how to develop a computer game using DarkBASIC Professional. Learning through game development is an extremely good approach because it makes the learning process fun. Since DarkBASIC Professional is a game development programming language, this instructional approach is perfectly suited.

This chapter's game project is the Dark Jokes game. As shown in Figure 1.1, this game will run within a typical application window, allowing it to be resized, minimized, or maximized, without affecting the look and feel of the game or altering the manner in which it executes.

FIGURE 1.1

The Dark Jokes game's opening screen.

Compared to many Windows games and applications, the Dark Jokes game is relatively simple. It consists of a single application window that is used to display text that tells humorous jokes, as demonstrated in Figure 1.2.

To advance from screen to screen, or joke to joke, the player only needs to press a keyboard key. Figures 1.3 through 1.6 show each of the jokes displayed by the game.

Once done, the game thanks the player for playing the game, as shown in Figure 1.7, and then automatically terminates its execution.

FIGURE 1.2

The first joke told by the Dark Jokes game.

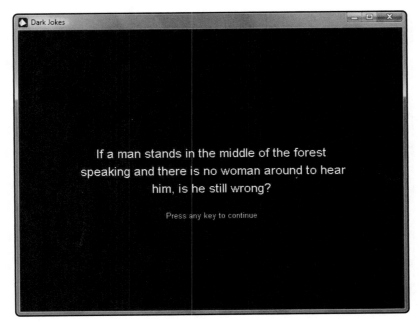

FIGURE 1.3

The second joke told by the Dark Jokes game.

FIGURE 1.4

The third joke told by the Dark Jokes game.

FIGURE 1.5

The fourth joke told by the Dark Jokes game.

FIGURE 1.6

The fifth joke told by the Dark Jokes game.

FIGURE 1.7

The Dark Jokes game's closing screen.

As you can see, the Dark Jokes game is very straightforward. All text is displayed in the middle of the screen. Text is automatically realigned in the event the player resizes the window. The game pauses each time new text is displayed and waits until the player instructs it to proceed by pressing one of the keys on the computer's keyboard. Once the last screen has been displayed and the player presses a keyboard key, the game closes its window and stops executing. By the time you have created and executed this game, you will have learned the basic steps involved in developing any DarkBASIC Professional game, and you will have established a foundation from which you can move on and tackle more advanced programming challenges.

A Quick Overview of DarkBASIC Professional

DarkBASIC Professional is a programming language created for the sole purpose of supporting the development of computer games. DarkBASIC Professional was created by the Game Creators (http://www.thegamecreators.com), a software development company based in Wigan, UK. Originally founded in 1999 by Lee Bamber, today the company sells a range of computer game development software tools and acts as a reseller for a number of third-party game development programs that complement its own line of products.

Even though DarkBASIC Professional's primary focus is on game development, many programmers also find it to be a useful programming language for creating small business applications and slideshows, and that it is also useful as a *RAD* or *rapid application development* language. As a RAD tool, programmers can quickly create an initial version of a new game to ascertain whether their initial idea translates well into a computer game before investing the time and energy required to build a complete version of the game using C++, Java, or some other high-end programming language.

DarkBASIC Professional provides you with all the tools necessary to create 2D and 3D computer games. These tools include an integrated compiler that creates standalone executable files for your DarkBASIC Professional projects and a built-in debugger that supports breakpoints, a step-through process, and the ability to monitor variable values. DarkBASIC Professional also provides a project editor with advanced features like syntax color coding, line numbering, integrated help, and function folding. Using these tools, you can build computer games of all types and even create multiplayer games that operate over networks and the Internet.

DarkBASIC Versus DarkBASIC Professional

DarkBASIC Professional is an advanced version of DarkBASIC, another programming language created by the Game Creators. DarkBASIC shares the same programming language syntax and basic set of commands as DarkBASIC Professional. Despite many similarities, DarkBASIC lacks a number of important game development features available in DarkBASIC Professional.

As you would expect, DarkBASIC costs less than DarkBASIC Professional. As of the writing of this book, when purchased online, DarkBASIC Professional costs $69.99, whereas DarkBASIC only costs $39.99. However, the Game Creators have released an enhancement pack for DarkBASIC that provides it with many new capabilities that are essential to modern game development. Purchasing it will cost you an additional $19.99, bringing your total cost up to $59.98 for DarkBASIC. Given the relatively small difference in price, DarkBASIC Professional is definitely worth the extra few dollars. However, DarkBASIC does offer a less expensive alternative and can certainly be used as a low-cost option for getting started.

Without the enhancement pack, DarkBASIC does not support multiplayer game development. Nor can it access the Windows registry. The enhancement pack provides DarkBASIC with these abilities. However, even with the enhancement pack, DarkBASIC does not support DVD playback or DirectX 9 or above. In addition, with or without the enhancement pack, DarkBASIC does not support any of the following game development features, all of which are supported by DarkBASIC Professional.

- Support for multiple cameras
- Animated sprites
- Transparent sprites
- 3D Math commands
- Pixel/vertex shaders
- Light, bump, and sphere mapping
- Terrain support
- Pixel locking

Don't worry if you are unfamiliar with the terminology listed above. This list represents a number of advanced topics, some of which are not covered in this book but are mentioned just to provide you with a feel for the comprehensive differences between DarkBASIC and DarkBASIC Professional.

One other key difference between DarkBASIC and DarkBASIC Professional is that DarkBASIC's source code is interpreted at runtime, resulting in slower initial execution, whereas DarkBASIC Professional's source code is compiled prior to execution, making it ready for immediate execution.

DEFINITION A *compiler* is a program that translates code statements written in a computer programming language into a format that can be executed by the computer operating system.

SETTING UP DARKBASIC PROFESSIONAL

Like most modern programming languages, DarkBASIC Professional requires a little work to get it up and running. The steps involved include not only installing DarkBASIC Professional but also ensuring that prerequisite software requirements are met. The following list outlines the different steps you may have to perform depending on your particular setup.

- **Installing DarkBASIC Professional.** Required on the computer that will be used to develop DarkBASIC applications.
- **Updating DarkBASIC Professional.** Required only if you are not installing the most current version of DarkBASIC Professional.
- **Installing ActiveX 9.0c.** Required only if the computer does not already have DirectX 9.0c installed.
- **Activating DarkBASIC Professional.** Required for any new DarkBASIC Professional installation.

In order to install DarkBASIC you must have an Internet connection. This is true even if you purchased the CD version of DarkBASIC Professional. The Internet connection is required for you to activate your copy of DarkBASIC Professional. Once activated, you won't need an Internet connection again (unless you need to download and install a DarkBASIC Professional update).

If you purchase DarkBASIC Professional online at www.thegamecreators.com, you will be presented with two different download options. At the time this book was written an 11MB download and a 90MB download were available. The primary difference between these two downloads is that the 90MB version includes more example files. The smaller download is intended to address the needs of customers with dial-up Internet access. Neither version provides the full collection of resources that comes with the DarkBASIC Professional CD.

Installing DarkBASIC Professional

Although DarkBASIC Professional can be purchased on CD-ROM, it is usually purchased and downloaded from the Game Creators' website at http://darkbasicpro.thegamecreators.com/?f=order. Once you have made your purchase, you will receive an e-mail with instructions on how to download your new copy of DarkBASIC Professional. The e-mail also includes an activation key, which you'll need to activate your copy of DarkBASIC Professional once it has been installed.

The following procedure outlines the steps involved in installing DarkBASIC Professional. This procedure assumes that you have downloaded your copy of DarkBASIC Professional, but it can also be applied to the installation of DarkBASIC Professional from CD-ROM as well.

1. Double-click on the Zip file containing DarkBASIC Professional. When the archive opens, you will see an executable file named something like dbpro_5-4-high.exe.
2. Double-click on this executable file to start the DarkBASIC Professional installation process.
3. Click on Run if Windows displays a Security Warning window to allow the installation process to continue.
4. Click on Allow if prompted by Windows to allow the installation program to continue running.
5. When prompted, click on Next to start the installation process.
6. When prompted, accept the DarkBASIC Professional license agreement and continue to click on the Next button when prompted to accept all remaining default options.
7. Click on the Finish button once the installation process completes.

Updating DarkBASIC Professional

DarkBASIC Professional is constantly being improved and updated. However, the Game Creators do not always update the downloadable installation version of DarkBASIC every time a new update is released. As a result, the version of DarkBASIC Professional that you download may not be the most current. You can determine the version number of your copy of DarkBASIC Professional by examining its filename. When this book was being written, the most current version of DarkBASIC Professional was 1.066, sometimes referred to as just 6.6. However, the version of DarkBASIC Professional that was available for download was 1.054. Therefore, the first thing that you will want to do after installing DarkBASIC Professional is determine if an update is available, which you can do by visiting http://darkbasicpro.thegamecreators.com/?f=upgrades.

If an update is available, you should download it. The download will be a Zip file. Inside that Zip file you will find a single executable program that when run, will update your copy of DarkBASIC Professional.

Installing DirectX 9.0c

The version of DarkBASIC Professional available at the time this book was written required that DirectX 9.0c be installed to execute properly. You can download a copy of DirectX 9.0c from http://www.microsoft.com/directx by clicking on the Get all DirectX downloads link. DirectX 9.0c can run on Windows 98, Me, 2000, XP, and Vista. Once downloaded, follow the instructions provided by Microsoft to install DirectX 9.0c.

Even though Microsoft Vista comes with DirectX 10 already installed, this version of DirectX is not backward compatible. As of the writing of this book, the current version of DarkBASIC is 6.6. This version did not support DirectX 10. It required DirectX 9.0c. Therefore, if the Game Creators have not released a DirectX 10-compatible version of DarkBASIC Professional by the time you make your purchase, you will have to download and install DirectX 9.0c if you are using a computer running Microsoft Vista.

Activating DarkBASIC Professional

Once DarkBASIC Professional has been installed and, if necessary, updated, you will find a new application group in the Windows Start menu named The Game Creators. Within this group, you will find a folder named DarkBASIC Pro Online. If you drill down into it, you will see the following items.

1. Activate from DBPro CD
2. DarkBASIC Pro Online
3. DarkBASIC Pro Online Setup
4. DarkBASIC Pro Website

Before you can begin using DarkBASIC Professional, you must activate it (which requires an Internet connection). To do so, click on Start > All Programs > The Game Creators > DarkBASIC > DarkBASIC Pro Online. Next, follow the steps outlined in the following procedure.

The following procedure assumes that you are installing a copy of DarkBASIC Professional that was purchased online and then downloaded to your computer. If you purchased a boxed copy of DarkBASIC Professional, click on the Activate from DBPro CD menu item instead of the DarkBASIC Pro Online option.

1. When DarkBASIC Professional is started for the first time, the DarkBASIC Professional IDE is displayed, as shown in shown in Figure 1.8.
2. To complete the activation process, you must have an active Internet connection. Once connected to the Internet, you can begin the registration process by clicking on the Activate/Register button located on the DarkBASIC Professional window.
3. If Microsoft Windows displays a popup window with a security message, click on the Allow link to allow the installation process to continue.
4. The DarkBASIC Professional Activation Service dialog appears. Click on the Enter Order Key button, as shown in Figure 1.9.

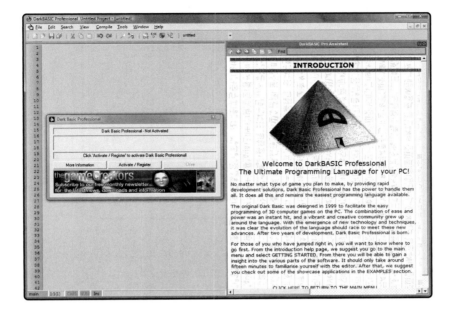

FIGURE 1.8

Starting
DarkBASIC
Professional for
the first time.

FIGURE 1.9

The DarkBASIC
Professional
Activation Service
will assist you in
activating your
copy of DarkBASIC
Professional.

5. Next, you are prompted to enter the e-mail address used when purchasing DarkBASIC Professional, as well as the activation key that was provided on the confirmation e-mail sent to you by the Game Creators after you completed your online purchase, as shown in Figure 1.10. Fill in this information and then click on the Next button.

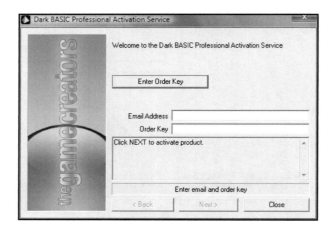

6. A message will display, informing you that it may take several minutes for the activation process to complete. Once the process has finished, your copy of DarkBASIC Professional is activated, as shown in Figure 1.11.

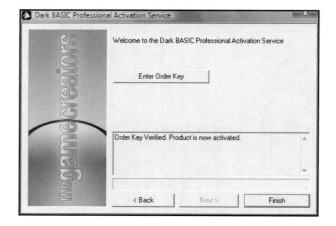

7. Click on the Finish button to close the DarkBASIC Professional Activation service window.

At this point, DarkBASIC is ready for use and the application's primary IDE window should be visible, as shown in Figure 1.12.

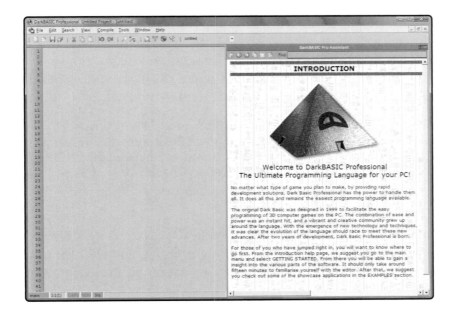

FIGURE 1.12

DarkBASIC Professional's default IDE provides you with access to the tools needed to create DarkBASIC Professional applications.

The Window that is initially displayed inside the IDE is the DarkBASIC Pro Assistant window. It displays a welcome message. At the bottom of the window is a line that, when clicked, displays DarkBASIC's Help menu. You can click on the DarkBASIC Pro Assistant window's close button to close it, maximizing the amount of available space within the DarkBASIC Professional IDE.

A QUICK DARK**BASIC** DEMONSTRATION

Okay, now that you have DarkBASIC Professional installed, let's start it up and take it for a quick test drive. By this, I mean let's use it to create and execute your first DarkBASIC Professional application. This application will not be anything too exciting. The program, when executed, will simply display the words Hello World! on the computer's screen. However, in developing this simple application, you will learn the basic steps involved in creating and executing any DarkBASIC Professional application. These steps include:

1. Creating a new project
2. Configuring project settings
3. Adding program code
4. Saving your application
5. Compiling and executing your new application

The DarkBASIC Professional *integrated development environment* or *IDE* is the tool that you will use to key in the code statements that make up your applications and store the application settings that you also specify. Application settings are application attributes that control a particular aspect of the application. Examples of application settings include the name assigned to your DarkBASIC Professional project and the resolution used to run your application. The IDE keeps track of the different files that make up DarkBASIC applications, including source code and any graphic or audio files that you may add.

> You will learn more about the DarkBASIC Professional IDE in Chapter 2, "Getting Comfortable with the DarkBASIC Development Environment." In addition to the default IDE, a number of alternate IDEs have been developed for DarkBASIC Professional. You will also learn about these in Chapter 2.

Creating a New DarkBASIC Project

The first step in creating a new DarkBASIC Professional application is to create a new project. To do so, start DarkBASIC Professional, if it is not already running, and click on the New Project menu item located on the File menu. The Create a New DarkBASIC Professional Project window appears, as shown in Figure 1.13.

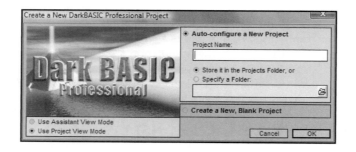

FIGURE 1.13

Creating a new DarkBASIC Professional project.

By default the Auto-configure a New Project option is selected. Beneath it, type in **Hello** in the Project Name file and then specify where you want your new project to be saved. Your choices are to either save it in DarkBASIC Professional Projects folder or to select the Specify a Folder option and then either type the name and path of the folder or click on the folder icon located in the right-hand side of the Specify a Folder field to browse and select a folder.

DEFINITION A *project* is a container used to store and manage the different types of files that make up a DarkBASIC Professional application.

Once you have specified a name for your project and the location where you want to store it, click on the OK button. In response, a new project is created for you, as demonstrated in Figure 1.14.

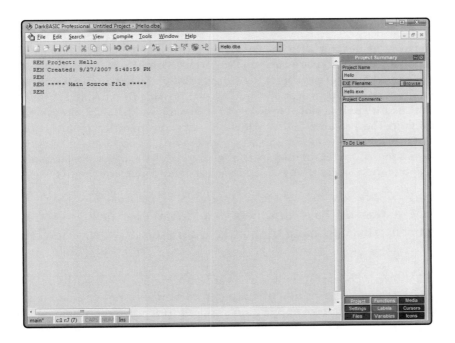

If you are using Microsoft Vista, you may run into trouble when you attempt to compile your application, depending on where you saved it. In particular, you may run into trouble if you try to store your DarkBASIC projects in DarkBASIC Professional's Projects folder (e.g., C:\Program Files\The Game Creators\DarkBASIC Professional Online\Projects). While this seems like a perfectly reasonable place to keep your DarkBASIC projects, and in fact *is* on a computer running a version of Microsoft Windows other than Microsoft Vista, the error shown in Figure 1.15 may appear when you attempt to compile a DarkBASIC project that has been saved in the Project folders using Vista.

The reason for this error is that DarkBASIC Professional lacks sufficient security permissions to save the compiled execution program for your application in this location. The easiest way of dealing with this situation is to store your DarkBASIC Professional script somewhere else. For example, you shouldn't run into any problems if you save your DarkBASIC Professional projects applications in your Documents folder.

Another way of dealing with this situation is to right-click on the DarkBASIC Professional Online icon and click on Properties from the context window that appears. From here you can select the Compatibility tab and then select the Run This Program as Administrator option. This will provide DarkBASIC Professional with the security permission it requires to save your DarkBASIC Professional applications in the Projects folder. However, I recommend against this option because it weakens Windows security and it is not a good idea to circumvent Windows security in this manner. Although DarkBASIC Professional is a safe and stable application, there is no reason to assign it administrative rights.

As you can see, five code statements have already been added to your new project. These statements serve as comments that document the name of your project as well as its creation date and time.

Each of the five code statements that are automatically added to your new project source code is a comment statement. Comment statements are statements embedded within an application's source code for the purpose of documenting the application and its source code. You can tell that each of these statements is a comment because each statement begins with the REM keyword. REM, which is short for remark, identifies any text that follows it as a comment. Comments are ignored when your project is compiled and therefore have no effect on the execution of your program.

Configuring Project Settings

If you look on the right-hand side of the screen, you will see the IDE's Project Panel window. At the bottom of this window are nine buttons. By default the Project button is selected and the Project Summary attributes associated with this project are displayed. As you look closely at Figure 1.14, you will see that your project is named Hello and that an executable file named Hello.exe will be created when you compile this project into a Windows application. You'll learn more about the Project Panel in Chapter 2.

Adding Program Code

Now that you have created a new project and configured its project settings, it is time to add the program code statements that will make your new DarkBASIC Professional application do something. For starters, the following code statements should already be visible in the DarkBASIC Professional IDE's code area.

```
REM Project: Hello
REM Created: 9/27/2007 5:48:59 PM
REM
REM ***** Main Source File *****
REM
```

As previously discussed, these five statements are comments that are automatically added to the code file when your project was created. As you can see, the first of these statements displays the name that you provided when the project was initially created.

It is up to you to add the programming statements required to make the application actually do something. This application, which displays the message Hello World! on a black background that takes up the entire display area, consists of just three additional programming statements, which are provided here:

```
PRINT "Hello World!"

WAIT KEY

END
```

 You will learn what each of these statements means in a few more pages; for now just type them in as shown.

Saving and Compiling Your Application

After adding the code statements to the end of the code file, you should save your application. To do this, click on the Save All option located on the File menu.

 When you execute the Save All option, changes made to your project settings, as well as any changes made to its source code are saved. Alternatively, you can use the Save Project option to just save changes to project settings or the Save Source option to just save changes made to the project's source code.

Once saved, you will find two files in your project folder. Both files will have the same names but different file extensions. In the case of the Hello project, you will find a file named Hello.dbpro, which is your application's project file. This file contains all of the configuration settings for your new project. The second file is named Hello.dba. This file contains a copy of your project's source code.

Once saved, you are ready to compile your project to create an executable file representing your new application. You can do this by clicking on the Check Syntax/Make EXE option located on the Compile menu. In response, DarkBASIC checks each statement in your project's source code for syntax errors. If none are found, an executable file is generated. Figure 1.16 provides a visual representation of the three types of files that are generated for every DarkBASIC Professional project.

FIGURE 1.16

DarkBASIC project, source code, and executable files.

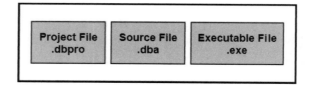

When you compile a DarkBASIC Professional project into a new application, the compiler checks the syntax of your application's code statements, and as long as it does not come across any errors, it translates your code statements into a format that can be executed by the computer system. It stores the resulting program, along with any graphics, sound, or other types of resources needed by the application, in an executable file with an .exe file extension.

In order to execute, this file needs access to the DarkBASIC Professional runtime library, which contains a library of functions required to run the application. To make things as simple as possible, the compiler automatically stores a copy of DarkBASIC Professional's runtime library inside each executable program. Therefore, all you have to do to run your DarkBASIC Professional application is to double-click on it. But don't forget that you still need DirectX 9.0c installed for your application to execute.

Executing Your New Creation

As long as you did not make any typos when keying in your new application's source code, it should compile without error. At this point, your application is ready to run. You can do so by double-clicking on the executable file that was created when you compiled your project into a standalone application, as demonstrated in Figure 1.17.

Hello World!

FIGURE 1.17

Running the Hello application.

When generated, this file is automatically assigned the same name as your project along with an .exe file extension. This file is stored in the application's project folder. This executable file is the file that you will want to make copies of when you are ready to distribute your new application.

TRICK

Since DarkBASIC Professional applications are stored inside individual executable files, you can share them by distributing a copy of their .exe files. To make them easier to distribute, you could zip them up in a Zip file, reducing the size of your distribution package. But remember, any computer on which your DarkBASIC application will run must have DirectX 9.0c installed.

A Few Basic Scripting Commands

In the previous DarkBASIC Professional project, you created a new application that filled the screen with a black background and displayed a message in white text in the upper-left corner. This message remained displayed until you pressed a keyboard key, at which time your application terminated its execution. In total, four different types of DarkBASIC Professional language statements were used to create this program. You will learn about each of these statements, as well as a few others, in the sections that follow.

Commenting Your Program Code

The REM statement was used to embed comment statements within the Hello program's source code. Adding comments to your DarkBASIC Professional source code is considered to be a good programming practice because it allows you to document why you did things a certain way. The syntax of the REM command is shown here:

```
REM Text
```

Text represents any character you want to add to your script file. Comments are ignored by the compiler and have no effect on the executable file that is generated. Therefore, it is always a good idea to make liberal use of comments within your program code. For example, the following statements demonstrate how you might use the REM statement to document the actions of another script statement.

```
REM The following statement displays a list of text on the screen
PRINT "Welcome to the world of DarkBASIC Professional programming!"
```

As an alternative to the REM statement, you can substitute the ` character using the syntax outlined here:

```
` Text
```

The ` character is located in the upper-left corner of your keyboard just above the Tab key. As the following example demonstrates, you can use the REM statement and the ` character interchangeably.

```
` The following statement displays a list of text on the screen
PRINT "Welcome to the world of DarkBASIC Professional programming!"
```

You can also use either the REM statement or the ` character to add a comment to the end of any statement, as demonstrated here:

```
PRINT "Welcome!"   `Display a greeting message
```

One last way to add comments to your source code is to use the REMSTART and REMEND statements. When used, these statements allow you to embed any number of statements after the opening REMSTART statement and before the closing REMEND statement, using the syntax outlined here:

```
REMSTART
    Text
    Text
    ...
REMEND
```

Displaying Text on the Screen

As was demonstrated in the previous exercise, the PRINT statement is used to display information on the screen. This statement has the following syntax.

```
PRINT [output, ... output] [;]
```

output represents one or more optional items to be displayed, each of which must be separated by a comma. By default, each PRINT statement prints its output on a new line. However, if you add the optional ; character to the end of a PRINT statement, any output displayed by a following PRINT statement will be appended to the end of the same line as the previous PRINT statement's output.

When used by itself, as demonstrated next, the PRINT statement displays a blank line.

```
PRINT
```

When used to display a text string, the string must be enclosed within a matching pair of quotes, as demonstrated here:

```
PRINT "Hello World!"
```

When executed, this statement displays the string Hello World!. Note that the quotation marks are not displayed, just the text that is inside them. When used to display a number, quotation marks are not required, as demonstrated here:

```
PRINT 1.5
```

When used to display two or more items, commas must be used to separate each item, as demonstrated here:

```
PRINT "Hello ", "World!"
```

When executed, this statement displays the following output.

```
Hello World!
```

By default, back-to-back PRINT statements print their output on separate lines, as demonstrated here:

```
PRINT "Once upon a time,"
PRINT "there were three bears."
PRINT "A daddy bear, a mommy bear, and a baby bear."
```

When executed, this statement displays the following output.

```
Once upon a time,
there were three bears.
```

```
A daddy bear, a mommy bear, and a baby bear.
```

However, by appending the ; character to the end of a PRINT statement, you can append the output of one PRINT statement to that of another PRINT statement on the same line, as demonstrated here:

```
PRINT "Once upon a time, ";
PRINT "there were three bears."
PRINT "A daddy bear, a mommy bear, and a baby bear."
```

When executed, this statement displays the following output.

```
Once upon a time, there were three bears.
A daddy bear, a mommy bear, and a baby bear.
```

As you can see, the PRINT statement is extremely flexible. As such, you'll find yourself using it a lot.

Pausing Program Execution

Depending on your application, you may want to pause application execution at different times in order, for example, to give the user the opportunity to read text that has been displayed. You might also want to provide a player with the ability to pause game execution at any point during the game play. To pause the application, you can execute the WAIT KEY statement. This statement pauses application execution until the user presses any keyboard key. The syntax of the WAIT KEY command is shown here:

```
WAIT KEY
```

Terminating Program Execution

By default, DarkBASIC Professional source code is processed sequentially, from beginning to end. Once the last statement has been processed, the application automatically terminates. Alternatively, you can also terminate your application's execution at any time by executing the END statement. The syntax of the END command is shown here:

```
END
```

That's all there is to this command. As you will learn in later chapters, this command can be used to control how and when your DarkBASIC Professional application terminates. In addition, it is a good programming practice to get used to adding an END statement to the end of your application's source code.

OTHER GAME BUILDING TOOLS PROVIDED BY THE GAME CREATORS

In addition to DarkBASIC and DarkBASIC Professional, the Game Creators have also developed a pair of specialized game creation applications named 3D Gamemaker and FPS Creator. 3D Gamemaker (t3dgm.thegamecreators.com) guides you through the creation of several different types of games such as a *Doom*-styled first-person shooter and car racing games. There is no programming involved. All you have to do is use your mouse to point and click your way through the creation of your game, selecting different scenarios, sounds, and objects. When you are done, you will end up with a standalone executable file. Since no programming is involved, you are limited in what you can do.

FPS Creator (www.fpscreator.com) is a specialized first-person shooter creation tool. Using its 3D editor, you can design different levels, placing walls, obstacles, lights, enemies, ammo, and weapons where you want them. You can choose from over 800 3D objects or upload custom objects of your own. Game actions are controlled by scripts, to which you have access and can modify, to customize your games. The end result of your efforts will be a *Doom*-styled, standalone executable program.

Both 3D Gamemaker and FPS Creator provide easy ways to quickly get a new computer game up and running quickly. However, both of these applications are inherently limited when compared to DarkBASIC Professional and there is only so far that you can go with them.

In the end, to create games that are uniquely your own, there is no substitute for DarkBASIC Professional. In addition to providing you with access to over 1,000 commands in its game engine, many of which are specifically designed to support 2D and 3D games, DarkBASIC Professional also provides you with access to all kinds of 3D models, bitmaps, sounds, icons, textures, and music. Of course, you can always create your own graphics and sounds but that can take time and a lot of work, not to mention specialized software. An easy option for getting your hands on high quality, professionally rendered graphics and audio resources is to purchase and download one of the many collections of graphics and audio files sold by the Game Creators. These packages include DarkMATTER, SkyMATTER, and SoundMATTER.

DarkMATTER

DarkMATTER (darkmatter.thegamecreators.com) is the name assigned to three collections of animated 3D objects that you can purchase and add to your DarkBASIC Professional games. Objects come equipped with pre-designed animated sequences that include running, jumping, driving, flying, and so on. You will find objects for all sorts of 3D cars, people, monsters, weapons, and much more.

You don't have to worry about licensing of any of the graphic objects. When you purchase them, you also get permission to distribute them as part of your games royalty-free. By purchasing DarkMATTER download packages, you provide yourself with immediate access to tons of professional-quality graphic objects, saving you an incredible amount of time since you won't have to design your own graphic objects. As a result, you can focus on the overall design of your DarkBASIC Professional games and the programming logic involved without getting bogged down in the role of graphic artist and animator.

SkyMATTER

SkyMATTER (skymatter.thegamecreators.com) is the name assigned to 10 collections of high-resolution textures that you can purchase and use in your DarkBASIC Professional games to provide realistic backgrounds. Like DarkMATTER, each SkyMATTER collection package provides you with royalty-free access to all textures.

Each SkyMATTER collection focuses on different types of scenarios. For example, some provide images of snow-filled mounts while others provide you with a desert scene or a strange alien landscape. Unless you are an exceptionally talented graphic artist, you'll find the landscapes provided in these packages to be an essential ingredient in your games.

SoundMATTER

SoundMATTER (soundmatter.thegamecreators.com) is the name assigned to thirteen collections of professional-quality sound effects that you can purchase and add to your DarkBASIC Professional games. Each SoundMATTER download package provides sound effects that focus on related topic categories. For example, you'll find SoundMATTER packs that provide sound effects for the following:

- **Arcade.** A collection of 75 arcade sounds.
- **Space Weapons.** A large collection of sci-fi sounds like laser beams, space cannons, and explosions.
- **Land Vehicles.** A collection of car, truck, and train sounds, including motors revving, horns, and brakes.
- **Aircraft.** A collection of sounds for planes, jets, and helicopters, including guns and bombing sounds.

You can use the audio effects that come with each SoundMATTER download package royalty-free to provide your DarkBASIC Professional games with the high-quality audio effects that today's computer gamers have come to expect.

Other Game Creation Resources

Download packages like DarkMATTER, SkyMATTER, and SoundMATTER provide easy access to professional-quality graphic and audio effects for your computer games and can be an invaluable resource for saving time and adding a professional look and feel to your computer games.

However, if you prefer the do it yourself approach and want to create all of your own graphics and audio effects, the Game Creators also sell software tools designed to provide everything that you need. For example, there is AC3D (www.thegamecreators.com/?f=ac3d), which is a 3D modeling program designed to facilitate the development of 3D game objects and characters. There is also 3D Canvas Pro (3dcanvas.thegamecreators.com), which is a software tool designed to facilitate the development of 3D models and animation.

If you need to develop textures for your games, the Game Creators offer Texture Maker 3 (texturemaker.thegamecreators.com). For explosions, you can purchase ExGen (exgen.thegamecreators.com) and create explosions, smoke, and other effects as both images and animation sequences. To create images and animate sequences for game characters, the Game Creators provide Pro Motion (www.thegamecreators.com/?f=promotion), which is a pixel-drawing program that you can use to create sprites and images. If you want to populate your game with greenery, the Game Creators offers an assortment of packages, including Blitztree, Blitzgrass, Plant Like, and TreeMagik G3 (www.aliencodec.com). If you cannot find a sound effect that suits your needs in one of the SoundMATTER packs, you can purchase SFXEngine (www.thegamecreators.com/?f=sfxengine) and use it to create your own audio effects.

OTHER DARKBASIC RESOURCES

In addition to all of the graphics, audio packages, and development tools available at www.thegamecreators.com, there are a number of excellent forums sponsored by the Game Creators where you can go to learn about the latest products and happenings with DarkBASIC Professional. You'll also find a helpful collection of DarkBASIC tutorials, covering a range of different topics, all waiting for you to download and review.

The Game Creator Forums

As of the writing of this book, the Game Creators website sponsors over two dozen forums (http://forum.thegamecreators.com/?m=forum), all dedicated to help members of the DarkBASIC Professional community share information. If you have a question in need of an answer or have run into a programming problem for which you need help overcoming, the odds are very good that you'll be able to get the answers you need at one of these forums. As of the publishing of this book, these forums had over 100,000 threads and more than 1,200,000 postings.

By keeping an eye on these forums, you can keep abreast of the latest products being developed by and for DarkBASIC. A partial list of the forums that will be of the most interest to DarkBASIC Professional programmers is provided here:

- **DarkBASIC Professional Discussion.** This board is dedicated to all things related to DarkBASIC Professional programming.
- **DarkBASIC Discussion.** This board is dedicated to all things related to the original DarkBASIC programming language.
- **Newcomers DBPro Corner.** This board provides a place for programmers new to DarkBASIC to meet and share their experiences and questions.
- **Code Snippets.** This board provides a place where you can post sample code that you created and get access to code posted by other programmers.
- **Bug Reports.** This board provides DarkBASIC programmers with a place to report bugs and to view entries posted by other programmers.

If you run into a problem that you cannot solve on your own, you can often get help from other DarkBASIC programmers by posting a description of your problem on one of these forums. However, if this does not work out, you can also send a message to the Game Creator's technical support area by visiting www.thegamecreators.com/?mlcontact_support and filling out the support form that is provided.

DarkBASIC Tutorials

The Game Creator's website also provides you with access to a collection of free tutorials, written in PDF format, located at http://developer.thegamecreators.com/?f=dbpro_tutorials. These tutorials address both beginner and advanced topics. A listing of the tutorials provided at the time this book was published is provided here:

- Screen Scrolling Techniques
- Rainbow Shading
- RGB Color Values
- Data Types
- Boxes
- Huge Dungeons
- 2D Star Fields
- 2D MemBlock Star Fields
- Sprites and the Blue Background
- Field of View

DarkBASIC Professional's Architecture

DarkBASIC Professional utilizes a collection of different components to create an outstanding game development environment. DarkBASIC Professional consists of the following components.

- The DarkBASIC scripting language
- The DarkBASIC game engine
- DirectX

The DarkBASIC Professional Scripting Language

The DarkBASIC Professional scripting language is based on a programming language named BASIC. *BASIC* is an acronym for *Beginners All-Purpose Symbolic Instruction Code*. BASIC was created in 1963 at Dartmouth College as a programming language designed to teach beginners how to program. As such, BASIC supports an easy and straightforward syntax and a set of language statements that makes the language ideal for anyone just starting out.

By basing DarkBASIC Professional on BASIC, the Game Creators were able to design a modern programming language that, when combined with the DarkBASIC Professional game engine, is both easy to learn and yet incredibly powerful, capable of creating world class software applications.

DarkBASIC Professional's programming language is a structured language. It relies on the use of procedures, also known as subroutines and functions, as a means of creating scripts that are modular and easy to manage. This distinguishes DarkBASIC Professional from other modern programming languages like Microsoft Visual Basic, which is object-oriented.

 An object-oriented programming language is a language that views everything as objects. This includes resources such as files and folders as well as custom defined objects representing real-world concepts like people, cars, and money. Objects contain attributes that describe their characteristics and program code called methods that are used to interact with and control the objects.

An object-oriented programming language like Microsoft Visual Basic is more difficult to learn than a procedure language like DarkBASIC Professional.

The DarkBASIC Game Engine

DarkBASIC Professional's game engine consists of over 1,000 commands, all of which were specifically created to support game development. These commands provide you with everything needed to display graphic images, collect player input, and play various types of sounds and music. The commands are all designed to work with a Microsoft technology called

DirectX, which is discussed in the next section. Each of these commands is really a C++ function, which can be executed from any DarkBASIC Professional program.

C++ is a programming language known for its power and speed. C++ is also known for its complexity and high learning curve. Because of its power and speed, C++ is well suited to game development. That's why it should come as no surprise that most games today are written in C++. Because C++ takes a long time to learn and master, it is very difficult to use it to create computer games. However, with the advent of DarkBASIC and DarkBASIC Professional and their game engines, things are beginning to change. Using DarkBASIC Professional, it is now possible to create games using a programming language that is relatively easy to learn, while also having access to an enormous collection of pre-written functions specifically designed to harness the power and speed of C++.

In addition to being written in C++, the commands that make up DarkBASIC Professional's game engine are specifically designed to work with DirectX, a Microsoft technology that facilitates high performance sound and graphics performance. By calling on the commands that make up DarkBASIC Professional's game engine, you are able to generate realistic games using all of the multimedia capabilities provided by DirectX, without having to know a thing about how DirectX works. As a result, DirectX is no longer a technology exclusively available to C++ programmers. This allows you to focus on what it is you are trying to create without having to get bogged down worrying about the inner workings of DirectX.

The DarkBASIC Professional game engine is also available as a separate, standalone C++ library known as the Dark Game GDK. C++ programmers can purchase the Dark Game GDK from the Game Creator's website (darkgdk. thegamecreators.com) and use it within their C++ applications, significantly simplifying the difficulty involved in developing games using C++.

DirectX

DirectX is a Microsoft Windows technology designed to facilitate the execution of high-end graphics and audio in multimedia applications and games. DirectX consists of a series of *application programming interfaces* or *APIs*. These APIs serve as an interface between application software and computer hardware, allowing these two resources to communicate and exchange information. By allowing direct access to hardware, DirectX supports the development of faster and more responsive games. DirectX's APIs have names like Direct3D, which is responsible for managing graphics, and DirectMusic, which is responsible for managing music playback. Collectively, all of these APIs are referred to as DirectX.

Direct3D is by far the most commonly referred to DirectX API. It is used by Microsoft Windows, Microsoft Xbox, and Microsoft Xbox 360. Often, you will see the term Direct3D and DirectX used interchangeably.

Hardware manufacturers design and create specific software drivers that allow their video and audio cards and other hardware products to work with specific versions of DirectX. DirectX also provides control over input devices like the mouse and keyboard as well as joysticks. Microsoft first introduced DirectX back in 1995. Since then, DirectX has been updated many times. As of the writing of this book, the current version of DirectX is DirectX 10.

DirectX 10 ships as part of Microsoft Vista. This replaces the previous version of DirectX, which was DirectX 9.0c. DirectX 10 provides more powerful and realistic graphics effects. As a result, game developers are going to be able to produce games that run on Microsoft Vista that have astoundingly realistic effects. Prior to DirectX 10, Microsoft ensured that previous versions of DirectX were backward compatible with older DirectX software drivers. However, due to major changes in the design of the Windows Display Driver model, DirectX 10 is not compatible with older DirectX hardware drivers.

As of the writing of this book, DirectX 10 was only available on Microsoft Vista and Microsoft does not appear to have any plans to provide a version of DirectX 10 for any of its previous operating systems. This means that on computers running Windows 98, Me, 2000, and XP, DirectX 9.0c is the most current version.

 At the time that this book was published, the current version of DarkBASIC Professional was 1.066 and required DirectX 9.0c to run. This version of DarkBASIC Professional does not fully support DirectX 10. Since Microsoft did not design DirectX 10 to be backward compatible, many DarkBASIC applications will not work with DirectX 10. However, this challenge is easily overcome since Microsoft allows you to install DirectX 9.0c along side DirectX 10. Therefore, if your computer is running Microsoft Vista, you'll need to download and install DirectX 9.0c, which you can do by visiting any number of websites, such as http://www.softwarepatch.com/windows/directx.html, that provide access to the DirectX 9.0c installation package. Once installed, you will be able to develop and run your DarkBASIC applications without any problems, and when the Game Creators come out with a new version of DarkBASIC Professional that supports DirectX 10, you'll also be ready to take advantage of any new DirectX features exposed by DarkBASIC Professional.

Putting All the Pieces Together

DirectX is a collection of different software APIs that abstract many of the components that make up your computer. Developing a strong understanding of DirectX requires a great deal of time and technical know-how and has traditionally been one of the reasons that game programming was off limits to all but the most talented and experienced programmers. However, with the advent of DarkBASIC Professional and, more specifically, its game engine, you no longer have to be a DirectX expert to become a world-class developer. As depicted in Figure 1.18, the DarkBASIC Professional game engine acts as a wrapper or interface between your DarkBASIC application or source code and DirectX.

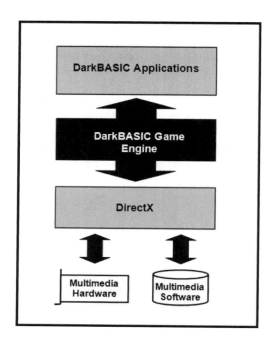

FIGURE 1.18

The architecture that supports the development and execution of DarkBASIC applications.

Thanks to the DarkBASIC Professional game engine, DarkBASIC programmers can spend their time focusing on the fun stuff, designing and testing computer games, without having to know anything about the inner workings and complexity of DirectX.

Back to the Dark Jokes Game

Now it is time to turn your attention to the development of this chapter's main project, the Dark Jokes game. Through the development of this game you will learn the basic steps involved in developing a DarkBASIC Professional application. Since you have yet to be introduced to all of the intricacies of the DarkBASIC Programming language, you should not get too bogged down in trying to understand what each programming statement in this application is doing. Although, because of the easy to understand nature of the BASIC programming language, upon which DarkBASIC Professional is based, you will probably be able to follow along.

As you work your way through the steps involved in developing the Dark Jokes games, try to place most of your focus on understanding the overall high-level process, without getting caught up in the details of the programming code. It will be made clearer to you as you work your way through this book.

Designing the Game

The overall design of the Dark Jokes game is very simple. However, the steps required to create and execute this game are fundamentally the same as those used to build larger and more complex games. This game will run within a window that contains minimize, maximize, and close buttons in its upper-right corner, just like any other typical application window. The window can also be resized, and the text displayed within that window will automatically adjust its size to provide the game with a professional look and feel.

As you follow along and create your own copy of this game, keep your focus on the overall mechanics and do not get caught up trying to understand the details of every programming statement. Any programming statements not already covered in this chapter will be reviewed as part of Chapter 2.

To help make things easy to understand, this game will be created by following a series of steps, as outlined here:

1. Create a new DarkBASIC project.
2. Specify game settings.
3. Document your application with comments.
4. Display a welcome message.
5. Tell the first joke.
6. Tell the second joke.
7. Tell the third joke.
8. Tell the fourth joke.
9. Tell the fifth joke.
10. Display a closing screen.
11. Save your new application.

Step 1: Creating a New DarkBASIC Project

The first step in creating a new DarkBASIC Professional application is to create a new project. To do so, start DarkBASIC Professional, and click on the New Project menu item located on the File menu. The Create a New DarkBASIC Professional project window appears.

Type **Hello** in the Project Name file, specify where you want your new project to be saved, and then click on the OK button. In response, a new project is created for you.

Step 2: Configuring Game Settings

With your new project now created, it is time to modify a few application settings. For starters, click on the Project button located at the bottom of the Project Panel window. This panel view displays information about the project being developed. By default, the following project settings should already be set.

- **Project Name.** Should be set to DarkJokes.
- **Exe Filename.** Should be set to DarkJokes.exe.

To help document this project, so that anyone who comes along after you will be able to identify the application's purpose, place the cursor in the Project Comments field and type **This application tells the player a series of five jokes**, as shown in Figure 1.19.

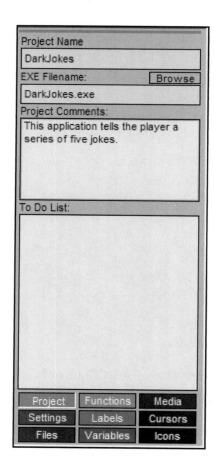

FIGURE 1.19

Providing high-level documentation about your DarkBASIC Professional project.

Next, click on the Settings button located at the bottom of the Project Panel window. This panel view displays property settings that you can use to specify whether the application will run inside a window or in full-screen mode. In addition, you can specify the screen resolution used by the game. By default, the Application Window Caption property, which stores a text string displayed in the application window's titlebar, is automatically set to DarkBASIC Pro Project. Change the contents of the Application Window Caption to Dark Jokes.

The default display setting for any new DarkBASIC Professional project is Windowed - Full Screen, which means that your application will take up the entire screen when executing. The Dark Jokes game will display its jokes within a window that used a resolution of 640 × 480. To set this up, select the Windowed option, as shown in Figure 1.20.

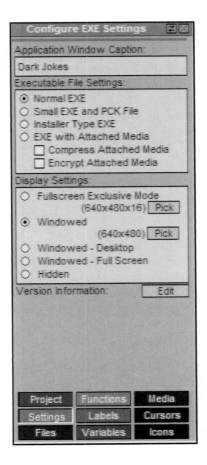

FIGURE 1.20

Configuring the window caption and resolution settings for the Dark Jokes game.

Step 3: Documenting Your DarkBASIC Application

Now that you have created a new project and configured its project settings, it is time to add the program code statements needed to make your new DarkBASIC Professional game run. By default, the following code statements should already be visible in the DarkBASIC Professional IDE's code area.

```
REM Project: DarkJokes
REM Created: 9/15/2007 2:55:01 PM
REM
REM ***** Main Source File *****
REM
```

As was previously explained, DarkBASIC Professional automatically adds these five statements to the beginning of the source code file for any new DarkBASIC Professional project. As you can see, all five statements are comments. The first of these statements displays the name that you provided when the project was initially created. Modify and add to these statements so that they look like the statements shown here:

Don't bother changing the second comment statement showing the date and time. Leave that statement as is to reflect the actual date and time that you created in your own copy of this game.

```
REM Project: DarkJokes
REM Created: 9/15/2007 2:55:01 PM
REM Executable name: DarkJokes.dba
REM Version: 1.0
REM Author: Jerry Lee Ford, Jr.
REM Description: This DarkBASIC application displays a series of humorous
REM              jokes.
```

As you can see, the comment statements have been modified to provide additional information about the game and its developer.

Step 4: Displaying a Welcome Message

The first thing the game does when started is display a welcome message and then pause, waiting for the player to read the message and then press the Enter key before continuing. This is accomplished by adding the following statements to the end of the script file.

```
SET TEXT FONT "Arial"  `Set the font type to Arial

SET TEXT SIZE 48  `Set the font size to 48 points
CENTER TEXT 320, 170, "Welcome to Dark Jokes!" `Display a welcome message
SET TEXT SIZE 16  `Set the font size to 16 points
CENTER TEXT 320, 250, "Press any key to continue"  `Display instructions
WAIT KEY  `Wait until the player presses a keyboard key
CLS  `Clear the display area
```

Although you will not be formally introduced to most of the statements used to develop this project's script file until Chapter 2, you can probably tell that the font type and size are first set to Arial 48 and a text string containing a welcome message is displayed. Next, the font size is set to 16 points and a second message is displayed. The WAIT KEY statement is then executed, pausing the program's execution until the player presses a keyboard key, after which the screen is cleared.

As previously stated, do not spend too much time trying to figure out what each code statement is doing. Instead, focus on the big picture for now. You will learn about the syntax of each of the programming statements used by this script soon enough.

Step 5: Displaying the Opening Joke

Once the player presses the Enter key, it is time to display the game's first joke. This is accomplished by adding the following code statements to the end of the script file.

```
SET TEXT SIZE 24  `Set the font size to 24 points
`Display the game's first joke
CENTER TEXT 320, 200, "Wear one watch and you will always know what time"
CENTER TEXT 320, 230, "it is."
CENTER TEXT 320, 260, "Wear two watches and you will never know."
SET TEXT SIZE 16  `Set the font size to 16 points
CENTER TEXT 320, 310, "Press any key to continue"
WAIT KEY  `Wait until the player presses a keyboard key
CLS  `Clear the display area
```

As you can see, no new statements have been introduced here. As with the previous set of statements, new text is displayed using different point sizes and the program's execution is paused to give the player a chance to read it, before allowing the program to resume its execution.

Step 6: Displaying the Second Joke

The code statements required to display the game's second joke are provided next and should be added to the end of the script file.

```
SET TEXT SIZE 24   `Set the font size to 24 points
`Display the game's second joke
CENTER TEXT 320, 200, "If a man stands in the middle of the forest"
CENTER TEXT 320, 230, " speaking and there is no woman around to hear"
CENTER TEXT 320, 260, "him, is he still wrong?"
SET TEXT SIZE 16   `Set the font size to 16 points
CENTER TEXT 320, 310, "Press any key to continue"
WAIT KEY   `Wait until the player presses a keyboard key
CLS   `Clear the display area
```

These statements are essentially identical to the statements used to tell the game's first joke; the only difference being the text string that contains the joke itself.

Step 7: Displaying the Third Joke

The code statements required to display the game's third joke are provided next and should be added to the end of the script file.

```
SET TEXT SIZE 24   `Set the font size to 24 points
`Display the game's third joke
CENTER TEXT 320, 200, "If people are not supposed to eat animals,"
CENTER TEXT 320, 230, "then why are they made of meat?"
SET TEXT SIZE 16   `Set the font size to 16 points
CENTER TEXT 320, 280, "Press any key to continue"
WAIT KEY   `Wait until the player presses a keyboard key
CLS   `Clear the display area
```

Step 8: Displaying the Fourth Joke

The code statements required to display the game's fourth joke are provided next and should be added to the end of the script file.

```
SET TEXT SIZE 24   `Set the font size to 24 points
`Display the game's fourth joke
CENTER TEXT 320, 200, "If you think that nobody cares whether you live or"
CENTER TEXT 320, 230, "die, try missing a couple of car payments."
SET TEXT SIZE 16   `Set the font size to 16 points
```

```
CENTER TEXT 320, 280, "Press any key to continue"
WAIT KEY  `Wait until the player presses a keyboard key
CLS  `Clear the display area
```

Step 9: Displaying the Final Joke

The code statements required to display the game's fifth and final joke are provided next and should be added to the end of the script file.

```
SET TEXT SIZE 24  `Set the font size to 24 points
`Display the game's fifth joke
CENTER TEXT 320, 200, "The early bird may get the worm,"
CENTER TEXT 320, 230, "but it is the second mouse that gets the cheese."
SET TEXT SIZE 16  `Set the font size to 16 points
CENTER TEXT 320, 280, "Press any key to continue"
WAIT KEY  `Wait until the player presses a keyboard key
CLS  `Clear the display area
```

Step 10: Displaying a Closing Screen

Now that the last of the game's jokes have been displayed, all that remains is to display a closing message and terminate the game's execution. This is accomplished by adding the following statements to the end of the script file.

```
SET TEXT SIZE 24  `Set the font size to 24 points
`Display the game's closing message
CENTER TEXT 320, 200, "Thanks for playing!"
SET TEXT SIZE 16  `Set the font size to 16 points
CENTER TEXT 320, 280, "Press any key to continue"
WAIT KEY  `Wait until the player presses a keyboard key

END
```

Step 11: Saving and Compiling Your Application

Okay, you have now seen all of the source code required to create the Dark Jokes game. Go ahead and save your new project by clicking on the Save All option located on the File menu. Now it's time to compile your new application. This time, rather than compiling your application and then finding and double-clicking on your application's new executable file, try clicking on the Make/EXE RUN option located on the Compile menu. When executed, this option checks your application for syntax errors and, if none are found, compiles and then executes your program, saving you the trouble of having to compile and execute your new application in two separate steps.

Once started, the Dark Jokes application should execute exactly as described at the beginning of this chapter. Once you have run your new application and ensured that everything works as expected, share a copy of your game with a few friends and solicit their input. Remember, you will find your application's executable file in the project folder that was created for you when you initially created your new DarkBASIC project. As Figure 1.21 demonstrates, you should find three files stored in the project folder.

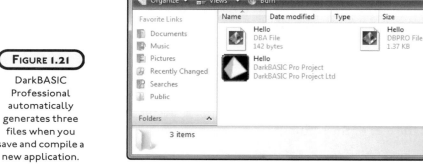

FIGURE 1.21

DarkBASIC Professional automatically generates three files when you save and compile a new application.

The Final Result

All right, you now have everything you need to create and execute the Dark Jokes computer game. Like all of the DarkBASIC games that will be presented in this book, the development of the Dark Jokes game was completed by following a number of steps. As with any programming endeavor, it is very easy to make typing errors or to accidentally skip one or more steps or parts of steps. This is especially true for beginning programmers or for programmers new to the programming language being used. To help ensure that things are as clear as possible, I have provided a full copy of the project's source code next. In the event you run into errors when trying to run your copy of the Dark Jokes game, you can use this fully assembled script to compare against your application's code statements and to look for any differences.

```
REM Project: DarkJokes
REM Created: 9/15/2007 2:55:01 PM
REM Executable name: DarkJokes.dba
REM Version: 1.0
REM Author: Jerry Lee Ford, Jr.
```

```
REM Description: This DarkBASIC application displays a series of humorous
REM             jokes.

REM ***** Main Source File *****

SET TEXT FONT "Arial"  `Set the font type to Arial

SET TEXT SIZE 48  `Set the font size to 48 points
CENTER TEXT 320, 170, "Welcome to Dark Jokes!" `Display a welcome message
SET TEXT SIZE 16  `Set the font size to 16 points
CENTER TEXT 320, 250, "Press any key to continue"  `Display instructions
WAIT KEY  `Wait until the player presses a keyboard key
CLS  `Clear the display area

SET TEXT SIZE 24  `Set the font size to 24 points
`Display the game's first joke
CENTER TEXT 320, 200, "Wear one watch and you will always know what time"
CENTER TEXT 320, 230, "it is."
CENTER TEXT 320, 260, "Wear two watches and you will never know."
SET TEXT SIZE 16  `Set the font size to 16 points
CENTER TEXT 320, 310, "Press any key to continue"
WAIT KEY  `Wait until the player presses a keyboard key
CLS  `Clear the display area

SET TEXT SIZE 24  `Set the font size to 24 points
`Display the game's second joke
CENTER TEXT 320, 200, "If a man stands in the middle of the forest"
CENTER TEXT 320, 230, " speaking and there is no woman around to hear"
CENTER TEXT 320, 260, "him, is he still wrong?"
SET TEXT SIZE 16  `Set the font size to 16 points
CENTER TEXT 320, 310, "Press any key to continue"
WAIT KEY  `Wait until the player presses a keyboard key
CLS  `Clear the display area

SET TEXT SIZE 24  `Set the font size to 24 points
`Display the game's third joke
CENTER TEXT 320, 200, "If people are not supposed to eat animals,"
CENTER TEXT 320, 230, "then why are they made of meat?"
```

```
SET TEXT SIZE 16  `Set the font size to 16 points
CENTER TEXT 320, 280, "Press any key to continue"
WAIT KEY  `Wait until the player presses a keyboard key
CLS  `Clear the display area

SET TEXT SIZE 24  `Set the font size to 24 points
`Display the game's fourth joke
CENTER TEXT 320, 200, "If you think that nobody cares whether you live or"
CENTER TEXT 320, 230, "die, try missing a couple of car payments."
SET TEXT SIZE 16  `Set the font size to 16 points
CENTER TEXT 320, 280, "Press any key to continue"
WAIT KEY  `Wait until the player presses a keyboard key
CLS  `Clear the display area

SET TEXT SIZE 24  `Set the font size to 24 points
`Display the game's fifth joke
CENTER TEXT 320, 200, "The early bird may get the worm,"
CENTER TEXT 320, 230, "but it is the second mouse that gets the cheese."
SET TEXT SIZE 16  `Set the font size to 16 points
CENTER TEXT 320, 280, "Press any key to continue"
WAIT KEY  `Wait until the player presses a keyboard key
CLS  `Clear the display area

SET TEXT SIZE 24  `Set the font size to 24 points
`Display the game's closing message
CENTER TEXT 320, 200, "Thanks for playing!"
SET TEXT SIZE 16  `Set the font size to 16 points
CENTER TEXT 320, 280, "Press any key to continue"
WAIT KEY  `Wait until the player presses a keyboard key

END
```

 You will also find a copy of this application's project file on this book's companion website, located at http://www.courseptr.com/downloads.

Running the Dark Jokes Application

Okay, that's it. Assuming that you have created your own copy of this game as you worked your way through each of the preceding steps, then your copy of the Dark Jokes game should be ready to run. Press the F5 key to compile and run your application. As long as you did not skip any steps or make any typos when keying in the code statements and you correctly modified the project level attributes as previously specified, the game should run exactly as was explained at the beginning of this chapter. If, however, the application fails to compile, then you will need to go back and retrace your steps.

SUMMARY

This chapter has provided you with an overview of DarkBASIC Professional. This includes learning how to install and upgrade it. This chapter showed you the basic steps involved in creating DarkBASIC Professional applications and provided a high-level overview of the architecture behind DarkBASIC Professional that makes application development possible. You also learned about other game development resources provided by the Game Creators that you can purchase and use to speed up and simplify game development. Last but certainly not least, you learned how to create your first computer game.

Before you move on to Chapter 2, I suggest you set aside a few additional minutes to try and improve the Dark Jokes game by implementing the following list of challenges.

CHALLENGES

1. The jokes that are displayed when the Dark Jokes game executes are admittedly not the funniest jokes ever told. To make the game better suit your sense of humor, consider replacing them with jokes of your own.

2. As currently written, the Dark Jokes game doesn't take very long for the player to complete. Consider making the game more fun by adding additional jokes to it. To accomplish this, just copy and paste the code statements that display one of the game's jokes and then modify the text strings that display new jokes.

3. Consider displaying additional text on the game's final screen that, in addition to thanking the player for playing, also promotes you and your website (if you have one). For example, you might publish your name, URL, and any other information that you think will help associate you with your application.

GETTING COMFORTABLE WITH THE DarkBASIC PROFESSIONAL INTEGRATED DEVELOPMENT ENVIRONMENT

I n this chapter, you will learn the ins and outs of working with the DarkBASIC Professional integrated development environment or IDE. This will include an overview of all the major components that make up the IDE, as well as an examination of available configuration settings. You will learn about some of the IDE's limitations and examine a number of alternative third-party IDEs that you can use in place of the default IDE. This chapter will also introduce to you a number of new commands that you can use to control the display and appearance of text. On top of all this, you will also learn how to create your next DarkBASIC Professional application, the Fortune Teller game.

Specifically, you will learn:

- About the different parts of the DarkBASIC Professional IDE
- How to access and modify IDE configuration options
- How to work with the Project Manager panel
- About alternative third-party IDEs
- How to work with different text, font, and color commands

PROJECT PREVIEW: THE FORTUNE TELLER GAME

This chapter's game project is the Fortune Teller game. This game simulates a session with a Fortune Teller. The player may ask as many questions as she wants. However, all questions must be able to be answered with a simple yes or no. When first started, the game displays the welcome message shown in Figure 2.1.

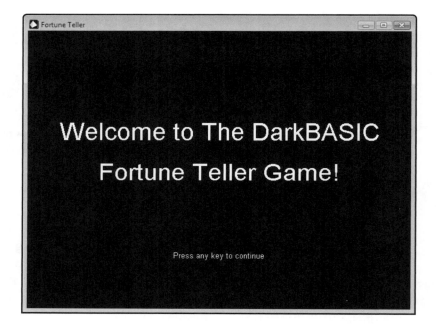

Fortune Teller

Welcome to The DarkBASIC
Fortune Teller Game!

Press any key to continue

FIGURE 2.1

The Fortune Teller game's welcome screen.

Next, instructions are presented, as shown in Figure 2.2, that tell the player how to properly format questions and how to stop game play.

 Although the player is told that game play can be terminated at any time by typing the word Quit, the game can, of course, also be terminated by clicking on the application window's Close button.

Next, the Fortune Teller instructs the player to ask a question, as shown in Figure 2.3.

Whenever the Fortune Teller speaks, her text is shown in yellow. The text that makes up the player's questions is shown in white, which helps to visually distinguish between who is talking. After entering a question, as demonstrated in Figure 2.4, the player must press the Enter key to continue.

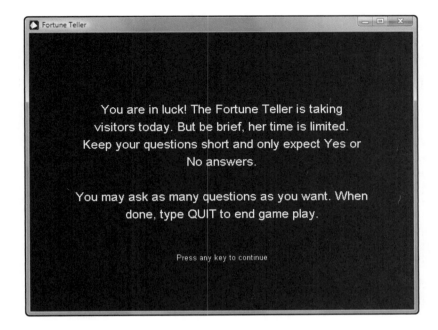

FIGURE 2.2

The rules for playing the game are simple and straightforward.

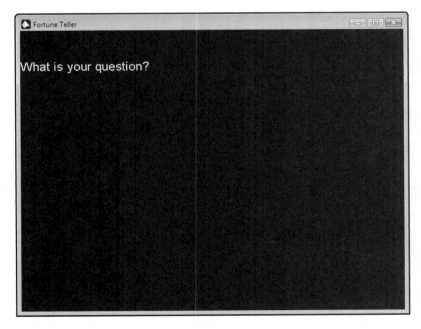

FIGURE 2.3

The player is prompted to ask a question.

To add a little drama to the game, the Fortune Teller's answer is provided in a series of three steps, separated by brief pauses. Figure 2.5 shows the Fortune Teller's initial response.

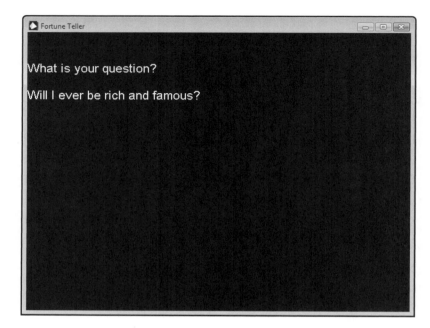

FIGURE 2.4

The Fortune Teller's text is shown in yellow and the player's input is displayed in white.

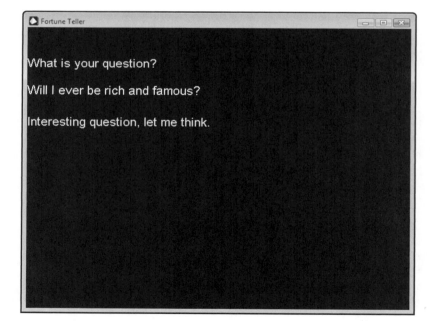

FIGURE 2.5

The Fortune Teller pauses to think about the player's question.

After three seconds have passed, the Fortune Teller speaks again, as shown in Figure 2.6.

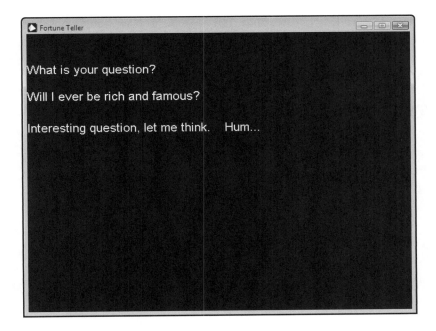

FIGURE 2.6

A little more deep thinking is required.

Finally, after two more seconds, the Fortune Teller provides the rest of her response, as demonstrated in Figure 2.7.

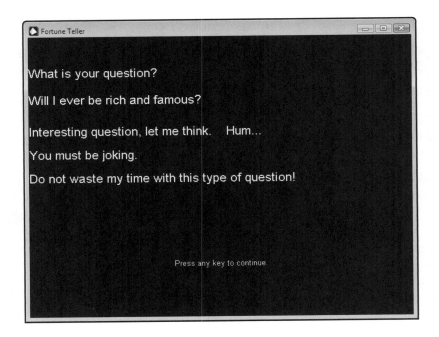

FIGURE 2.7

The Fortune Teller answers the player's question.

The Fortune Teller's responses are randomly generated and as such will continuously vary. Sometimes the answer will be Yes and sometimes it will be No. Other times, the Fortune Teller may report that she is unable to answer a particular question. From time to time, the Fortune teller may even get a little irritated and refuse to answer a question.

Mastering the DarkBASIC Professional IDE

The DarkBASIC Professional IDE is your primary interface for creating, testing, and compiling DarkBASIC Professional applications. It provides you with everything you need to write program code and to view and modify project settings like screen resolution and project level comments. When first started, DarkBASIC Professional opens in Assistant View mode, as shown in Figure 2.8.

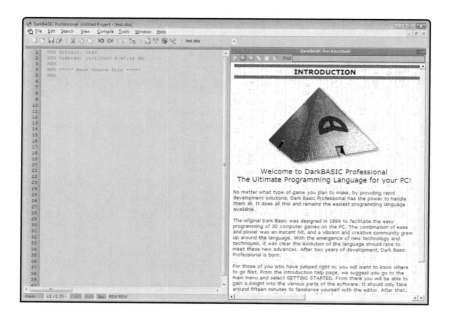

FIGURE 2.8

The Assistant View mode provides easy access to the Help system.

In Assistant View mode, the IDE is divided into two parts. The left-hand side of the IDE displays the code editing area, and the right-hand side displays the DarkBASIC Pro Assistant panel. If you scroll down to the bottom of the text that is initially displayed in the Assistant panel, you will see a link that when clicked provides easy access to the DarkBASIC Professional help system. The advantage of this mode is that it lets you easily reference online help while writing your program code. Although helpful for those just getting started, most programmers elect to work with DarkBASIC Professional's Project View mode. This mode replaces the DarkBASIC

Pro Assistant panel with the Project panel, which is much smaller, providing additional space in the code editing area.

Major IDE Components

DarkBASIC Professional's Project View mode, shown in Figure 2.9, is displayed by default any time a new DarkBASIC Professional project is created. In this mode, the IDE is organized into a number of distinct parts, as listed here:

- **Menu Bar.** Provides access to commands required to create, modify, and compile DarkBASIC Professional applications.
- **Toolbar.** Provides easy access to commonly used commands.
- **Code editor.** A full-featured text editor used to write and edit program code.
- **Status bar.** A bar located at the bottom of the IDE that displays status information about the current operation.
- **Project panel.** Displays project level settings and files and allows you to modify project settings.

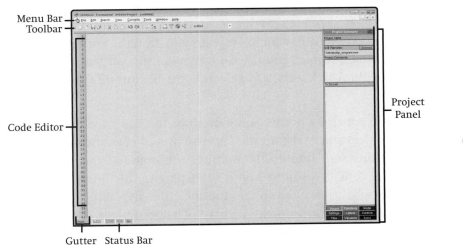

FIGURE 2.9

The Project View mode allows you to edit your project's code and to access and modify project settings.

DarkBASIC Professional's default IDE provides you with a basic set of editing capabilities. It includes all of the editing features that you would expect, including copy, cut, and paste. In addition, it provides a host of specialized commands that are designed to create, save, and compile DarkBASIC Professional applications. Like most editors, DarkBASIC Professional's default IDE is set up as the default application for any DarkBASIC Professional files (e.g., .dba and .dbpro files). As a result, if you double-click on a .dbpro project file, Windows will automatically start DarkBASIC Professional, if it is not already running, and load the project file into the default IDE.

TRAP DarkBASIC Professional's default IDE sometimes has trouble opening large project files using file association. If this happens to you, use the Open Project option located on the default IDE's File menu.

Navigating the IDE Menus

DarkBASIC Professional provides easy access to editor commands through its menu system, which consists of eight menus. The File menu provides access to commands that allow you to create new projects, open existing projects, and save and close projects. The Edit menu gives you access to commands that allow you to undo and redo actions, copy, cut, and paste code. The Edit menu also provides you with access to commands for setting and removing breakpoints, which is covered in detailed in Chapter 10, "Finding and Fixing Application Errors." Another command made available from this menu is the ability to set bookmarks, which are shortcuts or links that you can set up and then use to quickly jump around within a code file to any location where you have placed a bookmark.

The Search menu contains commands that you can use to perform a keyword search in a current source code file as well as perform search and replace operations. Other commands located on this menu include Go to Line #, which lets you reposition the current view within the code editor to a specific line number, and the Go to Bookmark command that you can use to jump to any bookmark that you have set, by selecting the bookmark from a drop-down list that will be displayed.

The View menu allows you to control whether some or all of the IDE's toolbar is displayed and to switch between the Project and Assistant modes. Also provided as options on the View menu are the Fold All Functions and Unfold All Functions commands. When executed, the Fold All Functions command tells the IDE to hide the display of all the code statements belonging to functions that you have defined within the code file, displaying only each function's name. This allows you to streamline the display of your project code statements, allowing you to focus on the overall controlling logic within your application. The Unfold All Functions command is the opposite of the Fold All Functions command, redisplaying the code statements for all folded functions.

HINT A *function* is a named collection of code statements that are called upon to execute as a unit. You will learn all about functions and how they work in Chapter 6, "Organizing Code Logic Using Functions."

Figure 2.10 shows an example of a small function as it would appear by default (unfolded) within the default IDE.

```
142  -|FUNCTION ProcessPlayerHits()
143
144      IF POINT(ballx, bally) > 0
145         speedx = speedx * - 1
146         PLAY SOUND 1
147      ENDIF
```

FIGURE 2.10

An example of an unfolded function.

Figure 2.11 shows how the IDE would display this same function once it had been folded.

```
142  +|FUNCTION ProcessPlayerHits()
```

FIGURE 2.11

An example of a folded function.

HINT

You will need to turn off function folding when you are developing functions within your code file. However, once you have developed and thoroughly tested all your application's functions, turning on function folding can make moving around in your code file a lot easier and less confusing, especially in larger projects.

The Compile menu contains commands that you will use to syntax check your source code and then generate a compiled application. In addition, the Compile menu provides you with access to commands that run your applications in debug mode and control the execution of program statements during a debug session. You will learn how to work with the debug commands in Chapter 10.

The Tools menu contains one menu item, System Options. When clicked, the System Options command displays the DarkBASIC Pro Options window, which allows you to view and modify a number of IDE configuration settings. You will learn more about how to work with the DarkBASIC Pro Options window later in this chapter.

The Window menu contains commands that allow you to control how windows are displayed within the IDE—cascaded or tiled horizontally or vertically.

The Help menu provides access to commands that display DarkBASIC Professional's Help files and links to different DarkBASIC Professional resources that are available online. More information on the DarkBASIC Professional help system is provided later in this chapter.

Getting Comfortable with the Toolbar

The DarkBASIC Professional default IDE's toolbar, shown in Figure 2.12, consists of a collection of 15 icons, each of which provides single-click access to commonly used IDE commands. Using the toolbar, you can create and save new projects, edit them, and then compile and execute them, all without having to use a single menu command.

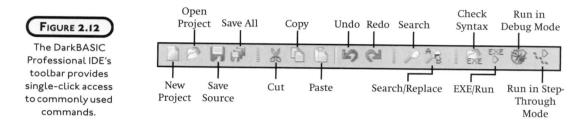

FIGURE 2.12

The DarkBASIC Professional IDE's toolbar provides single-click access to commonly used commands.

The default IDE's toolbar is static, meaning that unlike other third-party IDEs, you cannot add or remove toolbar icons. You can, however, hide and redisplay the toolbar using the Show Toolbar command located on the IDE's View menu.

Working with the Code Editor

The code editing area is essentially a sophisticated text editor that provides a number of advanced features specifically designed to assist in the development of DarkBASIC Professional source code. By default, the editor uses syntax statement color coding to highlight different language keywords, helping to make program code easier to read and understand. With the exception of an optional gutter (enabled by default) located on the left-hand side of the editing area, all of the space in the editing area is available for displaying code statements. The gutter is a vertical strip on the left-hand side of the editing area that displays line numbers. Line numbers are referenced in error messages and can be used to keep track of your location within code files.

Like any typical text editor, you can use menu and toolbar commands to edit any text displayed in the editing area. This includes copying, cutting, and pasting. The editor also supports code indentation, as demonstrated in Figure 2.13, and when enabled will assist you in indenting your program statements.

In addition to IDE menu and toolbar commands, you can right-click anywhere within the code editing area to access editing commands, as demonstrated in Figure 2.14.

FIGURE 2.13

The code editor supports syntax color coding and statement indentation.

FIGURE 2.14

The code editing area's context menu provides convenient access to common editing commands.

In addition to Cut, Copy, Paste, and Select All commands, you can also set and clear breakpoints when debugging your application. The editing area is highly configurable. Configuration settings are accessible on the DarkBASIC Pro Options window, which is accessed by clicking on the System Options item located on the IDE's Tools menu. The DarkBASIC Pro Options window is organized into two views. The Colors/Styles view, shown in Figure 2.15, lets you view and configure the font type and size used by the editor. In addition, you can specify the colors to be used when displaying keywords, strings, numbers, and comments.

The DarkBASIC Pro Options window's Editing view, shown in Figure 2.16, lets you access and control the execution of a number of optional IDE features, most of which are designed to control the operation of the code editor.

FIGURE 2.15

Modifying font type and color settings used by the code editor.

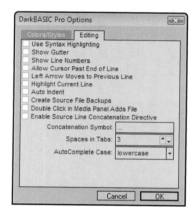

FIGURE 2.16

Modifying IDE code editor configuration settings.

As you can see, the DarkBASIC Pro Options window's Editing view lets you enable or disable syntax highlighting, the display of the gutter, line number display, cursor movement, auto indentation, and numerous other features. Take note of the AutoComplete Case option that allows you to specify how Intellisense functions when used. You can also optionally instruct the IDE how to format any text that it generates through Intellisense (all lowercase, all uppercase, or mixed case).

Intellisense is an editor feature that assists programmers in writing code by monitoring the current status of the function or statement that is currently being keyed, and then, when prompted, displaying suggestions on how to complete the function or statement. To use Intellisense, begin keying in a command and when you want assistance, press Ctrl+Spacebar. In response, the code editor will display a list of suggestions, as demonstrated in Figure 2.17. To apply a suggestion, click on it with your mouse.

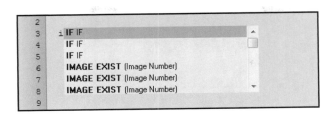

FIGURE 2.17

Letting
Intellisense help
you write code
statements.

TRAP

As was previously mentioned, DarkBASIC Professional's default IDE has a reputation for occasionally misbehaving, resulting in the unexpected loss of program
code that has not been saved. While this has not happened to me yet, I strongly
recommend that rather than allow yourself to fall prey to this unfortunate cir-
cumstance, you instead remember to save your work often.

The IDE Status Bar

DarkBASIC Professional's default IDE includes a status bar located at the bottom of the
IDE. The IDE uses the status bar to display context-sensitive information as you work with
the IDE. For example, the status bar displays information about the current location of the
cursor (column and row location). It also keeps track of whether the Caps Lock, Num Lock,
and Insert key have been pressed.

Configuring Project Settings Using the Project Manager Panel

DarkBASIC Professional projects have a number of settings that you can modify to affect
different aspects of application execution. These application settings are visible in the Project
Manager panel when you are working with the default IDE in Project View mode and include
settings that affect screen resolution, the display of text in window title bar text, and numerous other options.

By default, the Project Manager panel is displayed on the right-hand side of the IDE. You can
close it at any time by clicking on the Close button located in the upper-right corner of the
panel. If desired, you can redisplay the Project Manager panel by clicking on the Show Project
Manager option located on the View menu. You can also relocate the Project Manager panel
by clicking on the left and right arrow button located next to the panel's Close button. When
clicked, this button instructs the IDE to move the panel to the opposite side of the IDE.

In addition to application settings, the Project Manager panel also provides you with a means
of adding icons, cursors, and media files to your projects. Figure 2.18 shows how the Project
Manager panel looks for a project named Pong.

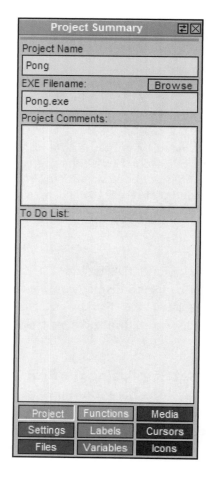

FIGURE 2.18

The Project view displays information about the name of your project, executable file, project comments, and a To Do List.

The Project Manager panel consists of nine different views. By default, the Project view is the initial view that is displayed. You can switch to other views by clicking one of the nine buttons located at the bottom of the Project Manager panel. I recommend that you take advantage of the Project Comments field in the Project view to provide a high-level overview of the application that you are developing. In addition, you should use the To Do List field to record information about future enhancements that you plan on making to the application.

The Settings view, shown in Figure 2.19, provides access to settings that control the display of the text string displayed in the application window's titlebar, the manner in which the application's executable file is created, and the resolution and window type used to display the application when it executes. You may display any text string you want in your application's titlebar by typing that string in the Application Window Caption field. Quotation marks are not required.

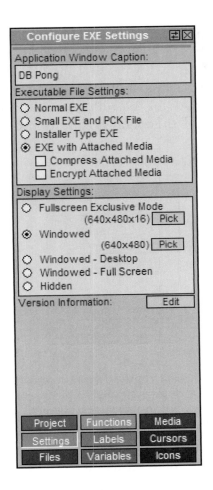

FIGURE 2.19

Configuring
execution and
display settings.

The Executable File Setting section of the Settings view allows you to specify how you want your application's executable file to be created. For this book, we'll just concentrate on the first three options, which are outlined here:

- **Normal EXE.** Creates a standalone executable file that also includes, embedded within itself, copies of any files required by the application.
- **Small EXE and PCK File.** Creates a standalone executable file and creates a separate file with a .pck file extension into which copies of any required files are embedded.
- **Installed Type EXE.** Creates an executable installed file that, when executed, creates a file containing a copy of your application.

The Display Setting section is used to specify whether you want your application to run full screen, in a window, or hidden. If you select the Fullscreen Exclusive mode, you will need to select the desired resolution and color depth. If you select the Windowed option, you will need to specify the screen resolution at which you want your application executed. For example, to specify a resolution and color depth for the Fullscreen Exclusive mode, you would select that display setting and then click on the option's Pick button, displaying the windows shown in Figure 2.20.

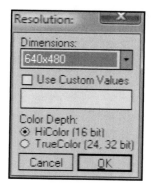

TRAP The computer upon which your application is run must be able to support any screen resolution and color depth you specify. Since not everyone has a state of the art computer, you may want to avoid using higher resolutions in conjunction with higher color depths.

The Settings view also lets you specify version information by clicking on the Edit button. Other Project Manager views, such as the Files, Media, Cursors, and Icons views, let you view, add, and delete audio and graphic files to your applications. For example, Figure 2.21 shows an example of the Media view in a project that uses two audio files.

As Figure 2.21 shows, new media files can be added to a project by clicking on the Add button located at the top of the panel and then specifying the name and path of the files. You can delete any media file by selecting it and then clicking on the Delete button.

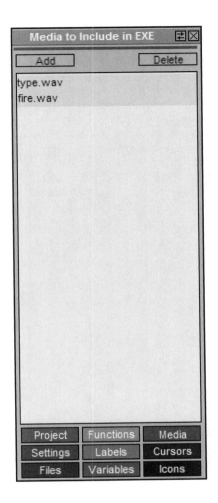

FIGURE 2.21

Adding media files to your DarkBASIC Professional project.

Other Project Manager views, including the Functions, Labels, and Variables view, do not allow you to edit their contents. Instead, these views let you keep an eye on all of the functions, labels, and variables that you have defined within your project. Each of these views can also be used as navigation tools. For example, Figure 2.22 shows an example of the Functions view for a project that contains ten functions. By double-clicking on any function in this list, the corresponding function is immediately located and displayed in the code editing section.

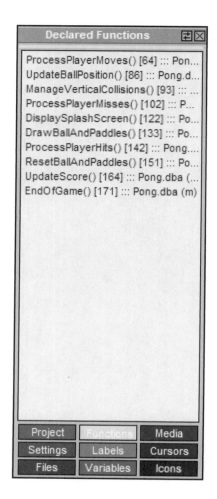

Declared Functions

ProcessPlayerMoves() [64] ::: Pon...
UpdateBallPosition() [86] ::: Pong.d...
ManageVerticalCollisions() [93] ::: ...
ProcessPlayerMisses() [102] ::: P...
DisplaySplashScreen() [122] ::: Po...
DrawBallAndPaddles() [133] ::: Po...
ProcessPlayerHits() [142] ::: Pong....
ResetBallAndPaddles() [151] ::: Po...
UpdateScore() [164] ::: Pong.dba (...
EndOfGame() [171] ::: Pong.dba (m)

Project	Functions	Media
Settings	Labels	Cursors
Files	Variables	Icons

FIGURE 2.22

Reviewing a list of all of the functions defined within a DarkBASIC Professional project.

Accessing Help

The DarkBASIC Professional's default IDE's Help menu provides access to DarkBASIC Professional help files and to links to various online resources. As Figure 2.23 shows, DarkBASIC Professional help files are presented as a series of menu items that you can click on to drill down and find information or help with a specific topic.

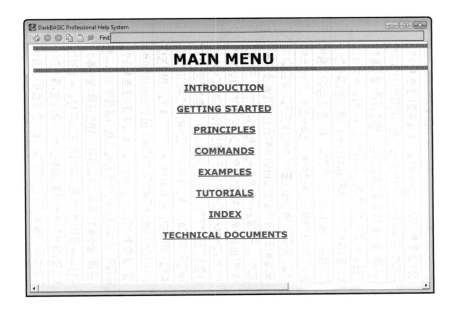

FIGURE 2.23

Accessing
DarkBASIC
Professional's
help files.

 You can click on the Help menu's About option to display DarkBASIC Professional's current version number.

CREATING NEW PROJECTS

As you have already seen, to create a new DarkBASIC Professional project, you need to click on the New Project option located on the File menu. Alternatively, you can click on the New Project icon located on the IDE toolbar or press Ctrl+N. In response, the Create a new DarkBASIC Professional Project window is displayed, as shown in Figure 2.24.

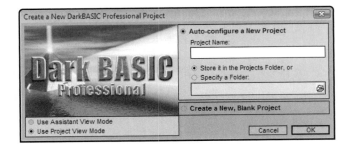

FIGURE 2.24

Creating a new
DarkBASIC
Professional
project.

DarkBASIC Professional projects are containers that store all of the files required to create new applications. These files includes both .dba and .dbpro files, as well as any icon, cursor, and media files that you may add to your application. By default, the Use Project View Mode option is always selected. However, you have the option of selecting the Use Assistant View Mode if you prefer. By default, the Auto-Configure a New Project option is also selected. As you have already seen, this option lets you specify a name for your new project and then specify the location where you want to store it. Alternatively, you can select the Create a New, Blank Project option. When selected this option creates a new DarkBASIC Professional project without a name or project folder. In addition, the default comments that are normally added to the beginning of each new project are not generated either. When the Create a New, Blank Project option is selected, it is up to you to assign a name and specify the location where you want to store your new project.

ALTERNATE INTEGRATED DEVELOPMENT ENVIRONMENTS

DarkBASIC Professional is a powerful, modern game development tool that puts the power of DirectX right in your hands. Its programming language is powerful, yet quite easy to use. Its game engine provides you with a wealth of resources that you can draw upon to create even the most advanced types of computer games. However, despite all of its bells and whistles, at the time this book was published, many DarkBASIC Professional programmers were not happy with the language's default integrated development environment or IDE.

DarkBASIC Professional's IDE is a little old school in its layout and design. It lacks a number of features found in many modern IDEs. For example, it only lets you open and work with one code file at a time. Although it supports opening a file through file associations, it does not, like most Windows applications, let you drag and drop a .dba or .dbpro file onto the IDE to open it. While it does support features like syntax color coding and automatic indentation and provides an integrated visual debugger, the default IDE does not provide features like project-wide searching and media viewing. Unlike many modern editors, which are filled with all kinds of highly configurable windows and tab-controlled panels, DarkBASIC Professional's main work area consists only of the code editing area and the Project Manager panel. As a result, the default IDE is less intuitive and slower to work with than the IDEs often used with other programming languages.

To make matters worse, the DarkBASIC Professional IDE has a reputation for being a little buggy and for occasionally losing program code. There has not been an update to the default IDE since 2002. There are no plans to update the default IDE; instead, the current direction that the Game Creators appear to be moving is to evaluate and adopt a replacement IDE from one of several community developed alternatives. However, as of the publishing of this book, no formal announcements or decisions regarding the future replacement of the default DarkBASIC Professional IDE had been announced.

However, as was just mentioned, a number of really good alternative IDEs, all of which are free, are currently available for DarkBASIC Professional. These alternative IDEs provide additional features and functionality not found in the default IDE and are modern in appearance and more intuitive to work with. A quick review of the major alternative IDEs that are currently available is provided in the following sections.

CodeSurge

CodeSurge is one of several free IDEs currently available as a replacement for DarkBASIC Professional's aging IDE. In addition to sporting a visually slick and modern interface design, CodeSurge provides a collection of editing commands that you would expect from any good IDE, including copy, cut, paste, find, replace, and so on. CodeSurge also supports syntax color coding and line indentation.

HINT

If you visit the Upgrades page at the Game Creators' website located at http://darkbasicpro.thegamecreators.com/?flupgrades, looking for an update to the default DarkBASIC Professional IDE (the last update for the default editor was published in October 2002), you will find that the Game Creators have posted an additional link for CodeSurge, advertising it as a fast, efficient, and professional alternative to the default IDE.

The CodeSurge IDE is organized into panels that can be moved around the IDE and docked to different sides of the IDE workspace. Using the Pin button displayed at the top of each panel, you can lock a panel into position or temporarily minimize it to a tab, displayed on the side of the IDE, where it can later be restored with a single click. Alternatively, you can undock these panels and work with them as independent windows.

In addition to the code editor, three different panels are available, as shown in Figure 2.25.

A brief description of what each panel does is provided here:

- **Code Explorer.** A panel that can be used to browse functions, labels, and types.
- **Project Explorer.** A panel that lets you quickly view project cursors, icons, media files, and source files.
- **Project Manager.** A panel that lets you view and modify project settings.

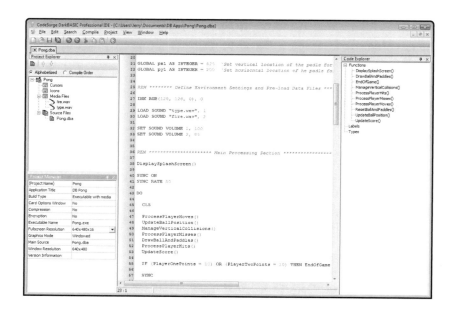

CodeSurge also features improved error reporting. For example, Figure 2.26 shows an example of the dialog window that is displayed whenever you compile a DarkBASIC Professional project in an application. During compilation, this window lets you know how far along it is by displaying the current line in the code file that is being processed. If an error is found, this window identifies the line number where the error was detected and the compile process terminates. Once you click on the OK button to dismiss this window, you will be returned to the main IDE where the specified line number will be highlighted, to help you hone in on the area within your script file where the error resides.

FIGURE 2.26

Compiling a
DarkBASIC
Professional
application using
CodeSurge.

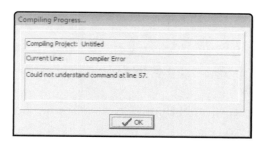

CodeSurge enjoys strong name recognition in the DarkBASIC Professional community. As of the writing of this book, you could download a free copy of CodeSurge by visiting the CodeSurge – DarkBASIC Professional IDE v1.0 thread located in the Program Announcements forum at the Game Creators' website (http://forum.thegamecreators.com/?m=forum_read&i=5).

Synergy IDE

The Synergy IDE boasts what its developer refers to as a Visual Studio look and feel. The Synergy IDE is designed to work with a number of different programming languages, include DarkBASIC, DarkBASIC Professional, and Omega Basic.

Synergy IDE works and operates very much like DarkBASIC Professional's default IDE. To create a new project, click on the New Project option located on the File menu and a popup dialog window displays that prompts you to specify the name of your new project. Once provided, you are presented with a new empty DarkBASIC Professional project. For the most part, you should not have any problems locating menu options, since they are pretty much organized the same way as with the default IDE.

Figure 2.27 shows an example of the Synergy IDE being used to edit a typical DarkBASIC Professional application. As you can see, the IDE contains both menus and a toolbar, which provide easy access to commonly accessed commands, much like the default IDE. The left-hand side of the IDE is used to display a series of different views, which are accessed via tabs located at the bottom of the IDE. In Figure 2.27, the Code View is displayed. From here you can easily view all of the current project's functions, types, labels, variables, errors, and constants.

FIGURE 2.27

The Synergy IDE is a multi-language IDE that also supports DarkBASIC Professional.

The right-hand side of the IDE is used to display the code editing area and an optional Output View, which displays information provided by DarkBASIC Professional whenever you save, compile, or execute your DarkBASIC applications. You should note that the Editing area allows you to open more than one file at a time and switch between the files by clicking on their associated tabs.

In working with the Synergy IDE, I found it to be both intuitive and highly reliable. Certainly, it is much less susceptible to crash than DarkBASIC Professional's default IDE. As Figure 2.28 shows, Synergy IDE is highly configurable—much more so than the default IDE.

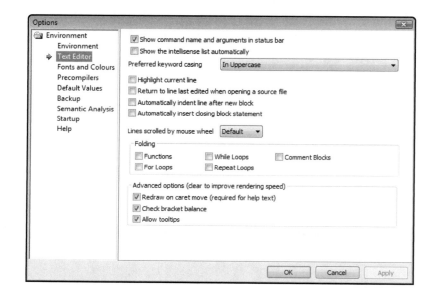

FIGURE 2.28

Synergy IDE provides a host of different configuration options.

As you would expect, Synergy IDE boasts a number of additional features, each of which is geared at simplifying project management and application development. These features include:

- Line numbering
- Syntax color highlighting
- Function, comment, while loop, for loop, and repeat loop folding
- Intellisense
- Tooltips
- Automatic indentation
- Error tracking and highlighting

You can download and learn more about the ongoing development of the Synergy IDE by visiting the Synergy Editor - FREE IDE for DarkBasic Professional thread located in the Work in Progress forum at the Game Creators' website (http://forum.thegamecreators.com/?m=forum_read&i=8).

> **HINT**
>
> As of the writing of this book, to download a free copy of the Synergy IDE, you could go to the Synergy Editor - FREE IDE for DarkBasic Professional thread located in the Work in Progress forum at http://forum.thegamecreators.com/?mlforum_read&il8 and scroll down until you locate the Synergy Editor - Available in the WIP forum posting, where you click on the Download button.

Unlike competing DarkBASIC Professional IDEs, Synergy IDE has a software dependency on Microsoft .NET Framework Version 2.0. In addition, the IDE also has a number of hardware requirements, which include

- 300 MHz Pentium III processor
- 6 MB hard disk space
- 64 MB of memory
- Windows 95, 98, Me, 2000, XP, and Vista

As you can see, none of these hardware requirements exceed those of DarkBASIC Professional and therefore should not pose any restrictions on your ability to use this IDE. All in all, Synergy IDE is an intuitive and reliable substitute for the DarkBASIC Professional default IDE and is certainly worthy of consideration as a substitute editor.

> **HINT**
>
> As of the publishing of this book, you could download a free copy of Microsoft Framework .NET 2.0 for free from the Microsoft Download Center located at http://www.microsoft.com/downloads/Search.aspx?displaylanglen.

BlueIDE

Blue IDE provides you with another alternative replacement for DarkBASIC Professional's default IDE. BlueIDE sports a slick user-friendly interface that provides easy access to all major functionality. BlueIDE is organized into a series of panels, each of which is controlled by tabs, allowing you to easily switch between different open files and application resources. As of the publishing of this book, the current version of BlueIDE, shown in Figure 2.29, was 2.00.13.

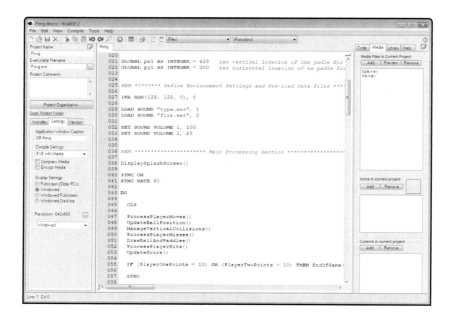

FIGURE 2.29

BlueIDE provides an intuitive and user-friendly integrated development environment.

As you would expect, BlueIDE provides a standard set of editor features, including:

- Line numbering
- Syntax color highlighting
- Function folding
- Intellisense
- Automatic indentation
- Error tracking and highlighting

In addition to these standard features, BlueIDE includes many unique features that differentiate it from competing IDEs, including:

- An option that lets you enable the automatic backup of your code and project files while you are working on them.
- An option that lets you instruct BlueIDE to automatically save your work every time you compile your application.
- A feature that allows you to create a library of commonly used code snippets that you can easily access and copy and paste into your code files.

- An advanced search feature that not only lets you search the file currently being edited but your entire project.
- A feature that allows you to set up shortcuts to functions and labels and then use these shortcuts as a way of moving around quickly within your program code file.

As previously mentioned, BlueIDE lets you enable Intellisense so that you can get assistance completing keywords or function calls by pressing the Ctrl+Space keys. In addition, BlueIDE can assist you in writing code statements by automatically completing loops and supplying matching parentheses and quotes. BlueIDE also provides the ability to preview both sound and graphic media files. For example, as demonstrated in Figure 2.30, BlueIDE's media browser lets you display 2D and 3D files, allowing you to see in advance how media files will look in your application.

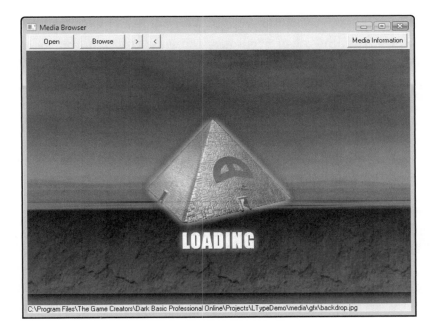

FIGURE 2.30

BlueIDE provides built-in media browsers that let you preview project media files.

To learn more about and download a free copy of BlueIDE, visit its homepage located at http://blueide.sourceforge.net. You can find additional information about BlueIDE by keeping an eye on the BlueIDE 2 thread located at the Game Creators' website Work in Progress forum (http://forum.thegamecreators.com/?m=forum_view&t=108639&b=8).

Operational Differences Between the IDEs

Each of the DarkBASIC Professional IDEs reviewed in this book shares a core set of basic functionality. In addition, each of the three third-party IDEs provides you with features not found in DarkBASIC Professional's default IDE. And of course, each of the three third-party IDEs has features that are unique to themselves.

One feature found in most Windows applications, but surprisingly lacking in all but one of the DarkBASIC Professional IDEs is the ability to open a project file by dragging and dropping it onto an open IDE. Specifically, the Synergy IDE supports this feature. However, the default IDE, BlueIDE, and CodeSurge do not.

Another difference in the ways the various IDEs operate is the manner in which they support the opening of DarkBASIC files using file associations. By default, if you double-click on a .dbpro file, Windows will start DarkBASIC Professional and load the file into it. However, the default IDE sometimes has trouble opening large project files using file association. This limitation can be overcome by opening the project to use the Open Project option located on the default IDE's File menu.

By default, none of the alternative DarkBASIC Professional IDEs override Windows file associations for DarkBASIC Professional files. However, both CodeSurge and BlueIDE supply you with the ability to modify DarkBASIC Professional file associations to associate them with these editors with the click of a mouse button. In CodeSurge, file associations can be automatically modified by clicking on the Associates DBPro Files with IDE option located on the IDE's File menu. In BlueIDE, file associations can be automatically modified to make BlueIDE the default program for DarkBASIC Professional files by clicking on the .dba and .dbpro buttons located on the Advanced tab of the IDE Options window, which is accessed by clicking on the Tools menu and selecting the IDE Options menu item. Although Synergy does not provide a means of changing DarkBASIC Professional file associations to set itself up as the default application, you can easily set this up yourself by right-clicking on any .dbpro files and selecting the Open with option from the context menu that appears and then selecting Synergy IDE. This step should be repeated twice, once for a .dbpro file and a second time for a .dba file.

TEXT, COLOR, AND GRAPHICS

In the last chapter and later in this chapter's game project, you work with a number of text, color, and graphics commands. For the most part, the commands are very intuitive. Still, a quick review of these commands, their purpose, and their syntax is required to ensure that you have a basic grasp of the concepts and programming methods involved.

Pixels and Text Placement

Within a DarkBASIC application, the text and graphics are written to the computer's screen based on a series of coordinates. Each coordinate position represents a *picture element*, commonly referred to as a *pixel*. A *pixel* is the smallest accessible point on the computer screen. It is made up of three color elements: red, green, and blue, also referred to as *RGB*.

 As you will learn a little later in this chapter, you can produce an incredible range of colors by controlling the brightness or intensity of the red, green, and blue colors.

The number of pixels available on the screen at any moment depends on the computer's current resolution setting. While all video graphics cards support a minimum resolution of 640×480, which equates to a screen displaying 640 columns along the x-axis and 480 rows across the y-axis, most video cards also support higher ranges such as 800×600, 1024×768, and 1600×1200.

As you can see, the coordinates have an x axis and a y axis. By specifying coordinate pairs you can target any individual pixel on the screen. For example, as demonstrated in Figure 2.31, coordinates 0, 0 represent the pixel located in the first row and first column position.

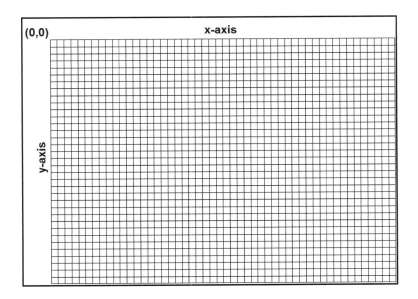

FIGURE 2.31

Text and graphics are drawn using a coordinate system.

Working with Text Commands

DarkBASIC Professional provides access to several commands that allow you to specify where text output is displayed on the computer screen. These commands include the SET, CURSOR, TEXT, and CENTER TEXT commands, each of which is reviewed in the sections that follow.

 In this book, I use all uppercase characters when typing in DarkBASIC Professional commands. However, DarkBASIC Professional is case-insensitive, meaning that you can use any combination of case that you want when typing in language keywords. However, I recommend that you select a particular style and stick with it. For example, in this book I will use all uppercase for language keywords.

Specifying Text Placement with the SET CURSOR Command

In previous examples, you have worked extensively with the PRINT command to display text on the computer screen. By default, the PRINT command begins displaying text using the system's default font starting at coordinates 0, 0. Additional PRINT statements are written beneath previous PRINT statements on different lines.

Rather than relying on DarkBASIC Professional's default behavior to determine where text output is placed, you can use the SET CURSOR command. This command lets you specify the x, y coordinates where you want the output of the next command to be written, and it has the following syntax.

```
SET CURSOR x, y
```

For example, using this command, the following examples display a text string of Once upon a time… starting at coordinates 50, 100.

```
SET CURSOR 20, 100
PRINT "Once upon a time ..."
```

Note the upper-left corner of the letter O begins at coordinates 20, 100.

Using the TEXT Command to Specify Text Placement

The PRINT command prints all text using the default system control. However, the TEXT command can be used to display text strings in a graphics mode that allows for different font types and sizes. The syntax for this command is shown here.

```
TEXT x, y, TextString
```

Here, x and y represent the coordinates where TextString should be displayed.

```
TEXT 20, 100, "Once upon a time ..."
```

As you can see, using the TEXT command, you can specify both the location where you want text to be displayed as well as the text itself, using a single command. Unlike the PRINT command, the TEXT command displays its output in a graphics mode. This allows it to use different font types and sizes.

Unlike the PRINT command, you cannot display numeric data using the TEXT command. Therefore the following statement would generate an error.

```
TEXT 200, 300, 5
```

To get around this issue, you could reformat the previous statement, as shown here:

```
TEXT 200, 300, "5"
```

Also, unlike the PRINT command, you can only display one string at a time using the TEXT command.

Using the CENTER TEXT Command to Center the Display of Text

The CENTER TEXT command is very similar to the TEXT command, except that instead of beginning the display of text output at a specified set of coordinates, the text string is centered horizontally around the specified location. The syntax for this command is shown here:

```
CENTER TEXT x, y, TextString
```

Here, x and y represent the coordinates around which *TextString* should be horizontally centered and displayed. For example, the following statement will display a text string in the middle of a window that has a resolution of 640 × 480, as demonstrated in Figure 3.32.

```
CENTER TEXT 320, 240, "Once upon a time ..."
```

Executing Font Commands

By default, DarkBASIC Professional displays text using the system's default font. However, you can set font type to any fonts installed on your computer. DarkBASIC Professional supplies a number of different commands that you can use to set font type and size when working with the TEXT and CENTER TEXT commands. In addition, DarkBASIC Professional also provides commands that you can use to set different font attributes, including bold, italic, and normal display attributes.

 DarkBASIC Professional commands that deal with font type, size, and attributes only work with the TEXT and CENTER TEXT commands and not with the PRINT command.

Displaying Text Using Different Font Types

The SET TEXT FONT command lets you specify the type of font you want to use when displaying text output. Of course, to use a given font, it must be installed on the computer where your DarkBASIC Professional application is executing. The syntax of the SET TEXT FONT command is outlined here:

```
SET TEXT FONT "FontName"
```

Note that the font type that you specify must be enclosed within a matching pair of double quotation marks. For example, the following statement demonstrates how to display a text string using a font type of Arial.

```
SET TEXT FONT "Arial"
CENTER TEXT 320, 240, "Once upon a time ..."
```

SET TEXT SIZE

The SET TEXT SIZE command lets you specify the size of the font that you want to use when displaying text output. Font size is specified in point, where each point equals 1/72 of an inch. Of course, if you specify a given font size, the font must support that size. The syntax of the SET TEXT SIZE command is outlined here:

```
SET TEXT SIZE PointSize
```

For example, the following statement demonstrates how to display text using an Arial font type and a font size of 18.

```
SET TEXT FONT "Arial"
SET TEXT SIZE 18
CENTER TEXT 320, 240, "Once upon a time ..."
```

Specifying Text Attributes

DarkBASIC Professional also supplies a small collection of commands that you can use to control different font attributes, including normal, italic, bold, and mixed bold and italic. The syntax of each of these commands is outlined here:

```
SET TEXT TO NORMAL
SET TEXT TO ITALIC
SET TEXT TO BOLD
SET TEXT TO BOLDITALIC
```

For example, the following statement demonstrates how to display text using an Arial font type set to font size of 18 with italics.

```
SET TEXT FONT "Arial"
SET TEXT SIZE 18
SET TEXT TO ITALIC
CENTER TEXT 320, 240, "Once upon a time ..."
```

Working with Color Commands

In addition to manipulating text type, size, location, and font attributes, you can also specify the colors you want to use when displaying text. This includes specifying both text color and background color. To do so, you need to learn how to work with two commands, the RGB command and the INK command.

Specifying Color Settings

To specify colors within a DarkBASIC Professional application, you must use the RGB command. This command accepts three arguments, which specify the values assigned to each of the three basic color elements (red, green, and blue). This command has the following syntax.

```
RGB(red, green, blue)
```

Here, *red*, *green*, and *blue* each represent a value between 0 and 255. A value of 0 specifies the absence of any color. A value of 255 specifies that color is set to its maximum intensity. Table 2.1 lists the values of a number of common colors.

Using Different Colors when Writing Text

To set background and foreground colors of the text that you want to display, you need to use the INK command. This command has the following syntax.

```
INK ForegroundColor, BackgroundColor
```

TABLE 2.1	COMMON RGB COLOR VALUES
Setting	**Color**
RGB(255, 255, 255)	White
RGB(0, 0, 0)	Black
RGB(255, 0, 0)	Red
RGB(0, 255, 0)	Green
RGB(0, 0, 255)	Blue
RGB(255, 255, 0)	Yellow
RGB(255, 128, 0)	Orange
RGB(128, 0, 128)	Purple
RGB(128, 64, 0)	Brown
RGB(128, 128, 128)	Dark Gray
RGB(192, 192, 192)	Light Gray
RGB(255, 128, 192)	Pink

ForegroundColor is the color that you want to be used when writing to the screen. *BackgroundColor* is the color to be displayed behind any text that is displayed on the screen. Note that for the background color to be displayed, you must also execute the SET TEXT TRANSPARENCY command, discussed later in this chapter. To get a better understanding of how to work with the INK command, take a look at the following example.

```
INK RGB(255, 255, 0), 0
CENTER TEXT 320, 240, "Once upon a time ..."
```

Here, a text string is written in yellow onscreen.

Clearing the Screen

You can clear the screen at any time using the CLS command. By default, DarkBASIC Professional clears the screen using a black background color. However, you can use the CLS command to clear the screen and display a background color of your choice. The syntax used by the CLS command is shown here:

```
CLS color
```

Here, *color* is any valid RGB value. For example, the following statement would clear the screen and display a solid blue background.

```
CLS RGB(0, 0, 255)
```

Erasing Text

There are a number of different ways that you can erase text once it has been written to the screen. You could, for example, use the CLS command. However, this would clear out the entire screen, which may not always be desirable. You could overwrite the string with a new string made up of blank spaces. However, you must be careful to ensure that you supply an adequate number of blank spaces to erase the desired text without accidentally supplying too many blank spaces and overwriting other parts of the screen. Perhaps the best way of deleting previously displayed text is to simply redisplay it after first changing its color to match the current background color, as demonstrated here:

```
CLS RGB(0, 0, 255)
INK RGB(255, 255, 0), 0
CENTER TEXT 320, 240, "Once upon a time ..."
WAIT KEY

INK RGB(0, 0, 255), 0
CENTER TEXT 320, 240, "Once upon a time ..."
```

```
WAIT KEY

INK RGB(255, 255, 0), 0
CENTER TEXT 320, 240, "in a far away land ..."
WAIT KEY

END
```

In this example, the screen is cleared and redisplayed with a blue background color. The INK command is then used to set the foreground color to yellow. A text string is then written to the screen. The example then pauses, waiting for a key to be pressed, after which the screen is again cleared and redisplayed with a blue background. Next, another INK command is executed, this time setting the foreground color to be the same color as the background color. The original text is then rewritten. Visually, this makes the original text disappear. The example again pauses and waits for a key to be pressed, after which a third INK command is executed, changing the foreground color back to yellow and a new text string is then displayed.

Executing Opaque and Transparency Commands

By default, DarkBASIC Professional prints all text using a transparent background. As a result, no matter what color you assign as an INK command background color, that background color is not used. However, you can override this behavior using the SET TEXT OPAQUE command. This command allows the background color assigned by the INK command to be seen. Any text that is then printed will be displayed on top of a solid background using the specified background color. The syntax of this command is outlined here:

```
SET TEXT OPAQUE
```

To get a better understanding of how to work with this command, take a look at the following example.

```
CLS RGB(0, 0, 0)
INK RGB(0, 0, 255), RGB(255, 255, 255)
SET TEXT FONT "Arial"
SET TEXT SIZE 48
SET TEXT OPAQUE
CENTER TEXT 320, 240, "Once upon a time ..."

WAIT KEY

END
```

Here, blue text with a white background is written on a screen whose background color is black, as shown in Figure 2.33.

Once upon a time ...

FIGURE 2.33

Displaying text with an opaque background.

If you want, you can reset DarkBASIC Professional's default behavior by executing the SET TEXT TRANSPARENT command. This command sets the background to allow text to be printed directly on top of any background color or image. The syntax of this command is outlined here:

```
SET TEXT TRANSPARENT
```

To get a better understanding of how to work with this command, take a look at the following example.

```
CLS RGB(0, 0, 0)
INK RGB(0, 0, 255), RGB(255, 255, 255)
SET TEXT FONT "Arial"
SET TEXT SIZE 48
SET TEXT TRANSPARENT
CENTER TEXT 320, 240, "Once upon a time ..."

WAIT KEY

END
```

Here, blue text with no background of its own is written on a screen whose background color is black, as shown in Figure 2.34.

FIGURE 2.34

Displaying text
with a transparent
background.

BACK TO THE FORTUNE TELLER GAME

Now it is time to turn your attention back to the development of this chapter's main project, the Fortune Teller game. Through the development of this game, you will get the opportunity to put your newfound understanding of working with graphic text commands to use. You will also learn how to work with several new commands, including commands required to generate random numbers, retrieve system time, and collect player input.

Designing the Game

The overall design of the Fortune Teller game is very straightforward. This game will run within a window that contains minimize, maximize, and close buttons in its upper-right corner, just like any other typical application window. As you follow along and create your own copy of this game, continue to keep your overall focus on the mechanics that are involved in creating DarkBASIC applications.

To help make things as easy as possible to understand and follow along, this game will be created by following a series of steps, as outlined here:

1. Create a new DarkBASIC project.
2. Specify game settings.
3. Document your application with comments.
4. Display a welcome message.
5. Display instructions.
6. Control game play.
7. Collect player questions.
8. Determine when to quit.
9. Generate answers.
10. Display a closing screen.
11. Save your new application.

Step 1: Creating a New DarkBASIC Project

The first step in creating the Fortune Teller game is to create a new project. Do so by starting DarkBASIC Professional and clicking on the New Project menu item located on the File menu. The Create a New DarkBASIC Professional Project window appears.

Type in **FortuneTeller** in the Project Name file and specify where you want your new project to be saved and then click on the OK button. In response, a new project is created for you.

Step 2: Configuring Game Settings

The next step in creating the Fortune Teller application is to modify a few application settings. Begin by clicking on the Project button located at the bottom of the Project Panel window. To help document this project, place the cursor in the Project Comments field and type **This game simulates a session with a Fortune Teller**.

Next, click on the Settings button. Type **Fortune Teller** in the Application Window Caption field. Select Windowed as display setting for this game and set the resolution to 640×480.

Step 3: Documenting Your DarkBASIC Application

With the project created and its project level settings now modified, it is time to add the program code statements needed to make your new application work. Begin by modifying the default comment statements that have been added to your application so that they match the statements shown here:

```
REM Project: FortuneTeller
REM Created: 9/15/2007 2:55:01 PM
REM Executable name: FortuneTeller.dba
REM Version: 1.0
REM Author: Jerry Lee Ford, Jr.
```

```
REM Description: This DarkBASIC application simulates a session with a
REM              Fortune Teller.
```

As you can see, the comment statements have been modified to provide additional information about the game and its author.

Step 4: Displaying a Welcome Message

Since the game is supposed to begin by displaying a welcome message, you next need to add the following statements to the end of the script file.

```
INK RGB(255, 255, 255), RGB(0, 0, 0)

SET TEXT FONT "Arial"

SET TEXT SIZE 48
CENTER TEXT 320, 150, "Welcome to The DarkBASIC"
CENTER TEXT 320, 220, "Fortune Teller Game!"
SET TEXT SIZE 16
CENTER TEXT 320, 380, "Press any key to continue"
WAIT KEY
```

As you can see, these statements begin by setting the foreground color to white and then setting the font type to Arial with a size of 48 points. Next, a welcome message is displayed using the CENTER TEXT command and another message is displayed. The WAIT KEY command is then executed, pausing application execution.

Step 5: Displaying Instructions

Once the player presses the key on the keyboard, the game displays instructions for playing. This is accomplished by adding the following statements to the end of the code file.

```
CLS
SET TEXT SIZE 24
CENTER TEXT 320, 120, "You are in luck! The Fortune Teller is taking"
CENTER TEXT 320, 150, "visitors today. But be brief, her time is limited."
CENTER TEXT 320, 180, "Keep your questions short and only expect Yes or"
CENTER TEXT 320, 210, "No answers."
CENTER TEXT 320, 270, "You may ask as many questions as you want. When"
CENTER TEXT 320, 300, "done, type QUIT to end game play."
SET TEXT SIZE 16
CENTER TEXT 320, 380, "Press any key to continue"
WAIT KEY
```

As you can see, after using the SET TEXT SIZE command to set the font size to 24, a series of strings is displayed. The font size is changed again and a final string is then displayed. The WAIT KEY command is executed again, pausing game play while the player reads the instructions.

Step 6: Setting Up a Loop to Control Game Play

The next step in the development of the Fortune Teller game is to set up a loop that repeatedly executes statements responsible for prompting the player to ask questions and for generating answers to those questions. To set this up, add the following statements to the end of the code file.

```
DO


LOOP
```

Any statements that you place within these two statements will execute over and over again. You will learn all about loops in Chapter 5, "Repeating Statement Execution Using Loops." For now, just add these two statements to the end of the code file.

Step 7: Collecting Player Questions

The next set of statements to be added to the code file is shown next and should be embedded inside the loop that you set up in the previous step.

```
CLS

INK RGB(255, 255, 0), RGB(0, 0, 0)

SET TEXT SIZE 24
TEXT 0, 50, "What is your question? "

INK RGB(255, 255, 255), RGB(0, 0, 0)

PRINT : PRINT : PRINT : PRINT
INPUT Question$
```

As you can see, these statements clear the screen, set the foreground color to yellow, and print out a string that serves as a prompt, instructing the player to enter a question. The INK command is then executed again, setting the foreground color to white. The player's question is then captured and stored in a variable named Question$.

The INPUT command displays an optional text message and pauses application execution to wait for the user to provide keyword input, allowing the application to resume execution when the Enter key has been pressed. The syntax of this command is shown here:

```
INPUT [string], variable
```

string represents an optional text string that if provided is displayed as a prompt, allowing you to display a message with instructions to the user as to what input is expected. *variable* represents a variable to which the user's input is assigned and stored. You will learn more about variables and their use in Chapter 3, "Working with Data Types, Variables, and Arrays."

Step 8: Determining Whether the Player Wants to Quit

The next set of statements to be added to the code file is shown next and should be embedded inside the application's loop, immediately after the previous set of statements.

```
IF QUESTION$ = "quit" or QUESTION$ = "Quit" or  QUESTION$ = "QUIT"
  EXIT
ENDIF
```

Here, an IF statement code block is used to check the player's input to see if the player entered the Quit command, and if this is the case, terminates the execution of the loop, allowing the rest of the statements in the code file to execute. You will learn all about the IF statement in Chapter 4, "Implementing Conditional Logic."

Step 9: Generating a Random Answer

The rest of the statements that make up the remainder of the programming logic in the application's loop are shown next and should be embedded inside the application's loop, immediately after the previous set of statements.

```
IF QUESTION$ <> ""

  seed = TIMER()
  RANDOMIZE seed

  answer = RND(4) + 1

  INK RGB(255, 255, 0), RGB(0, 0, 0)

  TEXT 0, 150, "Interesting question, let me think."
```

```
WAIT 3000

TEXT 330, 150, "Hum..."

WAIT 3000
SELECT answer
  CASE 1
    TEXT 0, 190, "Let's see. Ah, all is clear now."
    WAIT 2000
    TEXT 0, 230, "The answer to your question is yes."
  ENDCASE
  CASE 2
    TEXT 0, 190, "Give me a moment to focus on your future."
    WAIT 2000
    TEXT 0, 230, "It seems that the answer to your question is no."
  ENDCASE
  CASE 3
    TEXT 0, 190, "This is very strange."
    WAIT 2000
    TEXT 0, 230, "I cannot predict an answer to this question."
  ENDCASE
  CASE 4
    TEXT 1, 190, "You must be joking."
    WAIT 2000
    TEXT 0, 230, "Do not waste my time with this type of question!"
  ENDCASE
  CASE 5
    TEXT 0, 190, "Oh, yes I am seeing clearly now."
    WAIT 2000
    TEXT 0, 230, "The answer to your question is Yes"
  ENDCASE
ENDSELECT

SET TEXT SIZE 16
CENTER TEXT 320, 380, "Press any key to continue."

INK RGB(255, 255, 255), RGB(0, 0, 0)
```

```
WAIT KEY

CLS
```

```
ENDIF
```

For starters, all of these statements are embedded within an IF statement code block. The IF statement checks the player's input to ensure that the player did not just hit the Enter key when promoted to enter a question. Next, the TIMER() command is executed. This command retrieves the current time in milliseconds.

The TIMER() command is used to retrieve the computer's internal system time. This value is returned and assigned to a specified variable. The value that is returned is specified in milliseconds. 1,000 milliseconds represent a single second. The syntax of the TIMER() command is shown here:

variable = TIMER()

Here, *variable* represents the name of a variable to which the value returned by the TIMER() command will be assigned.

This value is used to generate a seed that is then used to generate a random number between 1 and 5.

The RANDOMIZE command is used to reseed DarkBASIC Professional's random number generator. If the random number generator is not seeded, it retrieves the exact same series of values. By passing a different seed each time your application is executed, you ensure that different numbers will be randomly generated. The syntax of this command is shown here:

RANDOMIZE *seed*

seed is a numeric value to be used by the random number generator. Many programmers use system time, retrieved using the TIMER() command, as the seed value.

The RND() command is used to generate a random number between 0 and a specified upper limit (integer). The syntax of this command is shown here:

Variable = RND(*UpperLimit*)

Here, *Variable* represents the name of a variable to which the value returned by the RND() command will be assigned, and *UpperLimit* is an integer value that specifies the maximum possible integer value that can be returned by the RND() command.

Next, the INK command is used to set the foreground color to yellow and then a text string representing the first part of the Fortune Teller's answer is displayed. The WAIT command is then executed, pausing application execution for three seconds. The next part of the Fortune Teller's response is then displayed followed by another three-second pause, after which one of five answers is displayed.

The answer that is selected for display depends on the value of the randomly generated number as analyzed by a SELECT code block. You will learn all about the SELECT statement in Chapter 4, "Implementing Conditional Logic." Finally, the SET TEXT SIZE command is executed and a text string instructing the player to press a keyboard key is displayed. The INK command is then used to set the foreground color to white and application execution is paused. Once the player presses a key, the screen is cleared and application execution resumes.

Step 10: Displaying a Closing Screen

The player can terminate game play at any time by either clicking on the application window's Close button or by entering the QUIT command. If the player enters the QUIT command, the game should clear the screen and display a final message, inviting the player to return and play again at a later date. This is accomplished by adding the following statements to the end of the script file.

```
CLS


SET TEXT SIZE 24
CENTER TEXT 320, 150, "So you have had enough. Very well, time is money"
CENTER TEXT 320, 180, "and there are others waiting to meet with the"
CENTER TEXT 320, 210, "Fortune Teller. Off you go. But feel free to"
CENTER TEXT 320, 240, "return at any time."
SET TEXT SIZE 16
CENTER TEXT 320, 380, "Press any key to continue"
WAIT KEY
CLS


END
```

Step 11: Saving and Compiling Your Application

At this point, your new application should be ready for testing. Before doing so, make sure that you save your work first by clicking on the Save All option located on the File menu. Once this has been done, click on the Make/EXE RUN option located on the Compile menu to try compiling and executing your application.

The Final Result

As long as you have not made any typos and you followed along with each step carefully, everything should work as described at the beginning of this chapter. To make things as clear as possible, I have provided a full copy of this application's source code next. If you run into any problems trying to run your copy of the Fortune Teller game, refer back to this copy of the game and use it to compare against your application's code statements and to look for any differences.

```
REM Project: FortuneTeller
REM Created: 9/29/2007 9:43:02 PM
REM Executable name: FortuneTeller.dba
REM Version: 1.0
REM Author: Jerry Lee Ford, Jr.
REM Description: This DarkBASIC application simulates a session with a
REM               Fortune Teller.


`Display white text on a black background
INK RGB(255, 255, 255), RGB(0, 0, 0)

SET TEXT FONT "Arial"  `Set the font type to Arial

SET TEXT SIZE 48  `Set the font size to 48 points
CENTER TEXT 320, 150, "Welcome to The DarkBASIC" `Display welcome message
CENTER TEXT 320, 220, "Fortune Teller Game!"
SET TEXT SIZE 16  `Set the font size to 16 points
CENTER TEXT 320, 380, "Press any key to continue"  `Display instructions
WAIT KEY  `Wait until the player presses a keyboard key
CLS  `Clear the display area

SET TEXT SIZE 24  `Set the font size to 24 points
`Display game instructions
CENTER TEXT 320, 120, "You are in luck! The Fortune Teller is taking"
CENTER TEXT 320, 150, "visitors today. But be brief, her time is limited."
CENTER TEXT 320, 180, "Keep your questions short and only expect Yes or"
CENTER TEXT 320, 210, "No answers."
CENTER TEXT 320, 270, "You may ask as many questions as you want. When"
```

```
CENTER TEXT 320, 300, "done, type QUIT to end game play."
SET TEXT SIZE 16  `Set the font size to 16 points
CENTER TEXT 320, 380, "Press any key to continue"
WAIT KEY  `Wait until the player presses a keyboard key

`This loop allows the player to ask an unlimited number of questions
DO

  CLS  `Clear the display area

  `Display yellow text on a black background
  INK RGB(255, 255, 0), RGB(0, 0, 0)

  SET TEXT SIZE 24  `Set the font size to 24 points
  TEXT 0, 50, "What is your question? "  `Prompt the player for a question

  `Display white text on a black background
  INK RGB(255, 255, 255), RGB(0, 0, 0)

  `By default, the PRINT statement begins displaying text at the top of
  `the screen. Execute four PRINT statements to ensure that the following
  `PRINT statement's output is properly placed
  PRINT : PRINT : PRINT : PRINT
  INPUT Question$  `Pause until the player types a question and capture
                   `the player's input

  `Check to see if the player has decided to quit playing
  IF QUESTION$ = "quit" or QUESTION$ = "Quit" or  QUESTION$ = "QUIT"
    EXIT  `Break out of the loop
  ENDIF

  `Do not allow the player to just press the Enter key without first
  `providing some input
  IF QUESTION$ <> ""

    seed = TIMER()  `Use the TIMER() function to retrieve a seed
    RANDOMIZE seed  `Seed the random number generator
```

```
answer = RND(4) + 1  `Generate a random number between 1 and 5

`Display yellow text on a black background
INK RGB(255, 255, 0), RGB(0, 0, 0)

`Begin responding to the player's question
TEXT 0, 150, "Interesting question, let me think."

WAIT 3000  `Pause for 3 seconds

TEXT 330, 150, "Hum..."  `Display a little more text

WAIT 3000  `Pause for 3 more seconds

`Use the randomly generated number to select and display an answer
SELECT answer
  CASE 1  `Display the following answer when the random number is 1
    TEXT 0, 190, "Let's see. Ah, all is clear now."
    WAIT 2000  `Pause for 2 seconds
    TEXT 0, 230, "The answer to your question is yes."
  ENDCASE
  CASE 2`Display the following answer when the random number is 2
    TEXT 0, 190, "Give me a moment to focus on your future."
    WAIT 2000  `Pause for 2 seconds
    TEXT 0, 230, "It seems that the answer to your question is no."
  ENDCASE
  CASE 3`Display the following answer when the random number is 3
    TEXT 0, 190, "This is very strange."
    WAIT 2000  `Pause for 2 seconds
    TEXT 0, 230, "I cannot predict an answer to this question."
  ENDCASE
  CASE 4`Display the following answer when the random number is 4
    TEXT 1, 190, "You must be joking."
    WAIT 2000  `Pause for 2 seconds
    TEXT 0, 230, "Do not waste my time with this type of question!"
  ENDCASE
  CASE 5`Display the following answer when the random number is 5
    TEXT 0, 190, "Oh, yes I am seeing clearly now."
```

```
      WAIT 2000  `Pause for 2 seconds
      TEXT 0, 230, "The answer to your question is Yes"
    ENDCASE
  ENDSELECT

  SET TEXT SIZE 16  `Set the font size to 16 points
  CENTER TEXT 320, 380, "Press any key to continue."

  `Display white text on a black background
  INK RGB(255, 255, 255), RGB(0, 0, 0)

  WAIT KEY  `Wait until the player presses a keyboard key

  CLS  `Clear the display area

 ENDIF

LOOP

cls  `Clear the display area

SET TEXT SIZE 24  `Set the font size to 24 points
`Display the game's closing message
CENTER TEXT 320, 150, "So you have had enough. Very well, time is money"
CENTER TEXT 320, 180, "and there are others waiting to meet with the"
CENTER TEXT 320, 210, "Fortune Teller. Off you go. But feel free to"
CENTER TEXT 320, 240, "return at any time."
SET TEXT SIZE 16  `Set the font size to 16 points
CENTER TEXT 320, 380, "Press any key to continue"
WAIT KEY  `Wait until the player presses a keyboard key
CLS  `Clear the display area

END  `Terminate game play
```

You will find a copy of this application's project file along with source code on this book's companion website, located at http://www.courseptr.com/ downloads.

SUMMARY

This chapter has provided you with a thorough review of the DarkBASIC Professional integrated development environment, pointing out major features and explaining how things work. This chapter also addressed a number of shortcomings of the default IDE and provided an overview of a number of alternative IDEs that not only address these shortcomings but also provide a host of additional advanced features. You also learned about a number of text and color display and manipulation commands.

Before you move on to Chapter 3, I suggest you set aside a few minutes to try and improve the Fortune Teller game by implementing the following list of challenges.

CHALLENGES

1. As currently written, the game's instructions are a little sparse. Make them more useful by adding text that provides a better understanding of how the game is played.
2. Currently, the Fortune Teller game only has five different answers from which to choose. It does not take long before this becomes obvious to the player. Consider making things a little more interesting by expanding the number of available answers from five to ten or more. Also, make an effort to make any new answers that you add as funny and distinct as possible.

Part II

Learning How to Write DarkBASIC Applications

WORKING WITH DATA TYPES, VARIABLES, AND ARRAYS

E ven the most simple computer application needs to store and access data in some manner. Sometimes this data may be embedded inside the application's source program code. However, most of the time at least some input is needed from the outside world. In the case of computer games, this means accepting and processing player input, which might be provided by the mouse, keyboard, or joystick. No matter where the data comes from, your DarkBASIC Professional application needs a place to store it. In this chapter, you will learn about a number of different ways in which you can store and retrieve data using computer memory. In addition, you will learn how to create your next computer application, the Number Guessing game.

Specifically, you will learn:

- How to store and retrieve data using variables
- The rules for naming variables
- How to create and work with constants
- How to work with groups of data using arrays
- About the different data types supported by DarkBASIC Professional

PROJECT PREVIEW: THE NUMBER GUESSING GAME

This chapter's game project is the Number Guessing game. This DarkBASIC Professional game demonstrates how to use variables to collect, process, and analyze data collected from the player during game play. Specifically, the game challenges the player to try and guess a randomly generated number between 1 and 100 in as few guesses as possible. When first started, the game displays the screen shown in Figure 3.1.

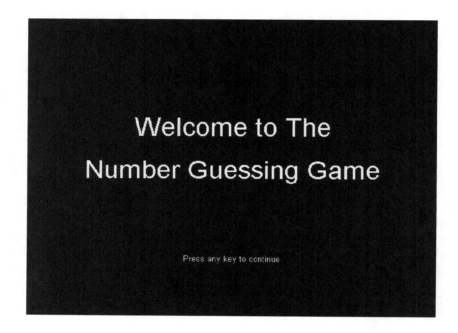

Welcome to The
Number Guessing Game

Press any key to continue

After pressing any keyboard key, game play begins and the player is prompted to enter a guess, as shown in Figure 3.2.

The game analyzes the player's guess to determine if the player has guessed the game's secret number. If the player has not guessed the secret number, the game displays a message informing the player that her guess was incorrect. Figure 3.3 shows the message that is displayed if the player's guess was higher than the game's secret number.

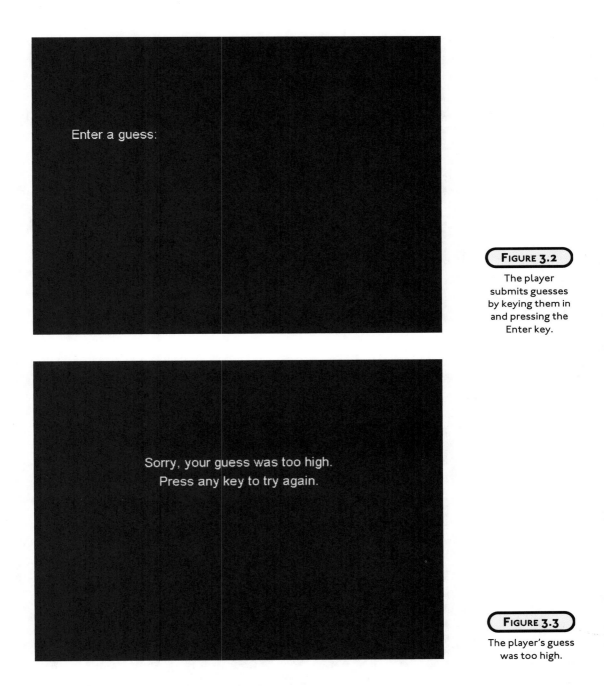

FIGURE 3.2

The player submits guesses by keying them in and pressing the Enter key.

FIGURE 3.3

The player's guess was too high.

Figure 3.4 shows the message that is displayed if the player's guess was lower than the game's secret number.

FIGURE 3.4

The player's guess was too low.

The player may make as many guesses as necessary to finally figure out the game's secret number. When the player has correctly guessed the game's number, the message shown in Figure 3.5 displays.

FIGURE 3.5

The player has guessed the secret number.

At the end of each round of play, the player is prompted to either quit or play another game, as shown in Figure 3.6.

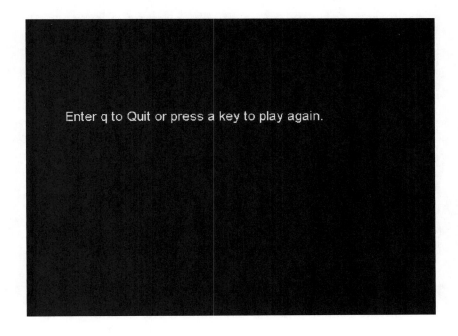

Enter q to Quit or press a key to play again.

FIGURE 3.6

The player can enter a q to quit the game or press any other key to play another round.

When the player has had enough and types q to quit, the screen shown in Figure 3.7 displays.

The game is played in full screen mode. In addition to typing a q to quit the game, the player can also press the Escape key to halt game play.

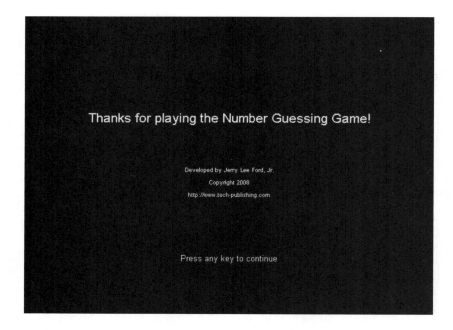

Thanks for playing the Number Guessing Game!

Developed by Jerry Lee Ford, Jr.

Copyright 2008

http://www.tech-publishing.com

Press any key to continue

FIGURE 3.7

The Number Guessing game's closing screen.

STORING AND MANIPULATING DATA

All computer games and applications manipulate data in some manner. *Data* is information that your application processes, collects, stores, modifies, and displays when it executes. For example, in a computer game, data can be the player's name, the number of points scored, or the amount of time left to play. DarkBASIC Professional supports three basic types of data.

- **Integer.** Any whole number.
- **Real.** Any number that includes a decimal point.
- **String.** Any set of characters enclosed within matching double quotation marks.

Data can be embedded inside your application, retrieved from files stored on the computer, passed to the program at runtime, or collected interactively from the player. For example, in a guessing game the player might be required to use the keyboard to submit guesses, whereas in an arcade-style game, input might come from a joystick, indicating which direction the player wants to move or when the player wants to shoot.

Data must be stored in the computer's memory to be used by your game or application. The location in memory where data is stored is referred to as an address. DarkBASIC Professional lets you store individual pieces of data in variables and to refer to the location in memory where the data is stored by simply referring to the variable's name.

Keeping Track of Your Program's Data

DarkBASIC Professional provides you with many different ways of storing data. Perhaps the simplest option is to hard-code literal values into your script statements, as demonstrated here:

```
PRINT "Today is 10/11/07."
```

As you can see, a text string containing a date is displayed using the PRINT command. Although effective for displaying static information that never changes, storing data in this manner is very limiting. Instead, DarkBASIC Professional lets you store data in a number of different ways, including variables, arrays, constants, DATA statements, and user-defined data types.

Variables are useful for storing individual pieces of data that may need to change during program execution. Arrays are used to store groups of related data, such as a list of items collected by the player during game play. Constants are used to store data that never changes. For example, the mathematical value of pi is an excellent candidate for a value that should be stored in a constant. DATA statements are lists of data that you can embed within your source code and then retrieve as individual data elements whenever you need them. A user-defined data type is an advanced structure that you define that can hold any number of related pieces of data. Each of these different options is uniquely suited to different types of situations, which will be explained as you make your way through this chapter.

Working with Integers, Real Numbers, and Strings

DarkBASIC Professional supports three basic types of data: integers, real numbers, and strings. DarkBASIC Professional treats integers, real numbers, and strings differently. For example, numbers can be added together to produce a new numeric value. Strings, on the other hand, can be concatenated together, resulting in a new, longer string. Numeric data can also be subtracted, multiplied, and deleted. No such operations can be performed on strings.

When it comes to working with numeric data, DarkBASIC Professional allows you to specify different data types. These data types, listed in Table 3.1, determine how much memory is required to store individual instances of data and determine the range of possible values that can be stored.

HINT

Computers use a binary language that is made up entirely of 0s and 1s. These 0s and 1s represent bits (binary digits). A bit can contain either of two values (0 or 1). A byte is made up of 8 bits and can be used to represent up to 256 (0 to 255) values. As Table 3.1 shows, using more bits allows you to store larger numbers.

Data Type	Bits	Range
TABLE 3.1		**DARKBASIC PROFESSIONAL DATA TYPES**
BYTE	8	0 to 255
WORD	16	0 to 65,535
DWORD	32	0 to 4294967295
INTEGER	32	−2,147,483,647 to 2,147,483,647
FLOAT	32	3.4E+/−38
DOUBLE FLOAT	64	1.7E+/−308
DOUBLE INTEGER	64	−9,223,372,036,854,755,808 to 9,223,372,036,854,755,807

To specify a numeric value's data type, you use the following syntax.

Variable AS *DataType*

Here, *Variable* represents the name of the variable being created. AS is a required keyword and *DataType* is placeholder representing one of the data types supported by DarkBASIC Professional. Once defined, you can assign a value to the variable, as shown here:

```
TotalScore AS INTEGER
TotalScore = 10
```

Alternatively, you can assign a value to a variable at the time that it is initially declared using the following syntax.

Variable AS *DataType* = *Value*

Using this syntax, you could rewrite the previous example as shown here and the result would be the same.

```
TotalScore AS INTEGER = 10
```

By specifying data type, you tell DarkBASIC Professional how much memory to set aside to store a piece of data. Smaller numbers require less memory than larger numbers. Therefore, by setting aside less memory, when appropriate, you can create more efficient program code that utilizes fewer system resources.

Proper specification of data type not only helps reduce the amount of memory required to store data but it also can have an impact on your program's data. For example, consider the following.

```
x AS INTEGER = 5
PRINT x
```

Here a variable named x is defined as an integer and assigned a value of 5, which is then displayed on the screen. Now, let's modify this example, as shown here:

```
x AS INTEGER
= 5.5
PRINT x
```

If you try to execute this example, an error will appear as demonstrated in Figure 3.8. The reason for the error is that it is illegal to assign a floating point number to an integer.

FIGURE 3.8

An error is generated if you attempt to assign a floating point to an integer when you initially declare it.

Now, let's modify this example one more time, as shown here:

```
x AS INTEGER
x = 5.5
PRINT x
```

This time the variable x is defined as an integer and then it is assigned a floating point value in a different statement. This time DarkBASIC Professional does not flag the assignment as an error. Instead, it allows the assignment. However, since x can only store an integer value, everything after the decimal point is lost, and as a result a value of 5 is stored. Therefore, it is very important that you consider the type of data that you will need to store in a variable when defining its data type.

Although not listed in Table 3.1, DarkBASIC Professional also supports a string data type. Strings are created by enclosing characters within matching pairs of double-quotation marks. A string can be of any length, limited only by the amount of available memory on the computer.

Unlike a number of programming languages, DarkBASIC Professional does not support date and time data types. Instead, it provides you with access to the GET DATE$ and GET TIME$ commands. The GET DATE$ command returns a string in a MM/DD/YY format. The GET TIME$ command returns a string formatted as HH:MM:SS. You can use the commands as demonstrated below.

```
PRINT "The current date is " ; GET DATE$()
PRINT "The current time is " ; GET TIME$()

WAIT KEY
```

When executed, output similar to the following will be displayed on the screen.

```
The current date is 10/11/08
The current time is 13:12:56
```

You can also assign the results returned by these commands to variables, as demonstrated here:

```
CurrentDate$ = GET DATE$()
CurrentTime$ = GET TIME$()

PRINT "The current date is " + CurrentDate$
PRINT "The current time is " + CurrentTime$

WAIT KEY
```

WORKING WITH VARIABLES

Anytime you need to collect, store, and modify data within your DarkBASIC Professional applications, you need to work with variables. A *variable* is a pointer to a location in memory where data is stored. Variables store individual pieces of data during program execution. Unlike many programming languages, DarkBASIC Professional does not require that you formally declare a variable and its type before you can assign data to it. Instead, DarkBASIC Professional lets you create variables on the fly by simply assigning data to them.

Defining New Variables

Every individual variable that you use must be uniquely named and must follow the variable naming rules, outlined a little later in this chapter. Unlike some programming languages, DarkBASIC Professional does not require that you explicitly declare a variable prior to using it. Instead, you can create a new variable by simply using it for the first time. In order to assign a value to a variable, you must use the = operator. For example, the following statement creates a new variable named InitialScore and assigns it a value of zero.

```
InitialScore = 0
```

Assuming that the `InitialScore` variable has not been previously defined, it would be automatically created as soon as this statement executed. The ability to create and work with variables on the fly allows for flexibility but it also allows for sloppy programming. It is important to check the spelling of all variable names that you use. If you accidentally mistype a variable name, instead of displaying an error, DarkBASIC Professional will happily create a new variable for you, which can lead to some much unexpected results, as demonstrated here:

```
TotalPoints = 10
NewPoints = 2

TotalPoints = NewPoint + TotalPoints
PRINT TotalPoints
```

Here, the intention was to increase the value of `TotalPoints` by adding it to the value of `NewPoints`. However, there is a typo on the third line. Here, `NewPoints` is mistyped as `NewPoint`. Rather than report that an error has occurred, DarkBASIC Professional instead creates a new variable on the fly named `NewPoint` and assigns it a default value of 0. As a result, the value assigned to `TotalPoints` remains set to 10.

Assigning Data to Your Variables

As with most programming languages, DarkBASIC Professional will assign a default value to any variables that you create if you do not assign an initial value yourself. Unassigned numeric variables are assigned a default value of 0. Unassigned string variables are assigned a default value of `""` (an empty string). To avoid default assignments and to make your program statements easier to understand, always explicitly assign an initial value to all variables.

Controlling Access to Variables

Depending on where and how variables are defined, you may find that you are unable to access them as expected. The reason for this is variable scope. *Scope* defines the location within your application's source code from which a variable can be accessed. Specifically, DarkBASIC Professional supports two types of scope, local and global, as outlined here:

- **Local.** Variable access is limited to the function within which a variable is created.
- **Global.** Variable access is available everywhere within the application.

Creating Global Variables

In DarkBASIC Professional, global variables are defined using the following syntax.

```
GLOBAL Variable AS DataType
```

GLOBAL is a required keyword that identifies the variable being global. *Variable* is a placeholder representing the name of the variable being defined. AS is another required keyword and *DataType* is a placeholder representing one of the data types supported by DarkBASIC Professional.

As an example of how to define a global variable, take a look at the following statement.

```
GLOBAL PlayerName$ AS STRING
```

Here, a variable named PlayerName$ has been defined that can be accessed from any location within the application.

 It is considered a good programming practice to limit access to variables whenever possible. This helps to conserve memory while also eliminating the possibility that the variable could be accidentally modified from a different location within the program.

Creating Local Variables

Local variables are accessible only within the function in which they are defined.

 A *function* is a named collection of code statements that are called upon to execute as a unit. You will learn all about functions and how they work in Chapter 6, "Organizing Code Logic Using Functions."

By default, any variable defined outside of a function or inside another function is not accessible from inside any of the application's other functions. In addition, any variable defined inside a function cannot be accessed from outside of the function. The following example demonstrates how to create a local variable within a function.

```
Test()
PRINT x
WAIT KEY
END

FUNCTION Test
  x = 5
  PRINT x
ENDFUNCTION
```

Here, a call is made to a function named Test. Within the function, a variable named x is created and assigned a value of 5, which is then displayed on the screen. Once the function has finished executing, a second PRINT statement is executed, this time outside of the function. Since x is a variable local to the Test function, it is not accessible outside of the function, so a value of zero is displayed.

Rules for Naming Variables

As you formulate names for the variables in your DarkBASIC Professional applications, make sure that you assigned names that are as descriptive as possible, without making them too long and cumbersome. This will help better document your source code. In addition to following this advice, DarkBASIC Professional has a number of rules that you must follow when assigning names to variables, as outlined here:

- Variable names must begin with a letter.
- Variable names can only contain letters, numbers, and the underscore characters.
- Variable names cannot contain blank spaces.
- Variable names cannot be DarkBASIC Professional language keywords.

DarkBASIC Professional variable names can be as long as you want. However, it is best to keep them as short as possible while still ensuring that they are descriptive. DarkBASIC Professional variable names are case-insensitive. Therefore, as far as DarkBASIC Professional is concerned, references to variables named Score, score, SCORE, and ScOrE are all references to the same variable.

DarkBASIC Professional supports three different types of variables: integer, real, and string. Integer variables follow all of the naming rules previously outlined. For example, the following statements assign a value of zero to an integer variable named InitialScore.

```
InitialScore = 0
```

Real variables, on the other hand, must end with the # character, as demonstrated here:

```
SubTotal# = 10.33
```

TRAP Be careful when performing calculations with real numbers. DarkBASIC Professional may round the result. As a result, while you might anticipate an assignment of 10.3, DarkBASIC Professional might assign a value of 10.29999.

Finally, string variable names must end with the $ character, as demonstrated here:

```
PlayerName$ = "Jerry"
```

In addition, the value assigned to a string variable must be enclosed inside matching double quotation marks.

While DarkBASIC Professional is case-insensitive and therefore sees SCORE and score as the same thing, it does not view any of the following variables as being the same.

Score
Score#
Score$

Instead, what DarkBASIC Professional sees is three separate variables, one integer variable, one real variable, and one string variable.

Converting Between Numbers and Strings

Depending on what your DarkBASIC Professional applications are designed to do, you may come across situations in which you want to convert a value from one data type to another. DarkBASIC Professional provides two commands specifically aimed at performing this task. These commands are outlined here:

- **VAL**. Converts a string to a real number.
- **STR$**. Converts an integer or real number to a string.

Converting a Number to a String

Using DarkBASIC Professional's STR$ command, you can convert any numeric variable into a string. This can come in handy in a situation such as when you want to print out numbers as strings on the screen. The STR$ command has the following syntax.

STR$(*number*)

To get a better feel for how the STR$ command works, consider the following example.

```
TotalScore# = 100
PRINT "Your score is " + STR$(TotalScore#)
```

Here, the value assigned to TotalScore# is converted to a string, appended to another string using the concatenation operator, and then displayed.

Concatenation is the process of creating a new string by appending two or more strings together. In DarkBASIC Professional, the + operator is used to perform concatenate operations on strings.

If you were to try and print the value of TotalScore# in the previous example, without first converting it to a string, as demonstrated here, an error would result and the error message shown in Figure 3.9 would be displayed.

```
TotalScore# = 100
PRINT "Your score is " + TotalScore#
```

FIGURE 3.9

An error occurs if you attempt to add a string to a numeric value.

Converting a String to a Number

Just as you can convert a number to a string, you can also convert a string to a number using the VAL command. However, in order to do so, the string that you are converting must be in a form that can be translated into a number. By this I mean that the string must be something like "12345" or "99.9" and not something like "apples" or "ninety nine." To convert a string to a number, you must use the VAL command, which has the following syntax.

```
VAL(string)
```

Here, *string* represents the text string to be converted. To get a better feel for how to work with the VAL command, take a look at the following example.

```
INPUT "Enter your age: ", Age$
PlayerAge = VAL(AGE$) + 1
PRINT "You are " + STR$(PlayerAge)
```

Here, the INPUT command is used to prompt the user to enter her age. The number entered by the user is then assigned to a string variable named Age$. Next, the player input is converted from a string to a number and then assigned to a variable named PlayerAge after being arbitrarily incremented by 1. Finally, the value assigned to PlayerAge is displayed. However, since PlayerAge is an integer, it must first be converted to a string before it can be displayed.

Doing a Little Arithmetic

Like most programming languages, DarkBASIC Professional provides access to a large number of commands designed specifically to assist in performing mathematical calculations. Table 3.2 provides a quick review of some of the numeric commands provided by DarkBASIC Professional.

TABLE 3.2	DARKBASIC PROFESSIONAL MATHEMATICAL COMMANDS	
Command	**Syntax**	**Description**
ABS	ABS(Value)	Returns the positive equivalent of any numeric value
SQRT	SQRT(Value)	Returns the square root of a specified numeric value
EXP	EXP(Value)	Returns the results of a number raised to the power
INT	INT(Value)	Returns the integer portion of a number

HINT

If you have experience with another programming language, you may have noticed that many of DarkBASIC Professional's commands are really just language functions. To stay consistent with DarkBASIC Professional terminology, this book will use the term "command" throughout.

Using these commands, you can perform a number of calculations without having to understand the complex mathematical formulas that are used behind the scenes. Using these commands, you can greatly simplify your program code. To use one of these commands, all that you need to do is to place the numeric value that you want to work with inside the command's parentheses, as demonstrated here:

```
Score# = 10.5
TotalScore = INT(Score#)
PRINT "Your score is " + STR$(TotalScore)
```

In this example, a value of 10.5 is assigned to a variable named Score#. The INT command is then used to retrieve the integer portion of the number and reassign it to TotalScore, which is then displayed.

Manipulating String Contents

As has been demonstrated a number of times already in this book, you can join or concatenate two strings together to create a new string using the + operator, as demonstrated here:

```
FirstNames$ = "Jerry"
LastName$ = "Ford"
FullName$ = FirstNames$ + " " + LastName$
PRINT FullName$
```

When executed, these statements display the following output.

```
Jerry Ford
```

In addition to supporting string concatenation, DarkBASIC Professional provides access to a number of string manipulation commands. Using these commands, you can extract portions of a string, convert characters from lower- to uppercase, and vise versa. Table 3.3 outlines a number of DarkBASIC Professional's more commonly used string commands.

TABLE 3.3   DARKBASIC PROFESSIONAL STRING MANIPULATION COMMANDS

Command	Syntax	Description
MID$	MID$(String, Position)	Retrieves a character from a string based on its position
LEFT$	LEFT$(String, Position)	Retrieves a specified number of characters from the left-hand side of a string
RIGHT$	RIGHT$(String, Position)	Retrieves a specified number of characters from the right-hand side of a string
LOWER$	LOWER$(String)	Converts all of the characters of a string to lowercase
UPPER$	UPPER$(String)	Converts all of the characters of a string to uppercase
SPACE$	SPACE$(Spaces)	Returns a string made up of a specified number of blank spaces
LEN	LEN(String)	Returns an integer value that represents the number of characters in a string

To get a better understanding of how to work with the commands listed in Table 3.3, take a look at the following example.

```
StoryText$ = "Once upon a time"

PRINT UPPER$(StoryText$)     `Displays ONCE UPON A TIME
PRINT LOWER$(StoryText$)     `Displays once upon a time
PRINT MID$(StoryText$, 2)    `Displays n
PRINT LEFT$(StoryText$, 4)   `Displays Once
PRINT RIGHT$(StoryText$, 4)  `Displays time

`Displays The variable is 16 characters long.
PRINT "The variable is " + STR$(LEN(StoryText$)) + " characters long."
```

The embedded comments show the results that are generated when each command is executed.

STORING DATA THAT NEVER CHANGES

As useful as variables are for storing all kinds of data, they are not appropriate for storing data that is not subject to change during program execution because the contents of variables can be accidentally modified. Instead, a better solution is to use constants. A *constant* is a descriptive name assigned to a value that is known as design time and which does not change when the program executes.

Data assigned to a constant cannot be changed. For example, if you developed an application that needs to perform complex mathematical calculations, you might assign the value of pi (3.14) to a constant at the beginning of your program file and then refer to it whenever necessary. Similarly, if you created a computer game that awarded an extra life when the player reached a certain score, you might save this value in a constant.

To define a constant within a DarkBASIC Professional program, you must use the #CONSTANT command, which has the following syntax.

```
#CONSTANT ConstantName [=] AssignedValue
```

Here, *ConstantName* is the name of the constant being defined and *AssignedValue* is the value that the constant will store. Note that the use of the equals sign is optional. As a demonstration of how to define a constant, take a look at the following statement.

```
#CONSTANT NewLife = 10000
```

Although constants can contain integers, real numbers, or strings, you are not allowed to end their names with the # or $ characters. Constant names can only consist of alphanumeric characters.

Here, a constant named NewLife has been defined and assigned a value of 10000. Alternatively, you could rewrite this statement as shown next and the result would be the same since the equals sign is optional.

```
#CONSTANT NewLife 10000
```

Not only are constants advantageous because their values cannot be accidentally changed, but when assigned a descriptive name, they can make your source code self-documenting. On top of all this, constants typically require less memory than variables, providing your application with additional efficiency gains.

EMBEDDING DATA IN YOUR CODE FILE

In addition to storing data in your program by hard coding individual pieces of data in variable or constant assignments, you can embed data within your DarkBASIC Professional program using the DATA statement, which has the following syntax.

```
DATA value1, … valueN
```

Here, *value1* through *valueN* represents a comma-separated list of values assigned to the DATA statement. For example, you might use a DATA statement in a computerized version of the hangman word guessing game as a way of storing a list of words that the game could draw upon. In this example, the DATA statement might look like the following.

```
DATA "House", "Capital", "Computer", "Tissue", "Car", "Window", "Mouse"
```

Here, a list made up of seven strings representing words to be used by the hangman game has been set up. If you want to expand the size of the word pool in the game you could do so by adding additional DATA statements, as demonstrated here:

```
DATA "House", "Capital", "Computer", "Tissue", "Car", "Window", "Mouse"
DATA "Pencil", "Desk", "Game", "Laptop", "Picture", "Tree", "Elephant"
DATA "Puppy", "Yard", "Summer", "Treadmill", "Glove", "Hat", "Stove"
```

When more than one DATA statement is added to a DarkBASIC Professional program, the contents of all DATA statements are combined and treated as one long statement. Although there is no effective limit on the amount of data that you can store using DATA statements, these statements are really only effective in small programs and can become difficult to maintain as the amount of data you want to define grows.

You can place DATA statements anywhere you want within your programs. However, it is a good idea to place them together at the beginning of your source code where they can be easily located and modified.

To retrieve data stored in a DATA statement, you must use the READ command, which has the following syntax.

```
READ variable
```

Here, *variable* represents a variable into which the individual data items are read. The first time a READ command is executed, it will retrieve the first item stored in a DATA statement. DarkBASIC Professional automatically keeps track of data as it is retrieved from DATA statements using the READ command. As a result, the second execution of a READ command will retrieve the second item stored in a DATA statement. As such, you do not have to worry about keeping track of things.

You can mix and match different types of data stored in DATA statements. However, when you later use the READ command to retrieve items from DATA statements, you must ensure that it is assigned appropriately the correct variable type (integer, real, or string).

As an example of how to use the READ command, consider the following.

```
DATA "House", "Capital", "Computer", "Tissue", "Car", "Window", "Mouse"
READ SecretWord$
PRINT "The secret word is: " + SecretWord$
READ SecretWord$
PRINT "The secret word is: " + SecretWord$
```

When executed, this example displays the following output.

```
The secret word is: House
The secret word is: Capital
```

Subsequent executions of the READ command would retrieve additional values from the DATA statement.

 An error will occur if your program executes a READ command and there is no DATA statement in your application. An error will also occur if a READ command is executed and all of the items stored in a DATA statement have already been previously retrieved. One way around this is to create DATA statements that contain a known arbitrary number of items and to keep count of the number of read operations that are performed. Another way of dealing with this challenge is to end your DATA statements with a value that signals the end of the list, as demonstrated here:

```
DO

  DATA "House", "Capital", "Computer", "Tissue", "Car", "Window", "END"
  READ SecretWord$

  IF SecretWord$ = "END"
    EXIT
  ELSE
    PRINT "The secret word is " + SecretWord$
  ENDIF

LOOP
```

Here, a loop and an IF statement code block are used to process all of the items stored in a DATA statement, stopping when the "END" word is found. "END" in this example, is not considered to be a data item but rather is a known value that signals that the end of the DATA statement has been reached. Loops and IF statements are not covered until Chapters 4 and 5. As such, you might want to bookmark this page and return once you have finished reading those chapters.

One last command that you should know about when working with DATA statements is the RESTORE command, which has the following syntax.

RESTORE

When executed, the RESTORE command instructs DarkBASIC Professional to reset the marker that it uses internally to keep track of the data items as they are retrieved by the READ command. As a result, once the RESTORE command has been executed, any subsequent READ commands will retrieve items starting at the beginning of the program's DATA statement.

STORING AND RETRIEVING COLLECTIONS OF DATA

If your application is only dealing with a few pieces of data at a time, then variables may be all you need to effectively manage the program's data. However, if you are working on an application that requires you to keep track of large amounts of information, you may be better served storing and managing program data using arrays. An *array* is an indexed list of data stored and managed as a unit. Data that you store inside an array is accessed by specifying the array's name and then the index position of the data that needs to be stored or retrieved. Arrays can be used to store any number of items, limited only by the available amount of computer memory.

Although similar in many respects to DATA statements, arrays are far more flexible, allowing you to collect, store, and modify data during application execution.

DarkBASIC Professional lets you create single- and multi-dimensional arrays. A single-dimensional array is like a list, whereas a two-dimensional array is like a spreadsheet made up of rows and columns. Although DarkBASIC Professional lets you create arrays with up to five dimensions, this book will focus on teaching you the basics of working with single-dimensional arrays.

Defining an Array

In DarkBASIC Professional, arrays can only store data that is of the same data type. In other words, you can create an array that contains strings or an array containing integers, but you cannot create an array that contains both. Like variables, you must end an array name that contains real numbers with the # character and an array that contains strings with the $ character. An array that contains integers does not have a mandatory ending character.

To define an array, you must use the DIM command, which has the following syntax.

```
DIM ArrayName(dimensions) AS DataType
```

Here, *ArrayName* represents the name of the array being created, *dimensions* represents a comma-separated list of values that specifies how many dimension the array has, and DataType specifies the type of data that the array can store. The following statements demonstrate how to define an array named Characters$() that is capable of storing five elements.

```
DIM Characters$(4)
```

Arrays are zero-based, therefore in the above example, the first element in the array begins at index position 0 and the fifth element ends at index position 4. Once defined, you can assign data to the array, as demonstrated here:

```
Characters$(0) = "King"
Characters$(1) = "Dragon"
Characters$(2) = "WhiteKnight"
Characters$(3) = "Wizard"
Characters$(4) = "Jester"
```

Accessing Data Stored in an Array

Once created and populated with data, you can refer to any element stored in an array by specifying its index position, as demonstrated here:

```
PRINT Characters$(3)
```

Here, the fourth element (Wizard) stored in an array named Characters$() is displayed.

 While you can certainly access array items one at a time as demonstrated above, this approach is not practical for large loops that may contain dozens, hundreds, or thousands of items. Instead, use a loop to process the contents of the array. Loops will be presented in many of the examples that follow and covered in greater detail in Chapter 5, "Repeating Statement Execution Using Loops."

Rather than accessing array items one at a time, it is usually more convenient and practical to set up a loop to iterate through every item in the loop. For example, the following statements create a loop and assign five items to it and then use a FOR...NEXT loop to iterate through the array and display its contents.

```
DIM Characters$(4)

Characters$(0) = "King"
Characters$(1) = "Dragon"
Characters$(2) = "WhiteKnight"
Characters$(3) = "Wizard"
Characters$(4) = "Jester"

FOR i = 0 TO 4
  PRINT Characters$(i)
NEXT i
```

 TRICK Instead of hard coding the size of the loop in the FOR loop, as was done in the preceding example, you can use the ARRAY COUNT() command to retrieve an integer value representing the index number of the last position in an array, as demonstrated here:

```
FOR i = 0 TO ARRAY COUNT(Characters$(0))
  PRINT Characters$(i)
NEXT i
```

Deleting an Array

If, after working with an array, it is no longer needed, you can delete it while your application is running using the UNDIM command, which has the following syntax.

```
UNDIM ArrayName(dimension)
```

Here, *ArrayName* identifies the array to be deleted and *dimension* represents the dimension of the array to be deleted. For a single-dimension array, the value of *dimension* will always be 0. For example, the following statement demonstrates how to delete an array named Characters$().

```
UNDIM Characters$(0)
```

By removing an array that is no longer needed, you free up memory and can potentially improve performance, depending on how much data was stored in the array.

Emptying an Array

You might want to keep the array but remove its contents, so that the array can be repopulated with new data, which might be the case if game play ends and the player elects to start a new round of play. To accomplish this you can use the EMPTY ARRAY command, which has the following syntax.

```
EMPTY ARRAY ArrayName(0)
```

For example, the following command demonstrates how to use this command to empty an array named Characters$().

```
EMPTY ARRAY Characters$(0)
```

INCREASING THE SIZE OF AN ARRAY

Using the ARRAY INSERT AT TOP command, you can add a new element to the beginning of an array. When executed, a new blank item is added to the beginning of the array (in index position 0) and the rest of the items in the array are pushed down by one index position to provide the needed room. The syntax required to use this command is outlined here:

```
ARRAY INSERT AT TOP ArrayName(dimension)
```

Here, ArrayName represents the name of the array being resized and dimension represents the dimension of the array that is being resized. To better understand how to work with the ARRAY INSERT AT TOP command, take a look at the following example.

```
DIM Characters$(4)

Characters$(0) = "King"
Characters$(1) = "Dragon"
Characters$(2) = "WhiteKnight"
Characters$(3) = "Wizard"
Characters$(4) = "Jester"

ARRAY INSERT AT TOP Characters$(0)
Characters$(0) = "Prince"

FOR i = 0 TO ARRAY COUNT(Characters$(0))
  PRINT Characters$(i)
NEXT i
```

Here, an array named Characters$() is defined and assigned five items. Next, the ARRAY INSERT AT TOP command is executed, adding a new blank item to the beginning of the array, which is then assigned a value of "Prince". The contents of the loop are then displayed, verifying that the new item has been added and the output shown below is displayed.

```
Prince
King
Dragon
WhiteKnight
Wizard
Jester
```

Using the ARRAY INSERT AT BOTTOM command, you can add a new element to the end of an array. When executed, a new blank item is added to the end of the array, resulting in a new index position. The syntax required to use this command is outlined here:

ARRAY INSERT AT BOTTOM *ArrayName*(*dimension*)

Here, *ArrayName* represents the name of the array being resized and *dimension* represents the dimension of the array that is being increased in size. To better understand how to work with the ARRAY INSERT AT BOTTOM command, take a look at the following example.

```
DIM Characters$(4)

Characters$(0) = "King"
Characters$(1) = "Dragon"
Characters$(2) = "WhiteKnight"
Characters$(3) = "Wizard"
Characters$(4) = "Jester"

ARRAY INSERT AT Bottom Characters$(0)
Characters$(5) = "Prince"

FOR i = 0 TO ARRAY COUNT(Characters$(0))
  PRINT Characters$(i)
NEXT i
```

Here, an array named Characters$() is defined and assigned five items. Next, the ARRAY INSERT AT BOTTOM command is executed, adding a new blank item to the end of the array, which is then assigned a value of "Prince". The contents of the loop are then displayed, verifying that the new item has been added and the output shown below is displayed.

```
King
Dragon
WhiteKnight
Wizard
Jester
Prince
```

INSERTING AN ELEMENT INTO THE MIDDLE OF AN ARRAY

Instead of adding a new blank item to the beginning or the end of an existing array, you can use the ARRAY INSERT AT ELEMENT command to insert a new blank item into any index position. When executed, the array element previously in that position, as well as any array elements that follow, are automatically shifted down by one position to make room for the new item. Once inserted you can assign a value to the newly added array item. The syntax required to use this command is outlined here:

```
ARRAY INSERT AT ELEMENT ArrayName(dimension), Index
```

Here, *ArrayName* represents the name of the array being modified, *dimension* represents the dimensions of the array that is being modified, and *Index* specifies the location within the array where the new entry is to be inserted. To better understand how to work with the ARRAY INSERT AT ELEMENT command, take a look at the following example.

```
DIM Characters$(4)

Characters$(0) = "King"
Characters$(1) = "Dragon"
Characters$(2) = "WhiteKnight"
Characters$(3) = "Wizard"
Characters$(4) = "Jester"

ARRAY INSERT AT ELEMENT Characters$(0), 2
Characters$(2) = "Prince"

FOR i = 0 TO ARRAY COUNT(Characters$(0))
  PRINT Characters$(i)
NEXT i
```

Here, an array named Characters$() is defined and assigned five items. Next, the ARRAY INSERT AT ELEMENT command is executed, inserting a new blank item at index position 2, which is then assigned a value of "Prince". The contents of the loop are then displayed, verifying that the new item has been added and the output shown below is displayed.

```
King
Dragon
Prince
WhiteKnight
Wizard
Jester
```

DELETING AN ARRAY ELEMENT

Instead of deleting an array using the UNDIM command or erasing all of its contents using the EMPTY ARRAY command, you can delete specific array items using the ARRAY DELETE ELEMENT command. When executed, this command removes the specified items, based on its index position from the array, and any array elements that follow it are automatically reassigned new index numbers. The resulting array is reduced in size by one element. The syntax required to use this command is outlined here:

ARRAY DELETE ELEMENT *ArrayName*(*dimension*), *Index*

Here, *ArrayName* represents the name of the array being modified, *dimension* represents the dimensions of the array that is being modified, and *Index* specifies the index position in the array that is to be removed. To better understand how to work with the ARRAY DELETE ELEMENT command, take a look at the following example.

```
DIM Characters$(4)

Characters$(0) = "King"
Characters$(1) = "Dragon"
Characters$(2) = "WhiteKnight"
Characters$(3) = "Wizard"
Characters$(4) = "Jester"

ARRAY DELETE ELEMENT Characters$(0), 2

FOR i = 0 TO ARRAY COUNT(Characters$(0))
  PRINT Characters$(i)
NEXT i
```

Here, an array named Characters$() is defined and assigned five items. Next, the ARRAY DELETE ELEMENT command is executed, deleting the item stored in index position 2. The contents of the loop are then displayed, verifying that the specified item has been deleted, as shown here:

```
King
Dragon
Wizard
Jester
```

CREATING USER-DEFINED DATA TYPES

Never being short on options, DarkBASIC Professional offers yet another way of storing and managing access to data in the form of *user-defined data types* or *UDTs*. A UDT is an advanced data type that you define yourself. UDTs can contain any number of different variables and are created using the syntax outlined here:

```
TYPE UDTName
  Variable AS DataType
  .
  .
  .
ENDTYPE
```

Here, *UDTName* represents the name being assigned to the user-defined data type. *Variable* is the name of a variable being defined within the UDT, and *DataType* represents the variable's data type. To better understand how to create a user-defined data type, take a look at the following example.

```
TYPE Player
  Name$ AS STRING
  Rank$ AS STRING
ENDTYPE

PlayerOne AS Player
PlayerOne.Name$ = "Jerry"
PlayerOne.Rank$ = "Expert"

PRINT "Welcome, " + PlayerOne.Name$
PRINT "Your current rank assignment is " + PlayerOne.Rank$
```

Here, a UDT named Player has been defined. The UDT has been assigned two string variables, representing the player's name and ranking. Once the UDT has been defined, you can use it as a template for creating new variables. Once you have created a new variable—in the example above the PlayerOne variable has been created—you can populate it with data. This is accomplished using dot notation in which a . character is appended to the end of the variable name, followed by the name of one of the variable definitions defined in the UDT. Once data has been assigned, you can work with it as appropriate.

HINT

UDTs are often used within 2D and 3D games as a means of defining and keeping track of various objects that make up the game (characters, cars, tanks, etc.).

BACK TO THE NUMBER GUESSING GAME

It is time to turn your attention back to the development of this chapter's main project, the Number Guessing game. The development of this game will demonstrate how to collect, store, and retrieve data using variables. This will include using variables to store the game's randomly generated numbers as well as the player's guesses. You will also get a sneak peak at how to implement conditional logic and how to set up loops to allow a DarkBASIC Professional application to repeatedly execute commands that control game play.

Designing the Game

Unlike the games that you developed in Chapters 1 and 2, the Number Guessing game will run in full-screen mode. As such, it won't display a window or any other controls associated with windows. Game play will continue until the player enters a specified quit command or until the player presses the Escape key, which by default automatically terminates a DarkBASIC Professional full-screen application.

To help make things as easy as possible to understand and follow along, this game will be created in a series of seven steps, as outlined here:

1. Create a new DarkBASIC project.
2. Specify game settings.
3. Document your application with comments.
4. Display a welcome message.
5. Develop the game's overall programming logic.
6. Display additional information about the game.
7. Save your new application.

Step 1: Creating a New DarkBASIC Project

The first step in creating the Number Guessing game is to create a new project. Do so by clicking on the New Project menu item located on the File menu. The Create a New DarkBASIC Professional Project window appears. Type in **NumberGuess** in the Project Name file and specify where you want your new project to be saved and then click on the OK button. In response, a new project is created for you.

Step 2: Configuring Game Settings

It is now time to modify a few application settings. Start by clicking on the Project button located at the bottom of the Project Panel window and then place the cursor in the Project Comments field and type **This game generates a random number between 1 and 100 and challenges the player to guess it in as few guesses as possible.** Next, click on the Settings button and type **Number Guessing Game** in the Application Window Caption field. Lastly, select Windowed – Full Screen as the display setting for this game.

Step 3: Documenting Your DarkBASIC Application

Now that you have created your new project and configured its project level settings, it is time to add the program code statements required to make your new application work. Begin by modifying the default comment statements that have been added to your application so that they match the statements shown here:

```
REM Project: NumberGuess
REM Created: 10/2/2007 9:48:35 PM
REM Executable name: NumberGuess.dba
REM Version: 1.0
REM Author: Jerry Lee Ford, Jr.
REM Description: This DarkBASIC game challenges the player to guess a
REM                secret number in as few guesses as possible
```

Step 4: Displaying a Welcome Message

The game begins by displaying a welcome message. To set up the display of this message, add the following statements to the end of the script file.

```
ForegroundColor = RGB(255, 255, 128) `Set color to yellow
BackgroundColor = RGB(0, 0, 0)  `Set color to black
INK ForegroundColor, BackgroundColor  `Apply color settings

SET TEXT FONT "Arial"  `Set the font type to Arial
SET TEXT SIZE 48  `Set the font size to 48 points
CENTER TEXT 320, 150, "Welcome to The" `Display welcome message
CENTER TEXT 320, 220, "Number Guessing Game"
SET TEXT SIZE 16  `Set the font size to 16 points
CENTER TEXT 320, 380, "Press any key to continue"  `Display instructions
WAIT KEY `Wait until the player presses a keyboard key
```

As you can see, these statements begin by setting the foreground color to yellow and the background color to black and then apply these color settings using the INK command. Next, the font type is set to Arial with a size of 48 points. A welcome message is displayed using the CENTER TEXT command. Font size is then set to 16 points and another message is displayed. Finally, the WAIT KEY command is executed, pausing application execution.

Step 5: Developing the Game's Overall Programming Logic

The code statements that control the actual game play, generating a random number and processing the player guesses, are shown next and should be added to the end of the code file.

```
do  `Loop forever

  NoOfGuesses = 0  `Initialize variable value

  `Generate a set and use it to retrieve a random number from 1 to 100
  seed = TIMER() :  RANDOMIZE seed :  RandomNo = RND(99) + 1

  do  `Loop forever

    CLS  `Clear the display area

    PRINT : PRINT : PRINT : PRINT : PRINT : PRINT  `Write six blank lines

    `Prompt the player to make a guess
    INPUT "         Enter a guess: ", Guess$

    Guess = VAL(Guess$)  `Convert guess from a string to a numeric value

    `Increment value used to keep track of the number of guesses made
    NoOfGuesses = NoOfGuesses + 1

    IF Guess = RandomNo  `Determine if the player's guess was correct
      CLS  `Clear the display area
      `Display the game's closing message
      CENTER TEXT 320, 150, "Correct. You guessed the secret number"
      CENTER TEXT 320, 180, "in " + STR$(NoOfGuesses) + " moves!"
      WAIT KEY  `Wait until the player presses a keyboard key
      EXIT
    ENDIF
    IF Guess <= RandomNo  `Determine if the player's guess was too low
      CLS  `Clear the display area
```

```
     CENTER TEXT 320, 150, "Sorry, your guess was too low."
     CENTER TEXT 320, 180, "Press any key to try again."
     WAIT KEY  `Wait until the player presses a keyboard key
   ENDIF
   IF Guess >= RandomNo  `Determine if the player's guess was too high
     CLS  `Clear the display area
     CENTER TEXT 320, 150, "Sorry, your guess was too high."
     CENTER TEXT 320, 180, "Press any key to try again."
     WAIT KEY  `Wait until the player presses a keyboard key
   ENDIF
 loop

 CLS
 PRINT : PRINT : PRINT : PRINT : PRINT : PRINT  `Write six blank lines
 `Prompt the player to quit or play again
 INPUT "          Enter q to Quit or press a key to play again. ", Reply$
 IF LOWER$(Reply$) = "q" THEN EXIT  `Analyze the player's response
```

Loop

These statements are controlled by a pair of DO loops. The outer DO loop controls the generation of random numbers at the beginning of each new round of play. It is also responsible for setting the value of NoOfGuesses to 0, to reset the variable's value and ready it for a new round of play. The inner DO loop is responsible for clearing the screen, processing the player's guesses, and determining when the game should be terminated.

Since you have not been introduced to the DO loop or the IF statements that are embedded inside these loops, I am not going to step through each of the statements in great detail. Instead, I'll simply point out that the game's randomly generated number is stored in an integer variable named RandomNo and that the player's guess is collected and stored in a string variable named Guess$. Because it is a string variable, the value of Guess$ must be converted to a numeric value using the VAL command and then stored in an integer variable named Guess.

The values stored in Guess and RandomNo are compared each time the player enters a guess. If the player's guess does not match the game's randomly generated number, a message is displayed, providing the player with a hint that helps the player make his next guess. Once the player finally guesses the game's number, a message is displayed showing how many moves it took for the player to win the game and the player is then prompted for permission to start a new round of play.

Step 6: Thanking the Player

Once the player types the letter q and presses the Enter key, the main loop terminates game play, allowing the following statements to execute.

```
CLS  `Clear the display area

SET TEXT SIZE 24  `Set the font size to 24 points
`Display the game's closing message
CENTER TEXT 320, 150, "Thanks for playing the Number Guessing game!"
SET TEXT SIZE 12  `Set the font size to 24 points
CENTER TEXT 320, 240, "Developed by Jerry Lee Ford, Jr."
CENTER TEXT 320, 260, "Copyright 2008"

ForegroundColor = RGB(128, 255, 255)  `Set color to light blue.
INK ForegroundColor, BackgroundColor  `Apply color settings

CENTER TEXT 320, 280, "http://www.tech-publishing.com"

ForegroundColor = RGB(255, 255, 128)  `Set color to yellow
INK ForegroundColor, BackgroundColor  `Apply color settings

SET TEXT SIZE 16  `Set the font size to 16 points
CENTER TEXT 320, 380, "Press any key to continue"
WAIT KEY  `Wait until the player presses a keyboard key
CLS  `Clear the display area

END  `Terminate game play
```

These statements should be added to the end of the code file. They are responsible for displaying the game's closing screen, which thanks the player for taking time to play the game. After reading the message that is displayed, the player must press a key to dismiss this screen, after which the game ends.

Step 7: Saving and Compiling Your Application

Assuming that you have followed along and created your own copy of the Number Guessing game, your new application should be ready for testing. However, before doing so, now would be a good time to save your project by clicking on the File menu's Save All option. Once this has been done, click on the Make/EXE RUN option located on the Compile menu to compile and execute your application.

The Final Result

That's it! Assuming that you have followed along carefully and that you have not skipped any steps or made any typing mistakes, your copy of the Number Guessing game should be ready to run and should work as described at the beginning of this chapter. If on the other hand, you run into an error, read the error message that is displayed carefully to see if it provides you with a clue as to where things went wrong and, if necessary, go back and review each of the steps that make up this programming project and look for any steps that you may have skipped or statements that you may have mistyped or left incomplete. Once you have everything running, be sure to test your new game thoroughly. This means entering both valid and invalid data to ensure that the game handles it properly.

 You will also find a copy of this application's project file along with source code on this book's companion website, located at http://www.courseptr.com/downloads.

Summary

In this chapter, you learned how to store and retrieve data using variables. You learned about the different data types supported by DarkBASIC Professional as well as how to define both local and global variables. You also learned how to store data that does not change in constants and how to embed data within your DarkBASIC Professional program using DATA statements. This chapter also showed you how to define your own custom user-defined data types, allowing you to store related information made up of different data types. On top of all this, you learned how to store and process collections of related items in arrays.

Before you move on to Chapter 4, I suggest you set aside a few additional minutes to try and improve the Number Guessing game by implementing the following list of challenges.

CHALLENGES

1. Consider modifying the game so that the player can select from a larger set of numbers, such as 1 to 1000.

2. Consider modifying the game so that the player can quit the game at any time and not just at the end of the current round of play.

3. Consider adding programming logic to the game that keeps track of the total number of games played, as well as the average number of guesses made per game.

IMPLEMENTING CONDITIONAL LOGIC

In order to create interactive computer games, you need to be able to develop programming logic that allows your games to evaluate data that is collected and then initiate different courses of action based on the result of those evaluations. This can be achieved through the use of conditional programming statements that incorporate comparison, mathematical, and logical operators. These tools provide everything needed to manipulate and analyze data. Through the application of conditional logic you will be able to build computer games and applications that alter their execution based on the input they are given. The end result will be an interactive and adaptive program capable of handling many different situations. In addition to learning all about the application of conditional logic, this chapter will guide you through the development of your next computer application, the Rock, Paper, Scissors game.

Specifically, you will learn:

- How to use different variations of the IF statement to set up conditional tests
- How to use the SELECT statement to set up conditional tests capable of comparing one condition to a range of values
- How to nest conditional statements to develop advanced conditional logic
- How to work with comparison, mathematical, and logical operators

PROJECT PREVIEW: THE ROCK, PAPER, SCISSORS GAME

This chapter's game project is the Rock, Paper, Scissors game. In this game the player is pitted against the computer in a computerized implementation of the popular children's game. As the name of the game implies, valid moves are Rock, Paper, and Scissors. When first started, the screen shown in Figure 4.1 is displayed.

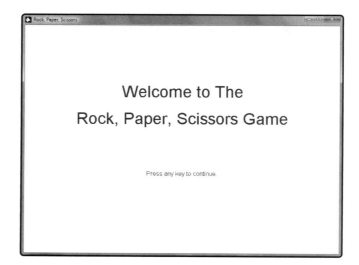

FIGURE 4.1

The Rock, Paper, Scissors game's welcome screen.

At the beginning of each new round of play, the player is prompted to make a move, as shown in Figure 4.2.

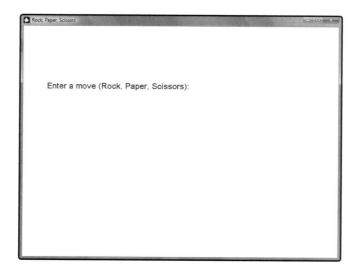

FIGURE 4.2

To make a move the player must enter Rock, Paper, or Scissors.

Once the player has made her move, the game generates a move on behalf of the computer. The player's move is then compared to the computer's move and a winner is determined based on the following set of rules.

- Rock crushes scissors
- Paper covers rock
- Scissors cut paper
- Matching moves are a tie

Figure 4.3 shows an example of a game that has been won by the player.

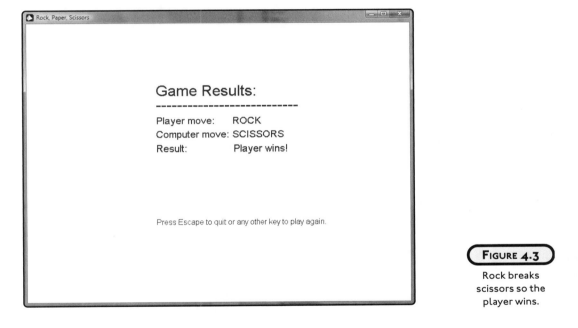

FIGURE 4.3

Rock breaks scissors so the player wins.

Figure 4.4 shows an example of a game that has been won by the computer.

FIGURE 4.4

Scissors cut paper so the computer wins.

Finally, Figure 4.5 shows an example of a game that has resulted in a tie.

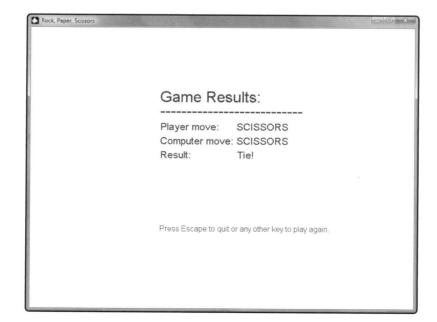

FIGURE 4.5

A tie occurs whenever the player and computer select the same move.

At the end of each round of play, the player is prompted to play again by pressing any key on the keyboard, except for the Escape key, which ends game play.

DEVELOPING GAMES THAT CAN ADAPT THEIR EXECUTION

In Chapter 1, you learned how to create the DarkJokes game. In this application, each programming statement was executed sequentially, beginning with the first statement and continuing to the last code statements. Given that this game simply displayed a consecutive series of jokes, this approach worked well for this game. There was no intricate programming logic involved. However, to develop applications of any degree of complexity, sequential processing doesn't cut it. Instead, you need the ability to analyze data collected by your program and then to specify what actions should occur based on that analysis.

As the game projects that you worked on in Chapters 2 and 3 demonstrated, the application of conditional programming logic is fundamental to just about any computer program. For example, most computer applications need to analyze the data that they are provided to determine if it is valid. In the Fortune Teller game that you created in Chapter 2, the following statements were used to determine whether to terminate the execution of the application.

```
INPUT Question$
IF QUESTION$ = "quit" OR QUESTION$ = "Quit" OR  QUESTION$ = "QUIT"
  EXIT
ENDIF
```

Here, the EXIT command, which immediately terminates an application's execution, is executed if the player types in the word quit, Quit, or QUIT. The analysis of the value assigned to QUESTION$ is performed by an IF statement. If the player did not enter quit, Quit, or QUIT, game play continues. Otherwise, it terminates.

Aside from becoming familiar with the syntax of the IF statement, which is reviewed later in this chapter, the application of conditional logic within a computer program is relatively easy. After all, you use conditional logic in one form or another all of the time as part of your normal daily routine. For example, every day that you are woken by your alarm clock, you are presented with either of two choices. You can turn off the alarm and go back to sleep or you can get up and begin your day. This decision and the two possible sources of action are outlined in Figure 4.6.

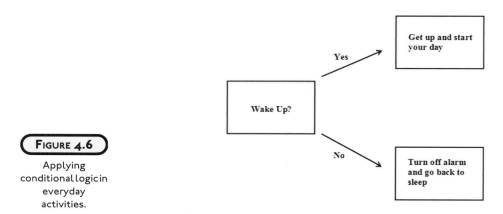

FIGURE 4.6

Applying
conditional logic in
everyday
activities.

 Figure 4.6 is an example of a simple flowchart. A *flowchart* is a graphical tool that is used to depict all or part of an application's logical flow. By developing a flowchart, you can outline the overall design of the logic required to develop your DarkBASIC Professional applications and potentially uncover any errors in your logic prior to beginning the coding process.

This same basic logic can be directly applied to your DarkBASIC Professional applications, as demonstrated in Figure 4.7.

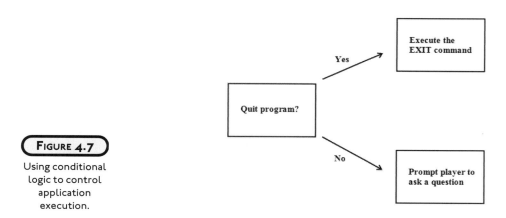

FIGURE 4.7

Using conditional
logic to control
application
execution.

In Figure 4.7, two different possible actions have been outlined. The execution of one of these actions depends on the player's decision as to whether to quit the application. Using the flowchart shown in Figure 4.7, you can translate the logic that is outlined into corresponding program statements, as demonstrated here:

```
PRINT "Enter Quit to stop playing or press any key to continue."
INPUT Question$
IF QUESTION$ = "quit" OR QUESTION$ = "Quit" OR  QUESTION$ = "QUIT"
  EXIT
ENDIF
```

Here, a PRINT statement is used to display a message prompting the player for permission to begin game play. The player's input is collected using the INPUT command and stored in a variable named QUESTION$. Once collected, the player's input is analyzed using an IF statement to see if the player entered the Quit command, in which case the EXIT command is executed and the game terminates. Otherwise, game play continues.

The fundamental result of any conditional analysis boils down to a determination as to whether the condition being evaluated is true or false. If the result of the analysis is true, one series of actions is taken. If the result of the analysis is false, a different series of actions is taken. DarkBASIC Professional provides you with two different programming statements that you can use to apply conditional logic. One is the IF statement that you have just previewed. The other statement is the SELECT statement. A brief description of both of the programming statements is outlined here:

- IF. Evaluates a condition and based on the result of that analysis, executes one of two possible actions.
- SELECT. Sets up a conditional analysis of one value against a range of matching values.

Working with the IF Statement

The IF statement is absolutely essential to the development of all but the most rudimentary applications. Using the IF statement, you can implement any type of conditional test that you need to perform. Because this statement is so important and so versatile, it merits a little extra attention. Let's begin by examining how this statement is used at a conceptual level using spoken English in place of programming language syntax by reviewing the following example.

```
IF I win the lottery
  I am going to retire
  I am going on a long vacation
ELSE
  I am calling in sick
  I am going to turn off my answering machine
ENDIF
```

Here, a pseudo code or English-like outline of a logical conditional has been developed. This example demonstrates how the IF statement can be used to analyze the thought processes that you might go through in your head just before you compare your lottery numbers to the week's winnings numbers.

In this example, the opening statement defines the condition that is to be evaluated. If the conditional evaluates as true, then the two statements that follow the IF statement are executed. If the conditional evaluates as false, then these two statements are skipped and instead the two statements that follow the ELSE keyword are executed.

Pseudo code is a programming term used to refer to an English-like outline of the programming logic that makes up all or part of a computer program. Programmers often use pseudo code as an intermediary step in the application development process because it provides a working outline from which to work. Because it is written in an English-like format, pseudo code allows the programmer to focus on the logic required to perform a task without getting bogged down with the syntax required to write individual statements. Once the basic logic has been outlined, you can then translate the pseudo code into specific programming statements.

Note in the above example that the IF statement has been used to create a logical test that consists of a number of statements, organized into a block of code beginning with the IF statement and ending with the ENDIF statement. This entire group of statements is often referred to as an IF statement code block.

Examining the Syntax of the IF Statement

The IF statement is used to evaluate a condition and then to initiate the action of one or more code statements based on the result of that analysis. The syntax of the IF statement is outlined here:

```
IF condition
     statements
ELSE
   statements
ENDIF
```

Here, *condition* is an expression that evaluates to a value of true or false. In most cases, the expression evaluates the relationship between two different values to see if they are equal or not equal. *statements* represents one or more code statements executed based on whether the value of *condition* is true or false. ELSE is an optional keyword that is used to specify an alternate set of programming statements that are executed in the event *condition* evaluates as being false. As you will see in the sections that follow, the IF statement is extremely flexible and can be used in several different variations, including:

- A simple if…then statement that fits on a single line
- An if…then code block that contains one or more embedded statements
- An if…then…else block that provides for an alternative course of action

Using Single-Line IF Statements

In its simplest form, the IF statement can be written on a single line using the syntax outlined here:

```
IF condition THEN statements
```

For example, the following statements use this version of the IF statement to conditionally execute the display of a text statement.

```
IF PlayerName$ = "William" Then PRINT "Welcome William!"
```

Here, an IF statement has been set up to examine the value assigned to a variable named PlayerName$ and if it is equal to "William", a PRINT statement is executed. Later in this chapter, when you work on the Rock, Paper, Scissors game, you will use a series of single-line IF statements as part of the process of generating a move on behalf of the computer.

```
seed = TIMER() :  RANDOMIZE seed :  RandomNo = RND(3)

IF RandomNo = 1 THEN ComputerM$ = "ROCK"
IF RandomNo = 2 THEN ComputerM$ = "PAPER"
IF RandomNo = 3 THEN ComputerM$ = "SCISSORS"
```

In this example, a random value between 1 and 3 is generated and assigned to an integer variable named RandomNo. Next, the IF statements analyze the value assigned to RandomNo to see if it is equal to 1, 2, or 3 and makes an assignment of ROCK, PAPER, or SCISSORS based on that analysis.

TRAP Note the absence of the ENDIF keyword at the end of each IF statement. ENDIF only applies to multi-line IF statement code blocks.

Single-line IF statements are perfect for setting up conditional tests in situations where you do not need to perform an alternative action in the event the test evaluates as false and when you are able to fit both the condition and the action to be taken on a single line.

Setting Up an IF Statement Code Block

If you need to execute more than one statement in the event an IF statement's condition evaluates as true, you need to create an IF statement code block, which you can do using the following syntax.

```
IF condition
  statements
ENDIF
```

 Note that unlike the single-line version of the IF statement, the multi-line code block does not permit the use of the THEN keyword.

Using this syntax, you can group any number of program statements together and conditionally execute them, as demonstrated here:

```
IF TotalScore >= 200
  PRINT "BONUS! You are awarded 50 extra points"
  TotalScore = TotalScore + 50
  PRINT "Your current score is " + STR$(TotalScore)
ENDIF
```

Here, a value assigned to a variable named TotalScore is checked to see if it is greater than or equal to 200, and if it is, the value of TotalScore is incremented by 50. In addition, two PRINT statements are executed.

Executing an Alternative Set of Statements

Using IF statement code blocks, the only way to control the conditional execution of different statements when testing a conditional is to set up multiple code blocks, as demonstrated here:

```
input "Enter your age? "; Age$
Age = VAL(Age$)

IF Age < 18
  PRINT "Sorry, but you are too young to play this game."
  WAIT KEY
  EXIT
ENDIF
```

```
IF Age >= 18
  PRINT "Great, let's play!"
ENDIF
```

Here, the user is prompted to enter her age. Next, an IF statement code block analyzes the value assigned to a variable named AGE to see if it is less than 18, and if it is, a message is displayed. Execution is then paused until the player presses a keyboard key, after which the EXIT command is executed, terminating the application. In order to conditionally execute a different set of statements when the value assigned to Age is greater than or equal to 18, a second IF statement code block had to be set up.

The disadvantage of using multiple IF statement code blocks, as demonstrated above, is even though the programming logic is mutually exclusive, meaning that one or the other but never both of the code blocks needs to execute, both code blocks are executed every time. A better way of handling this challenge is to use the optional ELSE keyword when formulating an IF statement code block. This version of the IF statement code block uses the following syntax.

```
IF condition
     statements
ELSE
   statements
ENDIF
```

When used, the ELSE keyword lets you specify an alternative set of code statements that will be executed in the event the condition evaluates as false. Thus, using the ELSE keyword, you could rewrite the previous example as shown here:

```
input "Enter your age? "; Age$
Age = VAL(Age$)

IF Age < 18
  PRINT "Sorry, but you are too young to play this game."
  WAIT KEY
  EXIT
ELSE
  PRINT "Great, let's play!"
ENDIF
```

Not only does this version of the IF statement code block require fewer lines of code but it is also more efficient, since the ELSE portion of the control block is executed only if the value of the condition is false.

Nesting IF Statements

Using the different forms of the IF statement that have just been discussed, you can set up any number of conditional tests. However, some situations require more complex conditional logic than can be written using individual IF statements. DarkBASIC Professional addresses this requirement by allowing you to embed or nest one IF statement or IF statement code block within another IF statement code block, as demonstrated here:

```
a = 1 : b = 2 : c = 3 : d = 4 : e = 5

IF a = 1
  IF b = 2
    IF c = 3
      IF d = 4
        IF e = 5
          PRINT "All systems are go!"
        ENDIF
      ENDIF
    ENDIF
  ENDIF
ENDIF
```

By embedding one IF statement code block within another IF statement code block, you can develop conditional logic that performs one test based on the result of a previous test. In the case of the preceding example, a series of five IF statements code blocks has been set up, each of which evaluates the value of a given variable. Only in the event that all five tests evaluate as being true will the PRINT statement execute.

TRAP

There is no limitation regarding the number of conditional statements that you embed. However, the deeper you go, the more difficult your application source code will be. In general, it is best to embed no more than two or three levels deep.

Working with the SELECT Statement

In addition to the different forms of the IF statement, DarkBASIC Professional also lets you apply conditional logic using the SELECT statement. The SELECT statement lets you replace multiple IF statement code blocks with a single SELECT code block. The SELECT statement is perfectly suited to situations where you want to compare one value against a series of possible matching values. The syntax for a code block based on the SELECT statement is outlined here:

```
SELECT expression
  CASE value, ... , value
    statements

        .
        .
        .

  ENDCASE
  CASE value, ... , value
    statements
  ENDCASE
  CASE DEFAULT
    statements
  ENDCASE
ENDSELECT
```

As you can see, the SELECT statement code block begins with the SELECT statement and ends with the ENDSELECT statement. You specify the value (or expression that evaluates to a value) that you want to match as an argument on the SELECT statement and then set up one or more embedded CASE statements with matching ENDCASE statements. Each individual CASE statement identifies one or more comma-separated values against which the value specified in the SELECT statement is compared. If a match occurs in one of the CASE statements, the statements embedded within that CASE statement and its ENDCASE statement are executed. If none of the CASE statements results in a match, then the statements embedded within the optional CASE DEFAULT statement, if present, and its associated ENDCASE statement are executed.

To better understand how to work with the SELECT statement, take a look at the following pseudo code example.

```
SELECT What is the movie rated?
  CASE If the movie is rated G
    You can go
  ENDCASE
  CASE If the movie is rated PG or PG-13
    You can go with a parent
  ENDCASE
  CASE If the movie is rated R
    You must wait until you are 18
  ENDCASE
 CASE DEFAULT
    If the movie is rated anything else you cannot ever go
```

```
  ENDCASE
ENDSELECT
```

Here you can see that a SELECT statement has been set up to compare the value of a movie's rating against a series of possible values, as specified by three CASE statements. The first CASE statement looks for a match with a rating of G. The second CASE statement looks for a match with a rating of PG or PG-13. The third CASE statement looks for a match with a rating of R. Finally, the CASE DEFAULT statement is executed in the event that none of the previous three case statements result in a match. Having designed a pseudo code outline of the logic involved, it is now an easy task of translating the rough outline into corresponding code statements as shown here:

```
PRINT "What is the movie rated? "
INPUT Rating$
Rating$ = UPPER$(Rating$)

SELECT Rating$
  CASE "G"
    PRINT "Of course you can go. Have Fun!"
  ENDCASE
  CASE "PG", "PG-13"
    PRINT "You can go see this movie with a parent."
  ENDCASE
  CASE "R"
    PRINT "Wait until you are 18."
  ENDCASE
  CASE DEFAULT
    PRINT "Don't even think about it!"
  ENDCASE
ENDSELECT
```

If you were to rewrite this SELECT code block using a series of IF statement code blocks, you would find that not only would it take more statements to write the IF statement code blocks, but the end result would be program code that was more difficult to read and follow.

WORKING WITH DIFFERENT RELATIONAL OPERATORS

Up to this point in the chapter, all comparison operators have relied on the = operator to determine whether two values were equal. In addition to the = operator, DarkBASIC

Operator	Description
=	Equal to
<>	Not equal
<	Less than
>	Greater than
<=	Less than or equal to
>=	Greater than or equal to

TABLE 4.1 DARKBASIC PROFESSIONAL RELATIONAL OPERATORS

Professional supports a number of different types of relational operators. These operators provide the ability to perform comparison operations that compare ranges of values. For example, rather than set up a whole series of tests to see if the value stored in a variable named x was 10, 11, 12, 13, ...100, you could instead set up a test that checks to see if x is greater than or equal to 10. DarkBASIC Professional supports the list of operators shown in Table 4.1.

Performing Numeric Comparisons

Using the relational operators listed in Table 4.1, you can compare both integer and real numbers. As you have already seen, the equals operator can be used to compare any two numbers, as demonstrated here:

```
x = 100
y = 50
IF x = y THEN PRINT "x is equal to y"      `False
IF x < y THEN PRINT "x is less than y"     `False
IF x > y THEN PRINT "x is greater than y"  `True
```

As you can see, three different types of comparisons have been set up, of which only the third one will result in a value of true.

Comparing Text Strings

DarkBASIC Professional only allows you to compare strings to other strings and numbers to other numbers (regardless of whether they are integer or real). For example, you can compare one string to another string to see if they are identical. Similarly, you can compare one number to another number to see if they are equal.

To compare strings, the strings must be identical in terms of both case and content for the results to be true. For example, the following comparison is false because of difference in case.

```
x$ = "Alexander"
y$ = "alexander"
IF x$ = y$ THEN PRINT "Welcome Alexander!"
```

You can just as easily check for inequality when comparing the value of two strings, as demonstrated here:

```
x$ = "Alexander"
y$ = "alexander"
IF x$ <> y$ THEN PRINT "Welcome Alexander!"
```

This time, the expression results in a value of true. DarkBASIC Professional also allows you to compare strings to determine if one string is greater than or less than another, as demonstrated here:

```
X$ = "A"
Y$ = "Z"
IF x$ < y$ THEN PRINT "A is less than Z"
```

In this example, a value of true is returned because the letter A is less than Z. DarkBASIC Professional adheres to a coding system known as ASCII (American Standard Code for Information Interchange) to represent different characters, including letters of the alphabet. According to the ASCII coding scheme, letters that occur earlier in the alphabet have a lesser value than letters that occur later in the alphabet. In addition, lowercase letters have a higher value than uppercase values. As a result, the following statement returns a value of true.

```
IF "a" <> "A" THEN PRINT "These letters are not equal to one another."
```

DOING A LITTLE MATH

Like all modern programming languages, DarkBASIC Professional provides the ability to perform addition, subtraction, multiplication, and division. It also provides an operator that makes it easy to perform exponentiation. For example, the following statement demonstrates how to use the + operators to add two numbers together.

```
x = 100
y = 50
z = x + y   `z equals 150
```

You can use negative numbers in your expressions by preceding a numeric value with the −character, with no intervening space, as demonstrated here:

```
x = 100
y = −50
z = x + y  `z equals 50
```

Here, y has been assigned a value of − 50.

Working with Different Arithmetic Operators

Table 4.2 outlines the different arithmetic operations supported by DarkBASIC Professional and provides an example of their use.

TABLE 4.2	DARKBASIC ARITHMETIC OPERATORS	
Operator	**Description**	**Example**
+	Addition	$x = 1 + 2$
−	Subtraction	$x = 4 − 2$
*	Multiplication	$x = 3 * 3$
/	Division	$x = 6 / 2$
^	Exponentiation	$x = 3 ^ 5$

Exponentiation is the process of multiplying a number by itself a specified number of times. $x = x$ ^ 5 is equivalent to 3 * 3 * 3 * 3 * 3, which equals 243. Be cautious when working with exponentiation. It is such a powerful mathematical concept that it does not take much to generate a numeric value that exceeds the limits of some of DarkBASIC Professional numeric data types.

Incrementing and Decrementing Values

One very common type of calculation performed in many games and computer applications is the increment of a value to keep track of the number of times that a particular event has occurred. For example, a game might keep track of the number of rounds played, and using reverse logic might decrement a number to keep track of the number of lives a player has remaining. Using the + and − operators, you can easily increment and decrement numeric values, as demonstrated here:

```
x = 0
x = x + 1
```

Here, the value of x is set to 0 and then incremented by 1, whereas in the following example, the value of y is set to 3 and then decremented by 1.

```
y = 3
y = y - 1
```

A different way to increment and decrement a number is to use the INC and DEC commands. The syntax of the INC command is shown here:

```
INC Variable, Increment
```

Here, *Variable* is the name of the value to be incremented, and *Increment* is the value by which *Variable* is incremented. By omitting the optional *Increment*, the INC command will automatically increase the value of the specified variable by one, as demonstrated here:

```
x = 10
INC x
```

The syntax of the DEC command is shown here:

```
DEC Variable, Increment
```

Like the INC command, you can omit the optional *Increment* parameter, and the DEC command will automatically decrease the value of the specified variable by one, as demonstrated here:

```
x = 0
DEC x
```

Understanding the Order of Operator Precedence

Just as you learned in grade school, you can combine the use of different operators to create mathematical equations, as demonstrated here:

```
x = 5 + 6 - 3 + 4 - 2 + 8    `x is set equal to 18
```

Like all programming languages, DarkBASIC Professional evaluates numeric expressions according to a specific set of rules referred to as order of precedence. Table 4.3 outlines the order of precedence that DarkBASIC Professional adheres to.

DarkBASIC Professional performs calculations from left to right in cases of equal precedence. The best way to understand the order of precedence is to work through an example, such as the one presented here:

```
x = 4 + 8 / 2 + 5 * 5 - 4 ^ 2
```

TABLE 4.3　DARKBASIC PROFESSIONAL ORDER OF PRECEDENCE

Operator	Description
^	Exponentiation occurs first
*, /	Multiplication and division occur second
+, −	Addition and subtraction occur last

When executed, DarkBASIC Professional processes this statement using the steps outlined here:

1. First, exponentiation is performed, so 4 ^ 2 is calculated resulting in a value of 16. At this point the status of the equation is as shown here:

   ```
   x = 4 + 8 / 2 + 5 * 5 − 16
   ```

2. Next, working from left to right, all multiplication and division operations are performed. As such, 8 divided by 2 yields 4 and 5 is multiplied by 8 yielding 25. At this point the status of the equation is as shown here:

   ```
   x = 4 + 4 + 25 −16
   ```

3. Lastly, addition and subtraction are performed in a left to right order and a final result of 17 is calculated and assigned to x.

Overriding the Order of Precedence

There may be situations where you want to instruct DarkBASIC Professional to perform mathematical expressions in a manner inconsistent with the order of precedence. To make this happen, you need to enclose the parts of the expression that you want to be evaluated first within parentheses, as demonstrated in the following example.

```
x = (4 + 8) / 2 + 5 * (5 −4 ^ 2)
```

This statement is very similar to the statement demonstrated in the previous example, except that this time two pairs of parentheses have been added to instruct DarkBASIC Professional to override the order of precedence. The end result is a completely different answer, as explained here:

1. Working from left to right, the part of the statements embedded inside each set of parentheses is calculated. In the first set of parentheses, 4 is added to 8, yielding a value of 12. In the second set of parentheses, 4 is first raised to a power of 2, yielding a value

of 16, which is then subtracted from 5, yielding a value of −11. At this point the status of the equation is as shown here:

```
X = 12 / 2 + 5 * −11
```

2. Next, multiplication and division is performed from left to right, so 12 is divided by 2, yielding a value of 6 and 5 is multiplied by −11, yielding a value of −55. At this point the status of the equation is as shown here:

```
X = 6 + −55
```

3. Finally, addition and subtraction are performed on a left to right order and ends in a final result of −49.

> You can include any number of parentheses within an expression. When more than one set of parentheses is included, they are evaluated on a left to right basis. In addition, if you embed one set of parentheses within another set of parentheses, the innermost set is evaluated first.

STREAMLINING CODE USING COMPARISON OPERATIONS

As you have already seen, you can embed any number of IF statements within one another to build complex tests. For example, the following statements use a set of IF statements to evaluate a user's name and determine whether to display a welcome message.

```
IF FirstName$ = "Jerry"
  IF MiddleName$ = "Lee"
    IF LastName$ = "Ford"
      PRINT "Welcome Mr. Ford."
    ENDIF
  ENDIF
ENDIF
```

As you can see, using IF statement code blocks, this example requires seven lines of code. More code means longer programs that are more difficult to understand and maintain. In addition, the more deeply you embed IF statements, the more difficult your code becomes to support. As a general rule, it is best not to nest conditional statements more than two, or at most three, layers deep.

To help you streamline the program statements that you use when implementing conditional logical, DarkBASIC Professional provides access to a number of logical operators, which you can use to combine logical tests and even reverse the results of those tests. These operators are listed in Table 4.4.

TABLE 4.4	DARKBASIC PROFESSIONAL LOGICAL OPERATORS	
Operator	**Type**	**Example**
AND	Both comparisons must be true	x > 1 and x < 4
OR	Either comparison must be true	x = 2 or x = 3
NOT	Reverses the result of a comparison	not (x < 10)

The first two operators shown in Table 4.4 are used to combine different comparison operations. For example, using the AND comparison operator, you could rewrite the previous example as shown here:

```
IF FirstName$ = "Jerry" AND MiddleName$ = "Lee" AND LastName$ = "Ford"
  PRINT "Welcome Mr Ford."
ENDIF
```

As you can see, this example required four less lines of code and is much easier to read and understand. The last operator in Table 4.4 is the NOT operator. When used, it reverses the value of a logical test. For example, the following statements analyze the value assigned to LastName$ and if it is equal to "Ford" (e.g., true), a test string is printed.

```
IF LastName$ = "Ford"
  PRINT "I need a job."
ENDIF
```

The following example uses the NOT operator to reverse the value of the text, returning a false value in place of a true value.

```
IF NOT (LastName$ = "Ford")
  PRINT "I need a job."
ENDIF
```

HINT

There is no limit to the number of conditions that you can use with logical operators. For example, the following statement tests four conditions, returning a result of true only if all four tests prove true. Otherwise, a value of false is returned.

```
IF x = 1 AND y = 5 AND a = 10 AND b = 20 THEN PRINT "True"
```

BACK TO THE ROCK, PAPER, SCISSORS GAME

Okay, now that you have learned how to work with different variations of the IF statement and the SELECT statement, as well as the different types of operators supported by DarkBASIC Professional, it is time to turn your attention back to the development of the chapter's application project, the Rock, Paper, Scissors game. This game pits the player against the computer. Its development gives you the opportunity to further explore the application of conditional logic.

Designing the Game

The Rock, Paper, Scissors game will run within a window that contains minimize, maximize, and close buttons in its upper-right corner, just like any other typical application window. As with all of the games that you have worked on so far in this book, you will interact with this game using the keyboard. To help make things as easy as possible to understand and follow along, I have broken the development of this project down into 11 distinct steps, as outlined here:

1. Create a new DarkBASIC project.
2. Specify game settings.
3. Document your application with comments.
4. Display a welcome message.
5. Set up a loop to control game play.
6. Prompt the player to make a move.
7. Validate player input.
8. Generate the computer's move.
9. Determine who won.
10. Display game results.
11. Save and compile a new application.

Step 1: Creating a New DarkBASIC Project

The first step in creating the Rock, Paper, Scissors game is to create a new DarkBASIC Professional project. To do so, start DarkBASIC Professional and click on the New Project menu item located on the File menu. The Create a New DarkBASIC Professional Project window will open.

Enter **RockPaperScissors** in the Project Name file and then specify the location where you want to store your new project and click on the OK button. In response, a new project is created for you.

Step 2: Configuring Game Settings

The next step in the creation of the Rock, Paper, Scissors game is to configure a few application settings. Begin by clicking on the Project button located at the bottom of the Project Panel window. To help document this project, place the cursor in the Project Comments field and type **This implementation of the Rock, Paper, Scissors game pits the player against the computer.** Next, click on the Settings button. Type **Rock, Paper, Scissors** in the Application Window Caption field. Select Windowed as the display setting for this game and set the resolution to 800×600.

Step 3: Documenting Your DarkBASIC Application

Now that your new project has been created and the project level settings have been configured, it is time to begin adding the program code statements required to make the game do something. Let's begin by modifying the default comment statements provided as part of your new DarkBASIC Professional project so that they match the statements shown here:

```
REM Project: RockPaperScissors
REM Created: 10/13/2007 1:45:51 PM
REM Executable name: RockPaperScissors.dba
REM Version: 1.0
REM Author: Jerry Lee Ford, Jr.
REM Description: This DarkBASIC Professional game pits the player against
REM              the computer in a game of Rock, Paper, Scissors
```

Step 4: Displaying a Welcome Message

Next, add the following statements to the end of the code file. These statements display the game's opening welcome screen.

```
CLS RGB(255, 255, 255)  `Set background color to white

ForegroundColor = RGB(0, 0, 160)       `Set foreground color to blue
BackgroundColor = RGB(255, 255, 255)   `Set background color to white
INK ForegroundColor, BackgroundColor   `Apply color settings

SET TEXT FONT "Arial"  `Set the font type to Arial
SET TEXT SIZE 48  `Set the font size to 48 points
CENTER TEXT 400, 150, "Welcome to The"  `Display welcome message
CENTER TEXT 400, 220, "Rock, Paper, Scissors Game"
SET TEXT SIZE 18  `Set the font size to 18 points
CENTER TEXT 400, 380, "Press any key to continue."  `Display instructions
WAIT KEY  `Wait until the player presses a keyboard key
```

These statements set the foreground color to blue and the background color to white and then apply these settings using the INK command. Next, the font type is set to Arial with a size of 48 points and a welcome message is displayed using the CENTER TEXT command. The font size is then changed to 18 and another string is displayed. The WAIT KEY command is then executed, pausing application execution to allow the player to read the screen before pressing a keyboard key to continue game play.

Step 5: Setting Up a Loop to Control Game Play

The overall logic required to control game play will be managed by a DO loop. You have not learned about loops yet, so for now just add the following statements to the end of the code file.

```
DO    `Loop forever
REM   Put all remaining code here

LOOP
```

HINT All of the code statements covered in steps 6 to 10 will be embedded within the DO loop that you have defined here, after the DO statement and before the LOOP statement.

Step 6: Prompting the Player to Make a Move

At the start of each new round of play, the player is prompted to enter her move, which is accomplished by keying in either Rock, Paper, or Scissors and pressing the Enter key. The code statements responsible for prompting the player to make a move and for collecting and storing moves are shown next and should be embedded within the DO loop that you created in the preceding step.

```
SET TEXT SIZE 24   `Set the font size to 24 points

CLS RGB(255, 255, 255)   `Set background color to white

PRINT : PRINT : PRINT : PRINT : PRINT : PRINT   `Write six blank lines

`Prompt the player to make a guess
INPUT "            Enter a move (Rock, Paper, Scissors): ", Move$

PlayerM$ = UPPER$(Move$)   `Convert player move to uppercase characters
```

After setting the font size to 24 points and clearing the screen, the INPUT command is used to prompt the player to enter a move, which is then stored in a variable named Move$. The Upper$ command is used to convert the player's input to all uppercase characters, which is then stored in a variable named PlayerM$.

Step 7: Validating Player Moves

The only valid moves allowed in this game are ROCK, PAPER, and SCISSORS. To prevent any invalid input from being accepted and causing errors, insert the following statements into the DO loop, immediately after the statements that you added in the previous step.

```
`Only accept valid moves
IF PlayerM$ = "ROCK" OR PlayerM$ = "PAPER" OR PlayerM$ = "SCISSORS"


ENDIF
```

These statements are the beginning of an IF statement code block and are designed to allow the code statement embedded within the code block to execute only if valid input was provided by the player. This way, any invalid move will not be ignored and the player will simply be prompted to make a new move when the game's loop re-executes.

 All of the code statements covered in steps 8 to 10 will be embedded within the IF statement code block that you have defined here.

Step 8: Generating a Move on Behalf of the Computer

Next, you need to add the following set of statements within the IF statement code block that you just set up.

```
`Generate a set and use it to retrieve a random number from 1 to 3
seed = TIMER() :  RANDOMIZE seed :  RandomNo = RND(3)


`Equate the random number to a computer move
IF RandomNo = 1 THEN ComputerM$ = "ROCK"
IF RandomNo = 2 THEN ComputerM$ = "PAPER"
IF RandomNo = 3 THEN ComputerM$ = "SCISSORS"
```

These statements are responsible for generating a move on behalf of the computer. To do so, a random number between one and three is generated and then that number is analyzed by a set of three IF statements that determine which move to assign to the computer.

Step 9: Analyzing Game Results

Now that the player has made her move and a move has been generated on behalf of the computer, it is time to analyze the result of the game. This is accomplished by adding the following statement to the end of the IF statement code block that you defined in step 7.

```
`Analyze the player and computer's moves and determine results
IF PlayerM$ = "ROCK"
  IF ComputerM$ = "ROCK" THEN Result$ = "Tie!"
  IF ComputerM$ = "PAPER" THEN Result$ = "Computer wins!"
  IF ComputerM$ = "SCISSORS" THEN Result$ = "Player wins!"
ENDIF

IF PlayerM$ = "PAPER"
  IF ComputerM$ = "ROCK" THEN Result$ = "Player wins!"
  IF ComputerM$ = "PAPER" THEN Result$ = "Tie!"
  IF ComputerM$ = "SCISSORS" THEN Result$ = "Computer wins!"
ENDIF

IF PlayerM$ = "SCISSORS"
  IF ComputerM$ = "ROCK" THEN Result$ = "Computer wins!"
  IF ComputerM$ = "PAPER" THEN Result$ = "Player wins!"
  IF ComputerM$ = "SCISSORS" THEN Result$ = "Tie!"
ENDIF
```

As you can see, these statements are organized into three separate IF statement code blocks, each of which is designed to process the results of the game based on the player's move. If, for example, the player's move was PAPER, then the second IF statement code block executes, comparing the computer's move to the player's move and then assigning a string to a variable named Result$ based on the result of that analysis.

Step 10: Displaying Game Results

With the result of the game now stored as a test string in the Result$ variable, it is time to display that result. This is accomplished by adding the following statements to the end of the IF statement code block that you defined in step 7.

```
CLS RGB(255, 255, 255)   `Set background color to white

SET TEXT SIZE 36   `Set the font size to 36 points
TEXT 270, 130, "Game Results:"
TEXT 270, 160, "---------------------------"
```

```
SET TEXT SIZE 24  `Set the font size to 24 points
TEXT 270, 200, "Player move:      " + PlayerM$
TEXT 270, 230, "Computer move: " + ComputerM$
TEXT 270, 260, "Result:             " + Result$
SET TEXT SIZE 18 `Set the font size to 18 points
TEXT 270, 420, "Press Escape to quit or any other key to play again."

WAIT KEY  `Wait until the player presses a keyboard key
```

As you can see, these statements display the results of the game on the screen. This includes displaying the player's and the computer's moves as well as the message stored in the Result$ variable. Note that the last statement shown above displays a text string that instructs the player to press the Escape key to terminate game play or to press any other key to play again.

Step 11: Saving and Compiling Your Application

Your new game should be ready to go. Before doing so, make sure that you save your work first by clicking on the Save All option located on the File menu. Once this has been done, click on the Make/EXE RUN option located on the Compile menu to try compiling and executing your application.

The Final Result

As long as you have not made any typos and followed along with each step carefully, everything should work as described at the beginning of this chapter. Once compiled, spend a little time testing your new application. For starters, test out every possible combination of moves that the player can make and ensure that the game is appropriately evaluating the results each time. In addition, make sure that you not only enter valid moves but that you also enter invalid moves to ensure that the game handles things properly.

 You will also find a copy of this application's project file along with the source code on this book's companion website, located at http://www.courseptr.com/downloads.

SUMMARY

This chapter has covered a lot of ground. You learned how to implement conditional programming logic using different variations of the IF statement. You also learned how to work with the SELECT statement and to use relational operators when analyzing data. You also learned how to work with DarkBASIC Professional's arithmetic operators to perform different types of calculations and to use parentheses to override the order of precedence. Logical operators were also discussed as a means of combining logical tests and producing program code that is easier to understand and maintain.

Before you move on to Chapter 5, I suggest you set aside a few additional minutes to try and improve the Rock, Paper, Scissors game by implementing the following list of challenges.

CHALLENGES

1. As currently written, the Rock, Paper, Scissors game does not provide any instruction on the rules of the game. Consider modifying the game to provide this information at startup.

2. Rather than requiring the player to key in entire words (Rock, Paper, Scissors), consider also accepting entries of R, P, and S as valid input.

3. Rather than simply allowing the player to play an endless series of games without providing any feedback on the player's overall success, consider collecting statistics regarding the number of games won, lost, and tied and displaying these statistics with the information that is already displayed at the end of each game.

REPEATING STATEMENT
EXECUTION USING LOOPS

In the last chapter, you learned how to perform conditional logic using the IF and SELECT statements. Now it is time to learn how to use loops in order to repeatedly execute blocks of statements. A loop provides you with a powerful tool that is essential to game development, helping to control animation sequences and allow the repeated execution of statements that are responsible for controlling game play. Loops also provide an efficient means for processing the contents of arrays. They also help to streamline code, allowing you to set up the repeated execution of any number of code statements using just two additional statements. This chapter will teach you how to work with all four of DarkBASIC Professional's loops and explain the situations to which each type of loop is best applied. On top of all this, you will also learn how to create your next computer application, the Slot Machine game.

Specifically, you will learn:

- How to set up DO…LOOP, REPEAT…UNTIL, FOR…NEXT, and WHILE…ENDWHILE loops
- About the dangers of accidentally creating endless loops
- How to exit out of loops

PROJECT PREVIEW: THE SLOT MACHINE GAME

This chapter's game project is the Slot Machine game, which simulates the execution of a Las Vegas-style slot machine. The development of this game will provide the opportunity to gain additional experience working with the different types of loops as well as additional experience in refining your understanding of how to apply conditional programming logic. When first started, the screen shown in Figure 5.1 displays.

FIGURE 5.1

The Slot Machine game's welcome screen greets the player.

Once the welcome screen has been dismissed, the screen shown in Figure 5.2 displays, providing the player with instructions for playing the game.

To proceed and initiate an initial spin of the slot machine, the player can press any keyboard key. The screen is then cleared and numbers representing dials on the slot machine are displayed. In all, a total of 20 numbers are displayed in an animated sequence that lasts four seconds, simulating the spinning of slot machine dials. Figure 5.3 provides a snapshot view of the screen during the middle of a typical animation sequence.

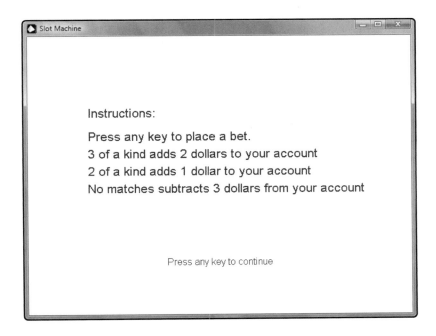

FIGURE 5.2

Before starting the game, the player must understand the rules of play.

At the end of the animation sequence, a final set of numbers is generated, representing the final result of the spin. Figure 5.3 shows the results of a spin in which the player has won.

FIGURE 5.3

Two or three of the same number results in a winning spin.

Money is automatically added or subtracted from the player's bank account after each spin. A pair results in one dollar being added to the player's account. Three of one number results in two dollars being added to the player's account. A spin with no matches results in a reduction of three dollars from the player's account. Figure 5.4 shows an example of a winning spin.

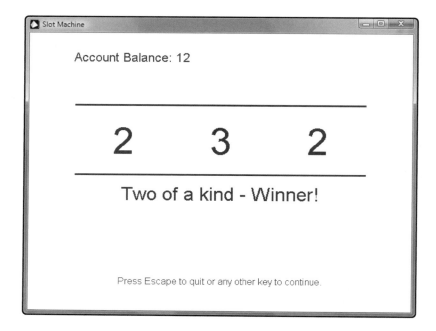

As long as the player has money in her account, she can elect to play the game indefinitely. In the player runs out of funds, as demonstrated in Figure 5.5, game play is immediately terminated.

However, if the player does not go broke and instead presses the Escape key or ends the game by clicking on the game window's close button, the screen shown in Figure 5.6 displays.

FIGURE 5.5

The player has gone broke.

FIGURE 5.6

The player is thanked for playing the game.

LEVERAGING THE POWER OF LOOPS

A *loop* is a block of code statements that repeatedly executes. Loops provide programmers with the ability to develop applications that are capable of processing large amounts of data. Loops also provide the ability to repeat the execution of groups of program statements while interacting with the user, as is the case with computer games. Without loops, you would be forced to create massive applications filled with redundant program statements to be able to process large amounts of data. Thanks to loops, you can write the program statements required to perform a particular task and then repeatedly execute as many times as necessary to control the play of a game, control any type of interaction with the user, or to process data stored in data statements, arrays, files, and so on.

As a quick demonstration of the power of loops and how they can be used to efficiently re-execute commands, take a look at the following example.

```
PRINT 1
PRINT 2
PRINT 3
PRINT 4
PRINT 5
PRINT 6
PRINT 7
PRINT 8
PRINT 9
PRINT 10
```

Here, 10 PRINT statements were required to display a list of 10 numbers. While retyping the same statements 10 times might not seem overly taxing, suppose you wanted to instead display 100, 1,000 or even 1,000,000 numbers? Obviously, you'd need a different way of addressing this challenge. The answer is to set up a loop and to let it do all of the heavy lifting for you. Consider the following example.

```
i = 1
DO
  PRINT i
  IF i = 10 THEN EXIT
  INC i
LOOP
```

Here, a DO...LOOP has been set up to display 10 numbers and then quit. When executed, this loop displays output that is identical to that produced by the previous example. However, only six statements were required to produce the desired result. When executed, this example displays the output shown in Figure 5.7.

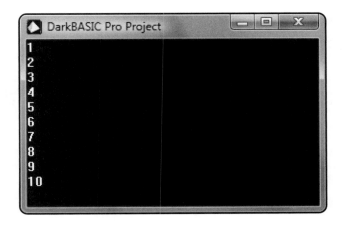

FIGURE 5.7

Using a DO Loop to count from 1 to 10.

Best of all, by modifying the embedded IF statement, you could adjust the loop to print 100, 1,000, or 1,000,000 numbers without requiring the addition of a single line of code.

DarkBASIC Professional provides a number of different types of loops, each of which is briefly outlined here:

- DO...LOOP. Sets up a loop that executes forever.
- REPEAT...UNTIL. Sets up a loop that repeats until a specified condition becomes true.
- FOR...NEXT. Sets up a loop that repeats a specified number of times.
- WHILE...WEND. Sets up a loop that repeats for as long as a specified condition remains true.

Although you can use any of the loops whenever you want, there are differences between them that make each type of loop better suited to address particular types of tasks. The rest of this chapter is dedicated to explaining how each of these different types of loops work and explaining the types of tasks that each loop is best suited to address.

Setting Up a DO...LOOP

The simplest loop to set up and work with is the DO...LOOP. This loop repeats a block of program statements forever. When you use this loop, it is up to you to provide for a way of terminating the loop's execution, which you can do using the EXIT command, which will be explained shortly. The syntax for the DO...LOOP is outlined here:

```
DO
    statements
LOOP
```

Here, *statements* represents one or more code statement to be executed each time the loop repeats its execution. Because the DO...LOOP does not provide a built-in mechanism for terminating its own execution, it is up to you to determine when you want to terminate the execution of the loop. For example, you might use a DO...LOOP to set up a loop to interactively prompt the player to provide any amount of input. As the following example demonstrates, you might set up the loop to terminate when the user enters a specific command, such as Quit or Exit, to signal the end of input.

```
PRINT "Christmas List Generator"
PRINT

DIM Presents$(0)
i = 0

DO

  CLS

  INPUT "What would you like for Christmas? ", Present$
  Present$ = UPPER$(Present$)

  IF Present$ <> "QUIT"

    Presents$(i) = Present$

    ARRAY INSERT AT BOTTOM Presents$(0)

    INC i

  ELSE

    CLS
    PRINT "Here is your Christmas list:"
    PRINT

    FOR Counter = 0 TO ARRAY COUNT(Presents$(0))
      PRINT Presents$(Counter)
    NEXT Counter
```

```
    WAIT KEY

    EXIT

  ENDIF

LOOP

END
```

In this example, a DarkBASIC application has been created that prompts the user to key in her Christmas wish list, one item at a time. Each time the user keys in a new item, the item is added to an item at the end of an array named Presents$(). Each time a new item is provided, it is added to the end of the array and the array is increased in size by one entry. The user is allowed to enter as many items as she wants. Data entry terminates when the user enters Quit and presses Enter, after which a FOR loop is executed. This loop processes every item stored in the Presents$() array. Figure 5.8 shows how this example looks when first started.

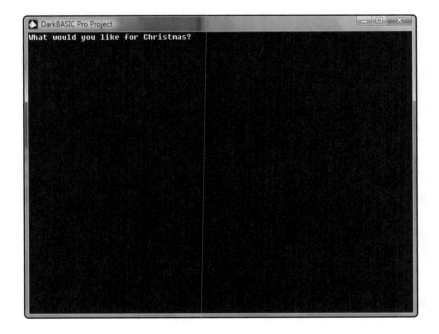

FIGURE 5.8

Using the DO…LOOP to collect user input.

Figure 5.9 shows an example of output generated by this DarkBASIC Professional application.

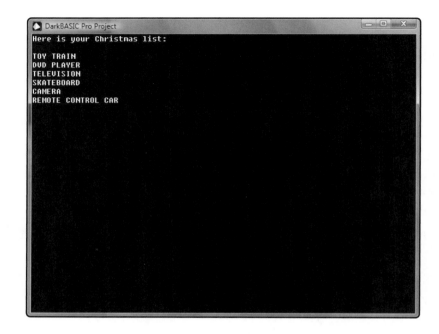

FIGURE 5.9

Displaying a list of six items that make up the user's Christmas list.

Working with the REPEAT...UNTIL Loop

The REPEAT...UNTIL loop is designed to execute as long as a tested condition continues to evaluate as false. The syntax of the REPEAT...UNTIL loop is outlined here:

```
REPEAT
  statements
UNTIL condition = true
```

Here, *statements* represents one or more code statements to be executed each time the loop repeats its execution, and *condition* represents an expression that is evaluated at the end of each execution of the loop. As long as the value of *condition* evaluates as false, the loop will repeat. However, if the value of *condition* evaluates as being true, the loop's execution is terminated.

Because the REPEAT...UNTIL loop's condition is not evaluated until the end of the loop, the loop will always execute at least once.

To develop a greater understanding of the DO...UNTIL loop, consider the following example.

```
i = 1

REPEAT

  PRINT i
  INC i

UNTIL i > 10
```

Here, a REPEAT...UNTIL loop that prints and increments the value assigned to a variable named *i* repeats 10 times, terminating only when the value of *i* exceeds a value of 10.

Working with the FOR...NEXT Loop

Another type of loop supported by DarkBASIC Professional is the FOR...NEXT loop. This loop is designed to address situations where programmers know in advance exactly how many times a loop must be repeated. As the FOR...NEXT loop executes, it automatically keeps track of the number of times that it executes using a variable, often referred to as a counter. The syntax for this form of loop is outlined here:

```
FOR counter = start TO end [STEP StepValue]
    statements
NEXT counter
```

Here, *statements* is a placeholder representing one or more code statements that should be executed each time the loop executes. *counter* is an integer variable that the loop will use to keep track of the number of times it executes. *start* is a numeric value used to assign an initial starting value to the *counter* variable. *end* is a numeric value that specifies the value that when reached by the counter variable, should terminate the loop's execution. *StepValue* is an optional parameter that is used to set the value that the loop will use when incrementing the value assigned to *counter* each time the loop repeats its execution. If the *StepValue* parameter is omitted, the FOR...NEXT loop will automatically increment the value of *counter* by one upon each iteration.

 Take note that *counter* is specified not only on the opening FOR statement but also on the closing Next statement. If you forget to add *counter* to the end of the Next statement, an error will occur.

The best way to get a good understanding of how to work with the FOR...NEXT loop is to look at a few examples. For starters, take a look at the following example.

```
FOR i = 1 TO 10
   PRINT i
NEXT i
```

Here, a FOR…NEXT loop is used to count from 1 to 10. The first time this loop executes, the value of i is set to 1 and then printed. Upon the next iteration of the loop, i is automatically incremented by 1. As a result a value of 2 is displayed. This process continues for another eight iterations, after which the value of i is set equal to 10, terminating the loop's execution.

As this example demonstrates, the FOR…NEXT loop performs the same types of tasks (including counting) that you can do using other types of loops. However, the FOR…NEXT loop differentiates itself from other loops by making the processing of data stored in loops an easy task, as demonstrated by the following example.

```
DIM ZooAnimals$(9)

ZooAnimals$(0) = "Lion"
ZooAnimals$(1) = "Zebra"
ZooAnimals$(2) = "Giraffe"
ZooAnimals$(3) = "Bear"
ZooAnimals$(4) = "Wolf"
ZooAnimals$(5) = "Python"
ZooAnimals$(6) = "Buffalo"
ZooAnimals$(7) = "Tiger"
ZooAnimals$(8) = "Eagle"
ZooAnimals$(9) = "Gorilla"

PRINT "Welcome to the Zoo. Today the following animals are on exhibit."
PRINT

FOR i = 0 TO ARRAY COUNT(ZooAnimals$())
  PRINT ZooAnimals$(i)
NEXT i

WAIT KEY

END
```

In this example, an array named ZooAnimals$() is set up and then 10 text strings are loaded into it. Next, a FOR…NEXT loop is used to print out all of the items that have been stored in the array. This is accomplished by setting the value of the loop's counter to 0 and then repeating the loop until its last element is processed. Rather than hardcode a value of 9, this example retrieved the index number of the last items stored in the array using the ARRAY COUNT command. When executed, this example displays the output shown in Figure 5.10.

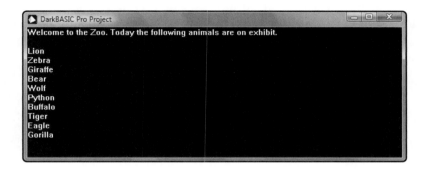

FIGURE 5.10

Using the FOR...NEXT Loop to process the contents of an array.

It you want, you can specify a negative number as the FOR...NEXT loop's *StepValue*, resulting in a loop that counts backwards, as demonstrated here:

```
DIM ZooAnimals$(9)

ZooAnimals$(0) = "Lion"
ZooAnimals$(1) = "Zebra"
ZooAnimals$(2) = "Giraffe"
ZooAnimals$(3) = "Bear"
ZooAnimals$(4) = "Wolf"
ZooAnimals$(5) = "Python"
ZooAnimals$(6) = "Buffalo"
ZooAnimals$(7) = "Tiger"
ZooAnimals$(8) = "Eagle"
ZooAnimals$(9) = "Gorilla"

PRINT "Welcome to the Zoo. Today the following animals are on exhibit."
PRINT

FOR i = 9 TO 0 STEP -1
  PRINT ZooAnimals$(i)
NEXT i

WAIT KEY

END
```

When executed, this example displays a list of all the elements stored in the ZooAnimals$() array, only unlike the previous example, this example prints out the contents of the array in reverse order.

Another interesting way of using the *StepValue* parameter when working with the FOR…NEXT loop is to assign a value other than 1 to it. For example, by assigning a value of 2 as the *StepValue* parameter, you could easily modify the FOR…NEXT loop used in the previous example to print out every other item stored in the ZooAnimals$() array.

```
DIM ZooAnimals$(9)

ZooAnimals$(0) = "Lion"
ZooAnimals$(1) = "Zebra"
ZooAnimals$(2) = "Giraffe"
ZooAnimals$(3) = "Bear"
ZooAnimals$(4) = "Wolf"
ZooAnimals$(5) = "Python"
ZooAnimals$(6) = "Buffalo"
ZooAnimals$(7) = "Tiger"
ZooAnimals$(8) = "Eagle"
ZooAnimals$(9) = "Gorilla"

PRINT "Welcome to the Zoo. Today the following animals are on exhibit."
PRINT

FOR i = 0 TO 9 STEP 2
  PRINT ZooAnimals$(i)
NEXT I

WAIT KEY

END
```

Figure 5.11 shows the output that will be displayed when this example is executed.

Setting Up a WHILE...ENDWHILE Loop

One last type of loop supported by DarkBASIC Professional is the WHILE...ENDWHILE loop. This loop is designed to repeat over and over again as long as the value of the specified condition continues to evaluate as being true. The syntax of the WHILE...ENDWHILE is outlined here:

```
WHILE condition = true
  statements
ENDWHILE
```

condition is a placeholder that represents an expression that the loop evaluates before it executes, and if the result of that evaluation is true, the loop executes. The loop will continue to execute until the value of the specified condition evaluates as false. For an example of the WHILE...ENDWHILE loop in action, take a look at the following statements.

```
i = 1

WHILE i <= 10
  PRINT i
  i = i + 1
ENDWHILE
```

When executed, this example counts from 1 to 10, at which time the i will equal 10 and the value of the text condition becomes false, ending the loop's execution.

GUARDING AGAINST ENDLESS LOOPS

Anytime you are working with a loop, you need to ensure that you do not accidentally set up an endless loop. An *endless loop* is a loop that is set up to run forever, without any means of terminating its own execution. Suppose for example, that you wanted to set up a loop to count from 1 to 100 as shown here:

```
i = 1

DO
   PRINT i
   INC i
LOOP
```

However, as currently set up, this loop has no means of terminating its execution when the value of i becomes equal to 100. As a result, the loop will repeat forever. To fix this error, you would rewrite it as shown here:

```
i = 1

DO
   PRINT i
   IF i = 100 THEN EXIT
   INC i
LOOP
```

As another example of how easy it is to accidentally set up an endless loop, take a look at this:

```
i = 1

WHILE i <= 100
   PRINT i
   i = i - 1
ENDWHILE
```

Here, the intention was to use a WHILE…ENDWHILE loop to count from 1 to 100. However, instead of incrementing the value of i by 1 at the end of each iteration of the loop, the value of i is accidentally decremented by 1, creating an endless loop.

When setting up a loop, it is very easy to accidentally mistype the • operator in place of the + operator. However, if you use the INC and DEC commands instead of the • operators, as demonstrated here, you are far less likely to mix things up.

```
i = 1

WHILE i <= 100
   PRINT i
   INC i
ENDWHILE
```

As the previous examples have demonstrated, loops provide the ability to repeatedly process a code block as many times as necessary using a minimum amount of program code statements. However, if you are not careful, the power of loops can be used to needlessly consume computer resources if you fail to set them up properly, creating an endless loop. It is therefore very important that you test every aspect of your program carefully, to ensure that you catch any possible mistakes, including endless loops.

Do not fret if you find that somewhere along the way, you create a DarkBASIC Professional application that contains an endless loop. Every programmer does it at least once. With proper testing, you should be able to identify an application with an endless loop before you share it with other people, protecting your reputation as a good programmer.

If during the testing of a DarkBASIC Professional application (when running it from within the DarkBASIC Professional default IDE) your program becomes unresponsive or begins repeating a series of actions without stopping, it may be stuck in an endless loop. You should be able to halt the execution by pressing the Escape key.

If, on the other hand, you are running a standalone copy of your application, you can halt the execution of your application using the Windows Task Manager window. The Task Manager window is accessed by pressing Ctrl + Alt + Del. Once opened, you can use the Task Manager to select your application from the list of active applications and click on the End Task button. In response, Windows will display a popup dialog that asks you to confirm the termination of your application. Of course, you still need to modify your application's source code to find and fix its endless loop and then compile a new standalone copy of your application.

Exiting Loops

As you have already seen, there are times when you will want to terminate a loop's execution early, based on the occurrence of a certain condition or value. This can be easily accomplished using the EXIT command, which has the following syntax.

```
EXIT
```

Once executed, the EXIT command immediately terminates the execution of the loop in which it is embedded, allowing processing to continue with the first statement that follows the loop, as demonstrated in the following example.

```
i = 1
DO
  PRINT i
  IF i = 10 THEN EXIT
  INC i
LOOP
```

Here, the EXIT command is used to terminate the execution of a DO...LOOP when the value of i becomes equal to 10.

 If you execute the EXIT command within a loop that is embedded inside another loop, only the inner loop's execution is halted. The outer loop will continue to run normally.

You can use the EXIT command to terminate the execution of any of the four types of loops supported by DarkBASIC Professional.

Back to the Slot Machine Game

Okay, it is time to turn your attention back to the development of this chapter's application project, the Slot Machine game. Through the development of this game, you will get further opportunities to work with different types of loops, including the DO...LOOP and FOR...NEXT loop. In addition, you will also have plenty of opportunity to apply conditional logic to the analysis of both player- and computer-generated data.

Designing the Game

The overall design of the Slot Machine game is relatively straightforward, using loops as the primary organizational structure for organizing and controlling application logic. The Slot Machine game will run within a window and is controlled via the keyboard. To help make things as easy as possible to understand and follow along, this game will be created by following a series of steps, as outlined here:

1. Create a new DarkBASIC project.
2. Specify game settings.
3. Document your application with comments.
4. Set up the player's account.
5. Display a welcome message.
6. Display game instructions.
7. Control game play with a loop.
8. Simulate the spinning of slot machine dials.
9. Generate final dial values.
10. Analyze spin results.
11. Display the player's adjusted account balance.
12. Terminate game play if the player goes broke.
13. Display a closing screen.
14. Save your new application.

Step 1: Creating a New DarkBASIC Project

The first step in creating the Slot Machine is the creation of a new DarkBASIC Professional project. Start DarkBASIC Professional and then click on the New Project menu item located on the File menu. In response, the Create a New DarkBASIC Professional Project window appears. Enter **Slot Machine** as the project name and then specify the location where you want to store your new project and then click on the OK button. In response, a new project is created.

Step 2: Configuring Game Settings

The next step in creating the Slot Machine application is to modify a few application settings. Begin by clicking on the Project button located at the bottom of the Project Panel window. To help document this project, place the cursor in the Project Comments field and type **This game simulates a Las Vegas slot machine**.

Next, click on the Settings button. Type **Slot Machine** in the Application Window Caption field. Select Windowed as the display setting for this game and set the resolution to 640×480.

Step 3: Documenting Your DarkBASIC Application

Now that you have modified the project's configuration settings, let's begin by modifying and adding the comment statements located at the beginning of the code file, as outlined here:

```
REM Project: SlotMachine
REM Created: 10/13/2007 9:58:53 PM
REM Executable name: SlotMachine.dba
```

```
REM Version: 1.0
REM Author: Jerry Lee Ford, Jr.
REM Description: This DarkBASIC Professional game simulates a Las Vegas
REM             Slot Machine
```

As you can see, the comment statements have been modified to provide additional information about the game and its author.

Step 4: Setting Up the Player's Account

At the beginning of the game, the player is assigned an account with ten dollars in it. To accomplish this, add the following statements to the beginning of the code file, as shown here:

```
`Assign ten dollars to the player's account
AccountBalance = 10
```

As you can see, an integer variable named AccountBalance has been created and assigned a starting value of 10.

Step 5: Displaying a Welcome Message

When first started, the game displays a welcome screen, which is created by adding the following statements to the end of the code file.

```
CLS RGB(255, 255, 255)  `Set background color to white

SET TEXT FONT "Arial"  `Set the font type to Arial
SET TEXT SIZE 48  `Set the font size to 48 points

ForegroundColor = RGB(0, 0, 160)      `Set foreground color to blue
BackgroundColor = RGB(255, 255, 255)  `Set background color to white
INK ForegroundColor, BackgroundColor  `Apply color settings

CENTER TEXT 320, 150, "Welcome to The"  `Display welcome message
CENTER TEXT 320, 220, "Slot Machine Game"
SET TEXT SIZE 18  `Set the font size to 18 points
CENTER TEXT 320, 380, "Press any key to continue."  `Display instructions

WAIT KEY  `Pause game play until the player presses a keyboard key
```

As you can see, these statements begin by clearing the screen and then setting the font type to Arial with a size of 48 points. Next, the background color is set to white and the foreground color to blue and then the game's welcome message is displayed using the CENTER TEXT command. Game play resumes after the player presses any keyboard key.

Step 6: Displaying Game Instructions

Once the welcome screen has been cleared, the game's instructions are displayed by adding the following code statements to the end of the code file.

```
CLS RGB(255, 255, 255)   `Set background color to white

SET TEXT SIZE 24   `Set the font size to 24 points
TEXT 100, 120, "Instructions:"
TEXT 100, 160, "Press any key to place a bet."
TEXT 100, 190, "3 of a kind adds 2 dollars to your account"
TEXT 100, 220, "2 of a kind adds 1 dollar to your account"
TEXT 100, 250, "No matches subtracts 3 dollars from your account"
SET TEXT SIZE 18 `Set the font size to 18 points
CENTER TEXT 320, 380, "Press any key to continue"  `Display instructions

WAIT KEY  `Pause game play until the player presses a keyboard key
```

The first statement sets the font size to 24 points using the SET TEXT SIZE command. Next a series of text strings is displayed and then the font size is changed to 18 points and a final string is then displayed. The WAIT KEY command is used to pause application execution, waiting for the player to first read the game's instructions.

Step 7: Controlling Game Play with a Loop

Overall game play is controlled by the repeated execution of a DO…LOOP, made up of the following statements

```
DO   `Loop forever

LOOP
```

These two statements should be added to the end of the project's code file. Except for the statements that are responsible for displaying the game's closing screen, all of the remaining code statements that make up this game are going to be placed inside this loop, allowing them to be re-executed as many times as the player wants to play the game.

Step 8: Simulating Spinning Slot Machine Dials

The first set of statements to be embedded within the game's DO...LOOP is shown next. These statements are responsible for simulating the spinning of dials on the lottery machine.

```
FOR i = 1 TO 19  `Iterate nineteen times

  ForegroundColor = RGB(0, 0, 160)       `Set foreground color to blue
  BackgroundColor = RGB(255, 255, 255)   `Set background color to white
  INK ForegroundColor, BackgroundColor   `Apply color settings

  CLS RGB(255, 255, 255)  `Set background color to white

  SET TEXT SIZE 36  `Set the font size to 36 points
  CENTER TEXT 320, 90, "_____"
  SET TEXT SIZE 72  `Set the font size to 72 points

  `Display random numbers representing slot machines dials
  CENTER TEXT 320, 150, STR$(RND(2) + 1) + "        " _
    + STR$(RND(2) + 1) + "          " + STR$(RND(2) + 1)

  SET TEXT SIZE 36  `Set the font size to 36 points
  CENTER TEXT 320, 210, "_____"
  SLEEP 200   `Pause game execution for a fifth of a second

NEXT
```

As you can see, a FOR...NEXT loop has been set up to execute 19 times. Each time the loop executes, it draws a line and displays three randomly generated numbers in the range of 1 to 3 followed by another line. In order to prevent the animation of the spinning numbers from occurring too quickly, and to properly simulate a real slot machine, the execution of the code statements in the FOR...NEXT loop has to be executed on a timed basis. This was accomplished using the SLEEP command.

 The SLEEP command pauses application execution for a specified amount of time and has the following syntax.

SLEEP *interval*

interval represents the number of milliseconds for which the application should be paused (1,000 milliseconds equals 1 second).

Take special note of the use of the underscore (_) character in the second occurrence of the CENTER TEXT command in the previous set of statements. This character is a continuation character, allowing you to write out a single statement over more than one line. Its use is entirely optional. This statement could have been easily written on a single line. However, doing so would have made the statement appear awkward. Splitting the statement up into two parts using the comment statement simply makes things easier to read by allowing the entire statement to be seen all at once, instead of letting it run off of the edge of the visible area of the screen.

TRAP

Unfortunately, the current copy of the default DarkBASIC Professional IDE does not support the use of the underscore continuation character. Neither does CodeSurge nor the Synergy IDE. However, BlueIDE does. If you are working with any code editor other than BlueIDE, you will have to avoid using the underscore continuation character.

Step 9: Generating Final Dial Values

Once the animated series of 20 dial spins has been completed, the FOR...NEXT loop ends, at which time a final 20th set of randomly generated numbers needs to be generated for each dial. It is these numbers that will be used to determine whether the player has received a winning or losing spin. The statement required to generate this final spin is shown next and should be embedded within the game's DO...LOOP, immediately after the FOR...NEXT loop that you just added.

```
SET TEXT SIZE 72   `Set the font size to 72 points
CLS RGB(255, 255, 255)  `Set background color to white

`Generate the final set of numbers representing dial values
DialOne = RND(2) + 1
DialTwo = RND(2) + 1
DialThree = RND(2) + 1

SET TEXT SIZE 36   `Set the font size to 36 points
CENTER TEXT 320, 90, "_____"
SET TEXT SIZE 72   `Set the font size to 72 points

`Display random numbers representing slot machine dials
CENTER TEXT 320, 150, STR$(DialOne) + "       " +  STR$(DialTwo) _
  + "        " + STR$(DialThree)

SET TEXT SIZE 36   `Set the font size to 36 points
CENTER TEXT 320, 210, "_____"
```

As you can see, this time the values of the three randomly generated numbers are assigned to variables named `DialOne`, `DialTwo`, and `DialThree`.

Step 10: Analyzing Spin Results

Now that the slot machine's three dial values have been generated, it is time to analyze the results of the spin and to determine whether the player won or lost money. This is accomplished by embedding the following statements inside the `DO…LOOP`, immediately following the previous set of statements that you just inserted.

```
`Add up the final result for each dial
Result = DialOne + DialTwo + DialThree

SET TEXT SIZE 36  `Set the font size to 36 points

`Look for a jackpot made up of 3 ones or 3 threes
IF (Result = 3) OR (Result = 9)
  CENTER TEXT 320, 260, "Three of a kind - Jackpot!"
  'Add 2 dollars to the player's account
  AccountBalance = AccountBalance + 2
ENDIF

IF Result = 6  `Look for a jackpot made up of 3 twos
  IF DialOne = DialTwo 'There are 3 twos
    CENTER TEXT 320, 260, "Three of a kind - Jackpot!"
    `Add 2 dollars to the player's account
    AccountBalance = AccountBalance + 2
  ELSE  `Look to see if a one, two, and three were generated
    CENTER TEXT 320, 260, "No matches - You Lose!"
    `Subtract 3 dollars from the player's account
    AccountBalance = AccountBalance - 3
  ENDIF
ENDIF

`Anything other than 3, 6, or 9 means a pair was generated
IF (Result <> 3) AND (Result <> 6) AND (Result <> 9)
  CENTER TEXT 320, 260, "Two of a kind - Winner!"
  `Add 1 dollar to the player's account
  AccountBalance = AccountBalance + 1
ENDIF
```

As you can see, the numeric value assigned to each dial is added together and assigned to an integer variable named Result. Next, a series of IF statement code blocks are executed that analyze the value assigned to Result. As Table 5.1 shows, by examining the value of Result, you can quickly ascertain the results of most spins.

TABLE 5.1   EVALUATING THE RESULTS GENERATED BY THE SLOT MACHINE

Value	Explanation
3	Three ones were generated
9	Three threes were generated
6	Three twos were generated or there was no match at all (e.g., a one and a two and a three were generated)
Other	Any other value indicates that a pair of matching numbers was generated

If Result has a value of three, this means that three ones must have been generated as the slot machine's final results. Similarly, the generation of three threes would result in a value of nine.

A final value of six means that either of two possible things has happened. Either three twos have been generated (2 + 2 + 2 = 6) or three different values have been generated (e.g., 1 + 2 + 3 = 6 or 1 + 3 + 2 = 6 or 2 + 1 + 3 = 6 or 2 + 3 + 1 = 6 or 3 + 1 + 2 = 6 or 3 + 2 + 1 = 6). The easier way of determining which of these two possible events has occurred is to examine the value of the first two dials. If Result equals 6 and the first and second dials have values of 2, then there is no need to even check on the value assigned to the third dial, since it must be 2. If the value of Result and the first two dials are not both 2s, then you know a losing spin has occurred (e.g., a spin with no matches).

Step 11: Displaying the Player's New Account Balance

Depending on the results of the spin, different amounts of money are automatically added or subtracted from the player's account. To notify the player of the changes to her bank account, the following statements are executed.

```
SET TEXT SIZE 24  `Set the font size to 24 points
`Display the player account balance
TEXT 75, 30, "Account Balance: " + STR$(AccountBalance)
SET TEXT SIZE 18  `Set the font size to 18 points
`Display instructions for continuing
CENTER TEXT 320, 420, "Press Escape to quit or any other key to continue."
```

These statements should be embedded at the bottom of the game's DO...LOOP. As you can see, they simply print out text strings that update the display of the player's account balance.

Step 12: Ending the Game if the Player Goes Bust

The last set of code statements to be included in the game's DO.....LOOP are shown next. These statements are responsible for checking on the value assigned to the AccountBalanace variable and for terminating game play in the event the player goes broke.

```
`End game play if the player has gone broke
IF AccountBalance <= 0

  SET TEXT SIZE 24  `Set the font size to 36 points

  ForegroundColor = RGB(255, 0, 0)       `Set foreground color to blue
  BackgroundColor = RGB(255, 255, 255)   `Set background color to white
  INK ForegroundColor, BackgroundColor   `Apply color settings

  `Notify the player that the game is over
  CENTER TEXT 320, 310, "G A M E   O V E R"
  CENTER TEXT 320, 350, "You have gone broke!"

  WAIT KEY  `Pause game play until the player presses a keyboard key

  EXIT  `Terminate the loop

ENDIF

WAIT KEY  `Pause game play until the player presses a keyboard key
```

As you can see, if the value of AccountBalance becomes less than or equal to zero, the EXIT command is executed, terminating the execution of the DO...LOOP.

Step 13: Displaying a Closing Screen

Once the game's DO...LOOP has finished its execution, the game needs to display its closing screen and then terminate. This is accomplished by adding the following set of statements to the end of the code file (outside of the DO...LOOP).

```
CLS RGB(255, 255, 255)  `Set background color to white

ForegroundColor = RGB(0, 0, 160)     `Set foreground color to blue
INK ForegroundColor, BackgroundColor  `Apply color settings

SET TEXT SIZE 24  `Set the font size to 24 points

`Display the game's closing message
CENTER TEXT 320, 150, "Thanks for playing the Slot Machine Game!"
SET TEXT SIZE 16  `Set the font size to 24 points
CENTER TEXT 320, 240, "Developed by Jerry Lee Ford, Jr."
CENTER TEXT 320, 260, "Copyright 2008"
CENTER TEXT 320, 280, "http://www.tech-publishing.com"

SET TEXT SIZE 18  `Set the font size to 16 points
CENTER TEXT 320, 380, "Press any key to end game."

WAIT KEY  `Pause game play until the player presses a keyboard key

END  `End the game
```

Step 14: Saving and Compiling Your Application

Assuming you created your own copy of the Slot Machine application as you followed along with the outlined steps, your new application should be ready for testing. Make sure you save your work by clicking on the File menu's Save All option and then click on the Make/EXE RUN option located on the Compile menu to compile and execute your new application.

The Final Result

Assuming that you have not made any typographical errors and that you followed each step carefully, everything should work as described at the beginning of this chapter.

> You will find a copy of this application's project file along with source code on this book's companion website, located at http://www.courseptr.com/downloads.

SUMMARY

In this chapter, you learned how to develop loops that repeatedly execute a block of statements. Loops are essential for the development of computer games. Loops facilitate the execution of programming statements that control a game's interaction with the user, collect player input, and then respond accordingly. DarkBASIC Professional provides access to many different statements that facilitate the creation of loops, including the DO...LOOP, REPEAT... UNTIL, FOR...NEXT, and WHILE...ENDWHILE loops. Loops also help to streamline program code by reducing the number of statements required to perform tasks that must be repeatedly executed. In addition to setting up different types of loops, this chapter also showed you how to prematurely terminate a loop's execution and advised you on the dangers of endless loops.

Before you move on to Chapter 6, I suggest you set aside a few additional minutes to try and improve the Slot Machine game by implementing the following list of challenges.

CHALLENGES

1. As currently written, the Slot Machine game only displays three different numbers. Because of this, it is very easy to generate spins that result in a tie. You might want to consider expanding the range of numbers used from 1 to 3 to 1 to 5 or more, thus increasing the game's level of difficulty.

2. Also, you might want to consider keeping track of the slot machine's previous spin and consider awarding double points whenever back-to-back matches occur.

3. If you elect to increase the range of numbers used by the game, you might also want to consider changing the values that are added and subtracted from the player's account. Because winning spins would be more difficult to generate, they should be increased in value.

ORGANIZING CODE LOGIC USING FUNCTIONS

Up to this point in the book, the only means that you have had for organizing the source code that makes up your DarkBASIC Professional applications are conditional code blocks and loops. While these constructs provide a means of grouping related code statements, they fall short as a tool for improving the overall organization of your code files. It is now time to learn how to organize your code statements using functions. Functions break down an application's source code into small parts, which work together like building blocks to create your code. This chapter will teach you how to create functions that can accept data passed to them as arguments and which can return a value back to the statements that call upon them to execute. You will also learn how to conditionally exit functions and to create external function libraries. On top of all this, you will learn how to create your next application project, the Tic, Tac, Toe game.

Specifically, you will learn how to:

- Improve the organization of your application source code using functions
- Create functions that accept and process data passed to them as arguments
- Return a value back to the statement that calls upon a function to execute
- Prematurely exit functions
- Create a function library and call upon functions stored in it
- Validate data passed to functions

PROJECT PREVIEW: THE TIC, TAC, TOE GAME

This chapter's game project is the Tic, Tac, Toe game. In this game, two players are pitted against each another in an effort to be the first player to line up three game board squares in a row (vertically, horizontally, or diagonally). When first started, the Tic, Tac, Toe game displays the welcome screen shown in Figure 6.1.

FIGURE 6.1

The Tic, Tac, Toe game's welcome screen.

When one of the players dismisses the welcome screen, the screen shown in Figure 6.2 displays.

Once a new game is started, the Tic, Tac, Toe game board is displayed, as shown in Figure 6.3. Players take turns making moves by specifying the coordinates of the square they want to select. Valid moves include: A1, A2, A3, B1, B2, B3, C1, C2, and C3.

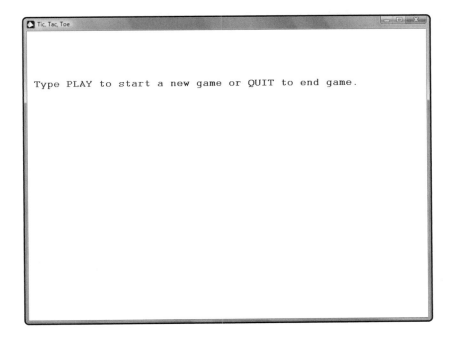

FIGURE 6.2

To start a new round of play, one of the players must type PLAY and press Enter.

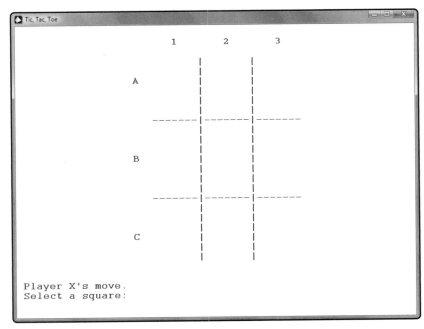

FIGURE 6.3

Player X always goes first.

Each time a player makes a move, the game evaluates it to ensure that it is valid. If a player enters a move that does not match one of the game board squares, the game disregards it, requiring the player to try again. If a player attempts to select a game board square that has already been selected, the message shown in Figure 6.4 displays.

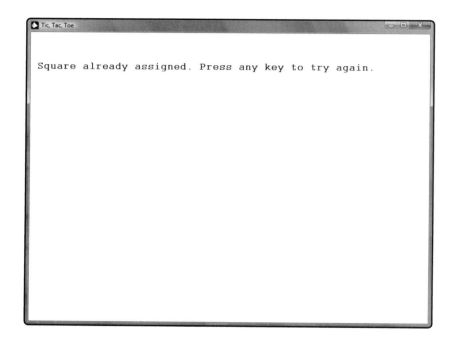

FIGURE 6.4

Players are not permitted to select a square that has already been assigned.

Game play continues until one player manages to successfully line up three consecutive game board squares or until every square on the game board is selected without either player winning. Figure 6.5 shows an example of a game that has ended with Player X winning.

At the end of each round, the players are prompted to play a new game or to quit. If the players elect to quit, the screen shown in Figure 6.6 displays, thanking the players for taking the time to play.

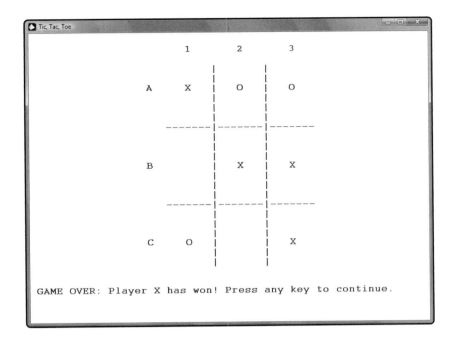

FIGURE 6.5

Player X has won the game by diagonally lining up three squares.

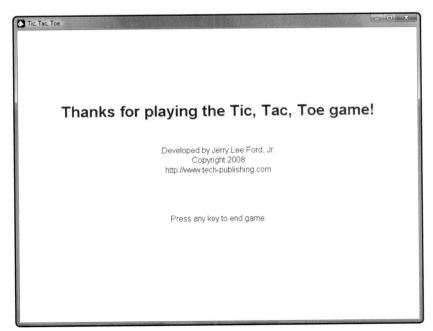

FIGURE 6.6

Game play has ended.

Improving Code Structure with Functions

As you learn more about DarkBASIC Professional and become a more proficient game programmer, it is inevitable that your application source code will grow longer and more complex. As such, it is important that you organize your source code to make it as manageable as possible. The best way of doing this is to break down your programming logic and corresponding program code into discrete parts, which you can then use as the basis for creating functions. A *function* is a procedure made up of a collection of programming statements that can be called upon to execute as a unit. Using functions, your DarkBASIC Professional source code is logically broken down into a series of mini applications, each of which performs a specific task. Like a complete application, individual functions are able to accept and process input and can produce output.

Most modern programming languages support two types of procedures: subroutines and functions. *Subroutines* are collections of programming statements called upon to execute as a unit. Subroutines can be passed data when called upon to execute. This data represents one or more *arguments*, which is then processed by the subroutine as it executes. *Functions* are basically the same things as subroutines, except that functions can also return a value back to the statement that called upon the function to execute.

DarkBASIC Professional does not make a distinction between these two types of procedures. Instead, it supports a single type of procedure, which it refers to as a function. However, depending on how you define them, DarkBASIC Professional functions can be made to act like either a subroutine or a function as defined in other programming languages.

Functions provide DarkBASIC programming with a number of different advantages. Primarily, they let you develop applications a section at a time. Each function that is added to an application should be designed to perform a specific individual task. By grouping statements that perform a particular task, functions facilitate code re-use, allowing all of the statements that make up a function to be called upon to execute whenever necessary. As a result, the use of functions can reduce the overall number of statements required to create an application.

By allowing you to develop your source code in a modular fashion, you can make your source code easier to understand and maintain. For example, suppose you developed a computerized version of the hangman word guessing game and put the code statements responsible for randomly retrieving a mystery word from an array of words in a function named RetrieveWord(). If, upon testing the game, you discovered that the game was repeatedly retrieving the same word, you should be able to identify the problem by locating the RetrieveWord() function and reviewing its statements. Since these statements are grouped within a single function, the task of locating and fixing the problem is significantly simplified. Obviously, by placing related code statements together into functions, you are able to isolate logical processes from one another.

DEFINING A FUNCTION

In DarkBASIC Professional, functions are declared using the FUNCTION and ENDFUNCTION statements using the syntax outlined here:

```
FUNCTION FunctionName([Parameter1,... ParameterN])
  statements
ENDFUNCTION [ReturnValue]
```

FunctionName represents the name assigned to the function. A function can accept and process any number of arguments passed to it when it is called upon to execute. Each argument that is to be accepted must be defined as individual, comma-separated parameters. *statements* represents any number of code statements that you want to execute when the function is called up for execution. *ReturnValue* is optional. When specified, it represents the value to be returned to the statement that called upon the function to execute. This value can be either a number or a string.

> Be sure that you assign unique names to any functions that you define within your DarkBASIC Professional applications. Function names must be unique and cannot be the same as other variable names that you have defined.

To get a better understanding of how to work with functions, take a look at the following example.

```
FUNCTION Greeting()
  PRINT "Good morning."
ENDFUNCTION
```

Here, a simple function named Greeting() has been defined. When called upon to execute, this function displays a text string. Once defined, the function can be called upon to execute from any location within a code file. When called, the function executes, after which control is returned back to the statement that called upon the function to execute.

Grouping Your Functions

DarkBASIC Professional is not able to execute a function unless it is explicitly called upon to execute. Therefore, you cannot locate your functions at the beginning or in the middle of your code files. If you forget and DarkBASIC Professional comes across a function that has not been explicitly called, an error occurs and the error message shown in Figure 6.7 displays.

To prevent an error from occurring, you must place all of your functions at the end of the code file, as demonstrated in the following example. As this example shows, you should precede any functions that are in your code file with the END command. This will ensure that your application is explicitly terminated and that an error will not occur.

```
REM Project: MyTest
REM Created: 10/21/2007 9:43:50 PM
REM
REM ***** Main Source File *****
REM

`Initialization Section

Global Name$ = "William"

`Main Processing Section

SayHello()
TalkAboutTheWeather()
GoodBye()

END

`Procedure Section

FUNCTION SayHello()
  PRINT "Well, hello " + Name$
  WAIT KEY
ENDFUNCTION

FUNCTION TalkAboutTheWeather()
  PRINT "Nice weather we are having, isn't it."
```

```
    WAIT KEY
    ENDFUNCTION

FUNCTION GoodBye()
    PRINT "Well, goodbye " + Name$
    WAIT KEY
ENDFUNCTION
```

Here, the source code file for a DarkBASIC Professional application is broken up into three main sections. The first section is used to define global variables used throughout the code file and it is where other application-wide initialization tasks should be placed. The second section is where the code statements that control the application's overall logical flow should be placed. The statements located in this section will also include calls to the application's functions. Finally, the third section (preceded by the END statement) is where functions should be placed.

As an alternative to placing all your application's functions at the end of its code file, DarkBASIC Professional provides the option of storing them in an external file, which you can then add to your project. You will learn how to set this up later in this chapter.

Executing Functions

So, now that you have seen how to define a simple function, it is time to learn how to call upon it to execute. If the function being called does not return a value, then you can call upon it using the following syntax.

FunctionName(Parameter1, ... ParameterN)

An *argument* is a value passed to a function for processing. This value can be a literal or a variable. A *parameter* is a variable defined within a function that corresponds to an argument that is passed to the function when it is called on to execute.

Here, *FunctionName* represents the name of the function that you want to execute. *Parameter1...ParameterN* represents any number of arguments that must be passed to the function.

An error will occur if you attempt to pass an argument to a function that does not accept them. Likewise, if you pass an argument of the wrong data type to a function, an error will occur.

As an example, suppose you added the following function to the end of a DarkBASIC Professional code file.

```
FUNCTION SayHello()
  PRINT "Well, hello."
ENDFUNCTION
```

To call upon this function, all you have to do is type its name, including its opening and closing parentheses, as shown here:

```
SayHello()
```

Passing Arguments to Functions

As has already been specified, you can define functions that are able to accept and process data passed to it as arguments. For example, the following function has been set up to accept a text string passed to it as an argument.

```
FUNCTION SayHello(Name$)
  PRINT "Well, hello " + Name$
  WAIT KEY
ENDFUNCTION
```

The following statement demonstrates how to call on this function.

```
SayHello("Molly")
```

 Arguments specified in functions are local to the function in which they are declared.

If you need to call upon a function that required two or more arguments, you can pass these arguments as a comma-separated list.

 DarkBASIC Professional provides the ability to specify the data type of any arguments that you specify when you are defining the function, as demonstrated here:

```
FUNCTION Greeting(Name$ AS STRING)
  PRINT "Good morning " + Name$
ENDFUNCTION
```

If you do not explicitly declare a function parameter's data type, DarkBASIC Professional will assign a default data type of integer.

Creating Functions That Return a Result

In addition to accepting and processing data passed to them as arguments, functions can also be set up to return a value back to a calling statement. To set this up, specify the value that you want to return by adding it to the end of the ENDFUNCTION statement, as demonstrated here:

```
FUNCTION RetrieveRandomNo()

  seed = TIMER() :  RANDOMIZE seed :  RandomNo = RND(3)

  IF RandomNo = 1 THEN ComputerM$ = "ROCK"
  IF RandomNo = 2 THEN ComputerM$ = "PAPER"
  IF RandomNo = 3 THEN ComputerM$ = "SCISSORS"

ENDFUNCTION ComputerM$
```

In this example, a function named RetrieveRandomNo() has been defined. Within the function, a random number between 1 and 3 is generated and assigned to a local integer variable named RandomNo. This value is then processed by three IF statements to determine which of three string values should be assigned to a variable named ComputerM$. The last thing the RetrieveRandomNo() function does when executing is return the value assigned to ComputerM$ to the statement that called on the function to execute.

Saving a Value Returned by a Function

When calling on a function that returns a value, you must use the syntax outlined next. Failure to do so will result in an error.

Variable = FunctionName(Parameter1, ... ParameterN)

Here, *FunctionName* represents the name of the function that you want to execute and *Parameter1 ... ParameterN* represents any number of arguments to be passed to the function.

For example, the following statement demonstrates how to call upon and execute the RetrieveRandomNo() function presented in the previous section.

```
ComputerMove$ = RetrieveRandomNo()
```

 Global variables offer an alternative to passing data as arguments to functions and setting up a function to return a value. However, the problem with using global variables in place of tightly controlled local variables is that it increases the possibility of accidentally changing the value assigned to a global variable. Limiting access to variables is considered to be a good programming practice.

PREMATURELY TERMINATING FUNCTIONS

Be default, a function processes all of its statements in a top to bottom order, terminating when the ENDFUNCTION statement is executed. However, there may be times in which you want to prematurely terminate the execution of a function. DarkBASIC Professional provides the EXITFUNCTION command, which has the following syntax.

```
EXITFUNCTION [ReturnValue]
```

Here, *ReturnValue* is optional, but if specified, it returns a value back to the statement that called upon the function to execute. To get a better understanding of how to work with this command, take a look at the following example.

```
INPUT "How old are you? " , PlayerAge

Continue$ = AgeCheck(PlayerAge)

IF Continue$ = "Rejected"
  PRINT "Sorry, but you are too young to play this game."
  EXIT
ELSE
  PRINT "OK, let's play!"
ENDIF

WAIT KEY
END

FUNCTION AgeCheck(Age)
  IF Age < 18 THEN EXITFUNCTION "Rejected"
ENDFUNCTION "Accepted"
```

Here, the user is asked to enter her age, which is stored in an integer value named PlayerAge. Next, the AgeCheck() function is called and passed the value of PlayerAge as an argument. The AgeCheck() function begins its execution by assigning the value passed to it to a local variable named Age. Based on the value assigned to Age, the function returns a value of "Accepted" or "Rejected" back to the statement that called upon it to execute.

VALIDATING DATA PASSED TO FUNCTIONS

In the preceding example, a value representing the player's age is passed to the AgeCheck() function. The function returns a string value back to the calling statement based on the value of the argument that is passed to it. However, what happens if the data passed to the function is not any good? For example, the user entered an age of 200 or -10. Neither of these arguments makes any logical sense when referencing a person's age.

Rather than accepting any data that is passed to it with blind faith, it is a good idea to validate the data, as demonstrated in the following example.

```
INPUT "Enter your name: " , PlayerName$
INPUT "Enter your age: " , PlayerAge

Greeting(PlayerName$, PlayerAge)

WAIT KEY
END

FUNCTION Greeting(Name$, Age)

  IF Name$ = "" THEN PRINT "Name not specified." : EXITFUNCTION
  IF Age < 1 or Age > 110 THEN Print "Age is out of range" : EXITFUNCTION

  PRINT "Hello " + Name$ + ". You are " + STR$(Age) + " years old."

ENDFUNCTION
```

The example begins by prompting the user to type in her name and then her age. These two pieces of information are then passed to the Greeting() function as arguments. Inside the function, these two arguments are mapped to local variables named Name$ and Age. Next, two IF statements analyze the validity of these two pieces of information. Specifically, the first IF statement checks to ensure that the user did not simply press the Enter key when prompted to type in her name. The second IF statement checks the numeric value assigned to Age to see if it falls within a valid range.

BUILDING A FUNCTION LIBRARY

If you find that over time you are copying one or more functions that you have created into many different applications, you might want to consider storing these functions in a code file of their own. You can then add this file to any application that needs access to one or more functions defined within that file. Once added to a project, DarkBASIC Professional automatically merges the contents of any files that you add to your project into a single source file.

There are a couple of different ways that you can create your own custom function library. One option is to create a new DarkBASIC project, naming it something like MyFunctionsLib and then adding your collection of functions to it. Later, when you are working on a DarkBASIC Professional project in which you want to include one of the functions stored in your function library, you can add your function library file to it. You can accomplish this by clicking on the Files button located at the bottom of the Project Panel. Once the Files view is displayed, you can add your function library file to your project by clicking on the Browse button located at the top of the panel. This will display a browser window, which you can use to locate and select your function library file. Once added to the project you are working on, you will see the file displayed on the Project Panel. In addition, using the drop-down list located on the DarkBASIC Professional IDE's toolbar, you will be able to switch between your project file and your function library file, as demonstrated in Figure 6.8.

FIGURE 6.8

Switching between a project file and a function library file.

Once you have added your function library file to your application, you can call on any function within it just as if the function were part of your project's main code file.

HINT

The DarkBASIC Professional IDE only displays information about files that you explicitly add to the Files panel. Your project's main or default project code file is not displayed in this panel.

The second way of creating and adding a function library file to a DarkBASIC Professional project is to click on the File button located at the bottom of the Project Panel and then click on the Add New files button located at the top of the panel. This opens a Save Source File To window in which you can enter the name that you want to assign to your new function library file and the location where you want to save it. Once created, you can add any functions that you want to the file and they will automatically be made available to your program code. In addition, since your new function library file is stored externally from your project file, you can easily add this file to other DarkBASIC Professional projects if you need to.

HINT

As the number of functions that you add to this file grows, you might want to consider grouping the functions into separate files, allowing you to better organize and manage them.

As your DarkBASIC Professional projects grow in size and complexity, the size of your project's source code can become difficult to manage. One way of managing this type of situation is to break down your project's source code into different files, which you can then manage and work with separately in your project. For example, you might group your project's functions into different groups, each of which could be stored in a separate file. If your application contains DATA statements, you could move them to an external file as well.

BACK TO THE TIC, TAC, TOE GAME

Okay, now it is time to turn your attention back to the development of the chapter's application project: the Tic, Tac, Toe game. This game's overall execution is controlled by a loop, which executes until the players decide to quit playing. The rest of the loop is organized into a collection of functions, each of which performs a specific task.

Designing the Game

The overall design of the Tic, Tac, Toe game is very straightforward. To help make things as easy as possible, this game will be created by following a series of steps, as outlined here:

1. Create a new DarkBASIC project.
2. Configure the game's project settings.
3. Document your application with comments.
4. Define the game's global variables.
5. Develop the game's overall controlling logic.
6. Create the Welcome_Screen() function.
7. Create the Set_Game_Font() function.
8. Create the Play_A_Round() function.
9. Create the Reset_Board() function.
10. Create the Play() function.
11. Create the Display_Board() function.
12. Create the Validate_Move() function.
13. Create the Post_Move() function.
14. Create the Analyze_Results() function.
15. Create the Closing_Screen() function.
16. Save your new application.

Step 1: Creating a New DarkBASIC Project

The first step in creating the Tic, Tac, Toe game is to create a new project. Do so by starting DarkBASIC Professional and clicking on the New Project menu item located on the File menu. The Create a New DarkBASIC Professional Project window appears.

Type in **TicTacToe** in the Project Name file and specify where you want your new project to be saved and then click on the OK button. In response, a new project is created for you.

Step 2: Configuring Game Settings

The next step in creating the Tic, Tac, Toe game is to modify a few application settings. Begin by clicking on the Project button located at the bottom of the Project Panel window. To help document this project, place the cursor in the Project Comments field and type **This is a two-player version of the Tic, Tac, Toe game**.

Next, click on the Settings button. Type **Tic, Tac, Toe** in the Application Window Caption field. Select Windowed as the display setting for this game and set the resolution to 800×600.

Step 3: Documenting Your DarkBASIC Application

Now that you have created and configured the project settings for the Tic, Tac, Toe game, let's begin the coding process by modifying and adding to the comment statements that have already been added to your project's code file, as shown here:

```
REM Project: TicTacToe
REM Created: 10/20/2007 11:10:26 AM
REM Executable name: TicTacToe.dba
REM Version: 1.0
REM Author: Jerry Lee Ford, Jr.
REM Description: This is a two-player version of the Tic, Tac, Toe game
```

As you can see, the comment statements have been modified to provide additional information about the game and its author.

Step 4: Defining the Game's Global Variables

The Tic, Tac, Toe game must keep track of and manage the values assigned to numerous variables, including variables representing all of the game board squares. Rather than trying to manage the passing of these variable's values as arguments to all of the project's functions, I have elected to define them as global variables as shown next. Each of these statements needs to be added to the end of the project's code file.

```
`Define the game's global variable and assign initial values
GLOBAL Player$ AS STRING = "X"    `Represents the current player
GLOBAL Winner$ AS STRING = ""     `Used to store game results
GLOBAL NoMoves AS INTEGER = 0     `Keeps count of the number of moves made
GLOBAL Message$ AS STRING = ""    `Used to display instructional messages
```

```
GLOBAL Choice$ AS STRING = ""    `Controls the execution of the main loop

`Define variables representing the squares on the game board
GLOBAL a1$, a2$, a3$, b1$, b2$, b3$, c1$, c2$, c3$ AS STRING
```

Step 5: Developing the Game's Overall Programming Logic

Because the programming logic required to play this game is organized into functions, the overall controlling logic required to manage the execution of the game, shown next, is not very long or complicated. Your next step is to add these code statements to the end of your project's code file.

```
Welcome_Screen()  `Call on the function that displays the welcome screen

Set_Game_Font()   `Call on the function that sets the game's default font

DO  `Loop forever

  `Call the function that prompts player for permission to start the game
  Choice$ = Play_A_Round()

  IF Choice$ = "PLAY"    `The player has elected to play a round
      Reset_Board()      `Call the function that prepares the game board
      Play()             `Call the function that controls game play
  ELSE                   `The player wants to end the game
    Closing_Screen()     `Call the function that displays the closing screen
    EXIT                 `Terminate the loop's execution
  ENDIF

LOOP

END  `Terminate the execution of this application
```

As you can see, the first two statements call on a pair of functions that are responsible for displaying the game's welcome screen and setting the game's global font settings. Next, a DO...LOOP is set up to control the repeated execution of the game. Each time the loop repeats, it calls upon the Play_A_Round() function, which asks the players if they want to play a game or quit. The result returned by the function is then analyzed by an IF statement code block. If the players elect to play a new game, the Play_A_Round() function returns a value of "PLAY" in which case the RESET_BOARD() and PLAY() functions are called upon to execute. These functions clear the game board and then manage the play of an individual round of play. If the players elect to quit the game, a value of "QUIT" is returned from the Play_A_Round() function, in which case the ClosingScreen() function is called on to execute and then the EXIT command is executed, terminating the DO...LOOP and ending the game.

Step 6: Displaying a Welcome Message

The code statements that make up the Welcome_Screen() function are shown next and should be added to the end of the project code file.

```
`This function displays the game's welcome screen
FUNCTION Welcome_Screen()

  CLS RGB(255, 255, 255)  `Set background color to white

  SET TEXT FONT "ARIAL"  `Set the font type to Arial
  SET TEXT SIZE 48  `Set the font size to 48 points

  ForegroundColor = RGB(0, 0, 160)      `Set foreground color to blue
  BackgroundColor = RGB(255, 255, 255)  `Set background color to white
  INK ForegroundColor, BackgroundColor  `Apply color settings

  CENTER TEXT 400, 150, "Welcome to the"  `Display a welcome message
  CENTER TEXT 400, 220, "Tic, Tac, Toe game"
  SET TEXT SIZE 18  `Set the font size to 18 points
  CENTER TEXT 400, 380, "Press any key to continue." `Display instructions

  WAIT KEY  `Pause game play until the player presses a keyboard key

ENDFUNCTION
```

When executed, this function displays a welcome message and prompts the players to press any keyboard key to continue.

Step 7: Developing the Set_Game_Font() Function

The code statements that make up the Set_Game_Font() function are shown next and should be added to the end of the project code file. This function is responsible for setting the font attributes that are used by the game when displaying the game board and the player's moves.

```
`This function sets default font and text settings
FUNCTION Set_Game_Font()

  SET TEXT FONT "Courier"  `Set the font type to Courier
  SET TEXT SIZE 24  `Set the font size to 24 points
  SET TEXT TO BOLD  `Set text to display in bold print
  ForegroundColor = RGB(0, 0, 160)     `Set foreground color to blue
  BackgroundColor = RGB(255, 255, 255)  `Set background color to white
  INK ForegroundColor, BackgroundColor  `Apply color settings

ENDFUNCTION
```

Step 8: Developing the Play_A_Round() Function

The code statements that make up the Play_A_Round() function are shown next and should be added to the end of the project code file. This function is responsible for asking the players whether they want to play a round of Tic, Tac, Toe or quit the game.

```
`This function prompts the player for permission to play a new game
FUNCTION Play_A_Round()

  DO  `Loop forever

    CLS RGB(255, 255, 255)  `Set background color to white
    PRINT : PRINT : PRINT : PRINT : PRINT     `Print five blank lines
    `Prompt the player for permission to start a new round of play

    INPUT " Type PLAY to start a new game or QUIT to end game. ", Reply$

    Reply$ = Upper$(Reply$)  `Convert the player's input to uppercase

    `Determine if valid input was provided
    IF Reply$ = "PLAY" or Reply$ = "QUIT"
      EXIT  `Exit the function
    ENDIF

  LOOP

ENDFUNCTION Reply$
```

As you can see, the statements within this function are controlled by a DO...LOOP. The first statement in the loop clears the screen. Next, five blank lines are printed and then the INPUT command is used to display a prompt that asks the players to enter PLAY to start a new game or QUIT to terminate the application. The player's response is stored in a variable named Reply$, which is then analyzed by an IF statement code block. If the players entered PLAY or QUIT, the EXIT command is executed, terminating the loop's execution. With nothing else to do, the function wraps up its execution as well, returning the string value that was entered by the players. However, if the players did not enter either PLAY or QUIT as their response, then invalid input was provided, in which case the loop repeats, prompting the players to supply an answer.

Step 9: Developing the Reset_Board() Function

The code statements that make up the Reset_Board() function are shown next and should be added to the end of the project code file. This function is responsible for resetting the value of variables representing each of the squares on the game board to a single blank space and then for resetting the values of a number of global variables back to their initial default values.

```
`This function readies the game for a new round of play
FUNCTION Reset_Board()

  `Clear out each game board square
  a1$ = " "
  a2$ = " "
  a3$ = " "
  b1$ = " "
  b2$ = " "
  b3$ = " "
  c1$ = " "
  c2$ = " "
  c3$ = " "


  `Reset default variable settings
  Player$ = "X"
  Winner$ = ""
  NoMoves = 0
  Message$ = ""

ENDFUNCTION
```

Take note of the fact that each of the nine variables used to represent game board squares is assigned a single blank space. A blank space indicates that the game board square is available for selection. Later, game board squares will be assigned to individual players by changing this blank space to an X or an 0.

Step 10: Developing the Play() Function

The code statements that make up the Play() function are shown next and should be added to the end of the project code file. This function is responsible for managing the steps involved in playing a complete round of Tic, Tac, Toe.

```
`This function is responsible for managing a round of play
FUNCTION Play()

  DO    `Loop forever

    IF Winner$ = "X"  `Player X has won the game
     Message$ = " GAME OVER: Player X has won! Press any key to continue."
     Display_Board()  `Display the Tic, Tac, Toe game board
     WAIT KEY     `Pause game play until the player presses a keyboard key
     EXIT          `Terminate the execution of the loop
    ENDIF

    IF Winner$ = "0"  `Player 0 has won the game
     Message$ = " GAME OVER: Player 0 has won! Press any key to continue."
     Display_Board()  `Display the Tic, Tac, Toe game board
     WAIT KEY     `Pause game play until the player presses a keyboard key
     EXIT          `Terminate the execution of the loop
    ENDIF

    IF Winner$ = "tie"   `The game has ended in a tie
     Message$ = " GAME OVER: Tie! Press any key to continue."
     Display_Board()     `Display the Tic, Tac, Toe game board
     WAIT KEY     `Pause game play until the player presses a keyboard key
     EXIT          `Terminate the execution of the loop
    ENDIF

    `Display message identify whose turn it is
    Message$ = " Player " + Player$ + "'s move."
```

```
Display_Board()  `Display the Tic, Tac, Toe game board

`Prompt the player to select a game board square
INPUT " Select a square: ", Move$
Move$ = LOWER$(Move$)  `Convert the input to all lowercase

`Only accept game board squares as valid input
If Move$ = "a1" OR Move$ = "a2" OR Move$ = "a3" OR Move$ = "b1" OR _
   Move$ = "b2" OR Move$ = "b3" OR Move$ = "c1" OR Move$ = "c2" OR _
   Move$ = "c3"

   `Call on the Validate_Move function in order to validate the player's
   `input
   ValidMove$ = Validate_Move(Move$)

   IF ValidMove$ = "True"  `The player's move was valid
     INC NoMoves  `Keep track of the number of moves made during the game
     Post_Move(Move$)  `Call on the function that assigns player moves
   ELSE  `the player's move was invalid
     CLS RGB(255, 255, 255)  `Set background color to white
     PRINT : PRINT : PRINT: PRINT: PRINT  `Print 5 blank lines
     PRINT " Square already assigned. Press any key to try again."
     WAIT KEY  `Pause game play until the player presses a keyboard key
   ENDIF

   `If all nine game board squares have been selected without a winner
   `being declared, then the game has ended in a tie
   IF NoMoves = 9
     Analyze_Results()  `Check for a winner
     If Winner$ = ""
         Winner$ = "tie"     `Declare a tie
     ENDIF
   ELSE
     Analyze_Results()  `Check for a winner
   ENDIF

   IF ValidMove$ = "True"  `Switch player turns
     IF Player$ = "X"
```

```
        Player$ = "O"
      ELSE
        Player$ = "X"
      ENDIF
    ENDIF

  ENDIF

  LOOP

ENDFUNCTION
```

As you can see, the statements within this function are controlled by a DO…LOOP. Three IF statement code blocks are set up at the beginning of the loop. Based on the value assigned to a global variable named Winner$, they determine whether the game is over. If the game is over, a message is displayed and the EXIT command is executed, terminating the loop's execution.

If, however, the game has not ended, then a string is assigned to Message$, indicating whose turn it is, and the game board is displayed by calling on the Display_Board() function to execute. Next, the INPUT command is used to prompt the current player to select a square. The player's input is then converted to all lowercase and assigned to a variable named Move$.

The rest of the loop is made up of a large IF statement code block, which executes only if the player specified a valid game board square as her input (A1-C3). If this is the case, then the Validate_Move() function is called and passed the player's move as an argument. This function is responsible for further validating the player's move. If the player's move is valid, the Post_Move() function is called and passed the player's move as an argument. If the player's move was not valid, an error message is displayed and the player is instructed to try again.

Once a valid move is received and processed, the value of an integer variable named NoMoves is examined to see if it is equal to 9, in which case the game is over because all of the game board squares have been selected. Therefore, the Analyze_Results() function is called. This function scans the game board to see if the last player to make a move has won and sets the value of a global variable named Winner$ to that player's corresponding letter. If the game has not been won, a tie is declared.

Even if all nine game board squares have not been selected, the Analyze_Results() function is still called to see if the game has been won. The last task performed within the loop is to switch between player turns whenever the current player has made a valid move.

Step 11: Developing the Display_Board() Function

The code statements that make up the Display_Board() function are shown next and should be added to the end of the project code file. This function is responsible for displaying the Tic, Tac, Toe game board.

```
`This function displays the Tic, Tac, Toe game board
FUNCTION Display_Board()

  CLS RGB(255, 255, 255)  `Set background color to white

  `Display the game board
  PRINT
  PRINT
  PRINT "                        1                2                3"
  PRINT
  PRINT "                                |                |"
  PRINT "                                |                |"
  PRINT "          A      " + a1$ + "    |    " + a2$ + "    |    " + a3$
  PRINT "                                |                |"
  PRINT "                                |                |"
  PRINT "                                |                |"
  PRINT "                    -------|------------------|-------"
  PRINT "                                |                |"
  PRINT "                                |                |"
  PRINT "                                |                |"
  PRINT "          B      " + b1$ + "    |    " + b2$ + "    |    " + b3$
  PRINT "                                |                |"
  PRINT "                                |                |"
  PRINT "                                |                |"
  PRINT "                    -------|------------------|-------"
  PRINT "                                |                |"
  PRINT "                                |                |"
  PRINT "                                |                |"
  PRINT "          C      " + c1$ + "    |    " + c2$ + "    |    " + c3$
  PRINT "                                |                |"
  PRINT "                                |                |"
  PRINT
  PRINT
  PRINT Message$    `Display anything stored in the Message$ variable

ENDFUNCTION
```

Note that the game board consists of blank spaces and regular text characters. You should also note that embedded within the game board (using string concatenation) are global variables representing each game board square. During game play, these blank spaces are replaced with the letters X and O, based on player moves. Also note that at the bottom of the game board the global variable Message$ is displayed. This variable is assigned different text string values during game play indicating whose turn it is or when the game has been won.

Step 12: Developing the Validate_Move() Function

The code statements that make up the Validate_Move () function are shown next and should be added to the end of the project code file. This function is responsible for ensuring that the current player has not attempted to select a game board square that has already been assigned. It is passed a text string argument when called, which is assigned to a local variable named Move$.

```
`This function is responsible for validating player moves
FUNCTION Validate_Move(Move$)

  ReturnValue$ = "False"  `By default return a value of false

  `Return a value of true if the selected square is available
  IF Move$ = "a1" AND a1$ = " " THEN ReturnValue$ = "True"
  IF Move$ = "a2" AND a2$ = " " THEN ReturnValue$ = "True"
  IF Move$ = "a3" AND a3$ = " " THEN ReturnValue$ = "True"
  IF Move$ = "b1" AND b1$ = " " THEN ReturnValue$ = "True"
  IF Move$ = "b2" AND b2$ = " " THEN ReturnValue$ = "True"
  IF Move$ = "b3" AND b3$ = " " THEN ReturnValue$ = "True"
  IF Move$ = "c1" AND c1$ = " " THEN ReturnValue$ = "True"
  IF Move$ = "c2" AND c2$ = " " THEN ReturnValue$ = "True"
  IF Move$ = "c3" AND c3$ = " " THEN ReturnValue$ = "True"

ENDFUNCTION ReturnValue$
```

As you can see, a series of nine IF statements are executed when the function is called. Each statement is designed to analyze the value assigned to a particular game board square. Only one of these IF statements actually execute each time the function is called. When executed, an IF statement checks to see if the value of the square's associated global variable is equal to a single blank space, in which case the square is available and a value of True is assigned to ReturnValue$. If, on the other hand, the global variable representing the game board square is not blank, then the square has already been assigned and a default value of False is assigned to `ReturnValue$`. Once the value of `Move$` has been analyzed, the value assigned to `ReturnValue$` is passed back to the statement that called upon the function.

Step 13: Developing the Post_Move() Function

The code statements that make up the `Post_Move()` function are shown next and should be added to the end of the project code file. This function is passed a text string representing one of the squares on the Tic, Tac, Toe game board. It then assigns the game board square associated with the variable that is passed to it to the current player.

```
`This function is responsible for displaying player moves
FUNCTION Post_Move(Move$)

  `Assigned the selected square to the current player
  IF Move$ = "a1" THEN a1$ = Player$
  IF Move$ = "a2" THEN a2$ = Player$
  IF Move$ = "a3" THEN a3$ = Player$
  IF Move$ = "b1" THEN b1$ = Player$
  IF Move$ = "b2" THEN b2$ = Player$
  IF Move$ = "b3" THEN b3$ = Player$
  IF Move$ = "c1" THEN c1$ = Player$
  IF Move$ = "c2" THEN c2$ = Player$
  IF Move$ = "c3" THEN c3$ = Player$

ENDFUNCTION
```

Remember, `Player$` is a global variable that contains a letter (X or 0) representing the current player whose move is being processed.

Step 14: Developing the Analyze_Results() Function

The code statements that make up the `Analyze_Results()` function are shown next and should be added to the end of the project code file. This function is responsible for analyzing the game board to see if the current player has won the game.

```
`When called this function analyzes the game board looking for a winner
FUNCTION Analyze_Results()

  `Check the first column for a winner
  IF a1$ = Player$ AND b1$ = Player$ AND c1$ = Player$
    Winner$ = Player$
  ENDIF
```

```
`Check the second column for a winner
IF a2$ = Player$ AND b2$ = Player$ AND c2$ = Player$
  Winner$ = Player$
ENDIF

`Check the third column for a winner
IF a3$ = Player$ AND b3$ = Player$ and c3$ = Player$
  Winner$ = Player$
ENDIF

`Check the first row for a winner
IF a1$ = Player$ AND a2$ = Player$ AND a3$ = Player$
  Winner$ = Player$
ENDIF

`Check the second row for a winner
IF b1$ = Player$ AND b2$ = Player$ AND b3$ = Player$
  Winner$ = Player$
ENDIF

`Check the third row for a winner
IF c1$ = Player$ AND c2$ = Player$ AND c3$ = Player$
  Winner$ = Player$
ENDIF

`Check diagonally from the top left corner to the bottom right corner
`for a winner
IF a1$ = Player$ AND b2$ = Player$ AND c3$ = Player$
  Winner$ = Player$
ENDIF

`Look diagonally from the bottom left corner to the top right corner
`for a winner
IF c1$ = Player$ AND b2$ = Player$ AND a3$ = Player$
  Winner$ = Player$
ENDIF

ENDFUNCTION
```

As you can see, this function is made up of eight IF statement code blocks, each designed to look for three consecutive matching squares, vertically, horizontally, or diagonally. If one of the IF statement code blocks finds three consecutive squares all assigned to the current player, it assigns the value of Player$ to another global variable named $Winner.

Step 15: Developing the Closing_Screen() Function

The last function in the Tic, Tac, Toe game is the Closing_Screen() function, which is responsible for thanking the players for playing the game and for displaying additional information about the game and its author.

```
`This function displays the game's closing screen
FUNCTION Closing_Screen()

  CLS RGB(255, 255, 255)  `Set background color to white

  SET TEXT FONT "ARIAL"  `Set the font type to Arial
  SET TEXT SIZE 36  `Set the font size to 36 points

  `Display the game's closing message
  CENTER TEXT 400, 150, "Thanks for playing the Tic, Tac, Toe game!"
  SET TEXT TO NORMAL  `Remove any text attribute settings
  SET TEXT SIZE 18  `Set the font size to 18 points
  CENTER TEXT 400, 240, "Developed by Jerry Lee Ford, Jr."
  CENTER TEXT 400, 260, "Copyright 2008"
  CENTER TEXT 400, 280, "http://www.tech-publishing.com"
  CENTER TEXT 400, 380, "Press any key to end game."

  WAIT KEY  `Pause game play until the player presses a keyboard key

ENDFUNCTION
```

Step 16: Saving and Compiling Your Application

Compared to any of the games created up to this point in the book, the Tic, Tac, Toe game is by far the most complex. Although not graphically challenging, the programming logic required to manage game play is fairly sophisticated. Assuming that you have been creating your own copy of this application as you followed along with this chapter, and that you did not accidentally skip any steps or make any typos, your copy of the Tic, Tac, Toe game should be ready for testing. But first, make sure you save all your work by clicking on the Save All option located on the File menu. Once this has been done, click on the Make/EXE RUN option located on the Compile menu to compile and execute your application.

The Final Result

As long as you have not made any typos and followed along with each step carefully, everything should work as described at the beginning of this chapter. Once your new game has been compiled, spend some time testing it and putting it through its paces. Once you are confident that everything is working correctly, find yourself a partner to play with and show off your new game.

 You will find a copy of this application's project file and source code on the book's companion website, located at http://www.courseptr.com/downloads.

SUMMARY

The focus of this chapter was on showing you how to improve the overall organization and manageability of your project source code through the use of functions. You learned the importance of breaking down your source code into discrete sections, each of which performs a particular task and serves as a building block in the development of the overall application. In learning to work with functions, you learned how to set them up to accept and process data passed to them as arguments. You also learned how to return a value from a function back to the program statement that called upon it to execute. To help make your project's source code even more manageable, you learned how to break up large code files into multiple files, which could be added to your project using the Files view of the Project Panel.

Before you move on to Chapter 7, I suggest you set aside a few additional minutes to improve the Tic, Tac, Toe game by implementing the following list of challenges.

CHALLENGES

1. As currently written, the Tic, Tac, Toe game makes the assumption that players are already familiar with the rules for playing the game. You might want to provide the player with access to game instructions, perhaps by adding a Help option.

2. Currently, the game displays a text message that informs the players when the game has been won. Consider enhancing the game to tell the players that it has been won and how it was won (e.g., diagonally, vertically across in column 3, horizontally in row B, etc.).

3. Since Player X and Player O are likely to want to play for a while, consider adding programming logic that keeps track of the number of games won, lost, and tied and making that information available to the players to determine the overall winner.

4. As currently written, the game is set up so that Player X always goes first. Consider modifying the game to allow the players to determine who goes first. Alternatively, consider arbitrarily setting up the game so that Player X and Player O alternate going first.

Part

III

Advanced Topics

WORKING WITH GRAPHICS AND SOUND

Up to this point in the book, the primary focus has been on teaching the fundamental principles of computer programming. With this foundation now in place, it is time to begin focusing on DarkBASIC Professional's support for graphics programming. This chapter will introduce commands that can be used to draw dots, lines, and different shapes. You will also learn how to work with bitmap images. This will include learning how to create and draw new bitmap images as well as how to load and display existing bitmap images. This chapter will discuss the importance of loops in controlling the game execution. You will learn how to control the rate at which the screen is refreshed and animation occurs and how to use collision detection as a means of controlling the movement of objects in action-oriented computer games. You will also learn how to add sound effects.

Specifically, you will learn how to:

- Use different DarkBASIC Professional commands to draw graphics
- Work with bitmap images and to apply special effects to them
- Control the rate at which graphics are drawn in action-oriented games
- Use collision detection as a means of determining when objects interact with one another in games
- Add sound effects to your games

PROJECT PREVIEW: THE PONG GAME

This chapter's application project is the DB Pong game. This game is loosely based on the original *Pong* video game developed by Atari in 1972. In this version of the game, the first player to reach 10 points wins. Points are scored when the other player fails to deflect the ball back with the paddle.

As Figure 7.1 shows, DB Pong begins by displaying a welcome screen that instructs the players to press any keyboard key to begin game play.

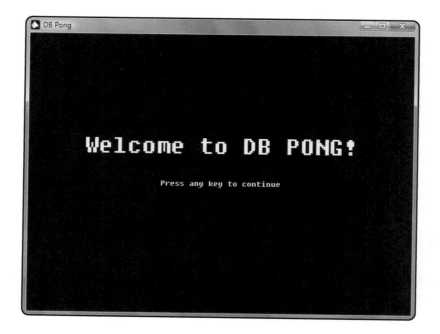

FIGURE 7.1

The DB Pong game's welcome screen.

Players deflect the ball, bouncing it back in the opposite direction, using yellow paddles. Player 1 controls her paddle using the Shift key to move her paddle upwards and the Ctrl key to move it downwards. Player 2 uses the keyboard's up and down arrow keys to control her paddle. Figure 7.2 shows an example of the game being played. Note that this is the first point in the game (neither player has scored yet).

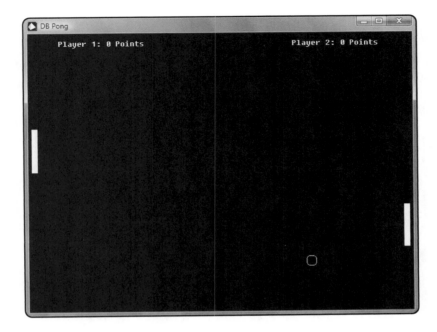

FIGURE 7.2

An example of the DB Pong game in action.

Figure 7.3 shows another screen shot from later in the game. At this point, Player 1 is winning 3 to 2.

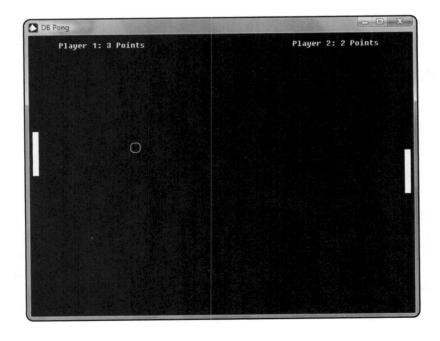

FIGURE 7.3

Player 1 is winning the game.

As soon as one of the players reaches 10 points, the game ends and the screen shown in Figure 7.4 displays.

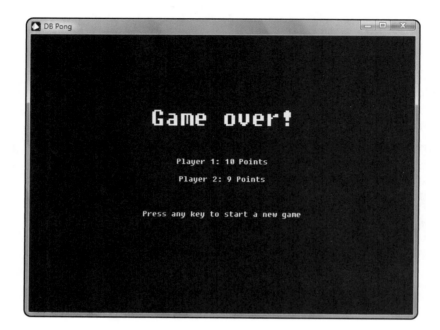

FIGURE 7.4

A new game can be started by pressing a keyboard key.

Game play can be terminated at any time by pressing the Escape key or by clicking on the game window's close button.

A Few Quick Words About Graphics Programming and Animation

While the creation of computer games and animation has traditionally required advanced technical knowledge and programming skills, the advent of DarkBASIC Professional is changing the playing field. DarkBASIC Professional provides all of the tools needed to develop professional quality computer games and does not require an advanced computer science degree to be able to understand how to use it.

DarkBASIC Professional's game engine, composed of over 1,000 commands, allows you to take advantage of the power of DirectX, without requiring you to understand that technology's inner workings. Specifically, DarkBASIC Professional's game engine makes it easy for you to utilize Direct3D, which is capable of handling all aspects of 2D and 3D graphics programming.

TRAP Starting with this chapter, the book's focus now turns to graphics programming. In order to be able to reproduce all of the examples and game projects in this chapter as well as those in the rest of the book, you must have DirectX 9.0c installed, as was described in Chapter 1. Also, if you have not already done so, you need to make sure that you are running DarkBASIC version 6.6 or higher to ensure that all remaining game projects will work as described.

DRAWING YOUR OWN GRAPHICS

When working with graphics, DarkBASIC Professional lets you draw directly to the screen or to bitmap images that you create or load. As was discussed in Chapter 2, "Getting Comfortable with the DarkBASIC Development Environment," the pixel is the smallest addressable location on the computer screen and is the foundation upon which graphics are based. As with drawing text, drawing graphics involves the placement of dots, lines, and shapes on the computer screen or on bitmap images that are mapped out using a coordinates system whose origin begins at the upper-left corner (0,0), as demonstrated in Figure 7.5.

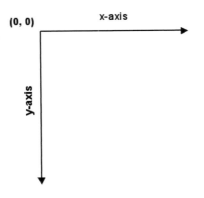

FIGURE 7.5

Graphics are drawn by using a coordinate system that contains an x-axis and a y-axis.

By default, DarkBASIC Professional draws all graphics in white on a black background. Unless you change it, the default background is the screen. You can modify color settings using the INK command in conjunction with the RGB command. You can use the CLS command to clear the display area using the current background color. DarkBASIC Professional provides many additional graphics commands in addition to the INK, RGB, and CLS commands, including commands that allow you to draw directly to the screen or upon other graphic images. These commands include:

- DOT
- LINE
- BOX
- CIRCLE
- ELLIPSE

Drawing Dots

Using the DOT command, you can draw a single dot or pixel at any location on the screen or on a graphic image. By default, the dot is drawn using the current INK color settings. Placement of the dot is specified using X and Y coordinates. The syntax for this command is outlined here:

```
DOT X, Y [, Color]
```

X is a coordinate along the x-axis and *Y* is a coordinate along the y-axis. *Color* is optional. When specified, *Color* sets the color that is used to draw the dot.

As an example of how to work with the DOT command, look at the following statement. Here, a single yellow dot is drawn at coordinate location 200, 200.

```
DOT 200, 200, RGB(255, 255, 0)   `Draw a yellow dot
```

Drawing Lines

Using the LINE command, you can draw a line anywhere you want on the screen or on a graphic image. By default, the line is drawn using the current INK color setting. Placement of the line is specified using two pairs of X and Y coordinates. The syntax for this command is outlined here:

```
LINE X1, Y1, X2, Y2
```

X1 and *Y1* identify the starting coordinate for the line, and *X2* and *Y2* identify its ending coordinate.

Unlike the DOT command, the LINE command does not accept a color argument. Instead, the LINE command uses the current INK settings when rendering its output. As an example of how to work with the LINE command, look at the following statements. Here, a series of six consecutive lines are drawn, each of which is a little longer than its predecessor.

```
LINE 50, 100, 200, 100
LINE 50, 125, 250, 125
LINE 50, 150, 300, 150
```

```
LINE 50, 175, 350, 175
LINE 50, 200, 400, 200
LINE 50, 225, 450, 225
```

Figure 7.6 shows the output these commands produce when executed.

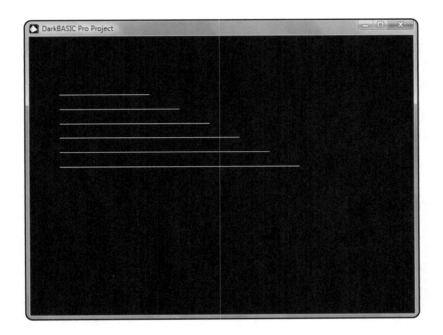

FIGURE 7.6

Drawing a series of lines using the LINE command.

Creating Rectangle Shapes

Using the BOX command, you can draw a box shape anywhere you want on the screen or on a graphic image. By default, the box is filled in with color using the current INK color settings. Placement of the box is specified using two pair of X and Y coordinates. The syntax for this command is outlined here:

```
BOX Left, Top, Right, Bottom
```

As you can see, this command requires that you provide it with the upper-left and lower-right corner coordinates of the rectangle.

As an example of how to work with the BOX command, look at the following statements. Here, three rows of boxes have been drawn on the screen.

```
`Draw the first row of squares
BOX 75, 75, 175, 175
BOX 275, 75, 375, 175
BOX 475, 75, 575, 175

`Draw the second row of squares
BOX 175, 175, 275, 275
BOX 375, 175, 475, 275

`Draw the third row of squares
BOX 75, 275, 175, 375
BOX 275, 275, 375, 375
BOX 475, 275, 575, 375
```

Figure 7.7 shows what the output of these commands looks like when displayed.

FIGURE 7.7

Using the BOX command to draw a checkerboard background.

Creating Circles

Using the CIRCLE command, you can draw a circle shape anywhere you want on the screen or on a graphic image. By default, the circle is drawn using the current INK color setting. Placement of the center of the circle is based on the specification of a pair of X, Y coordinates and an argument representing the circle's radius. The syntax for the CIRCLE command is outlined here:

```
CIRCLE X, Y, Radius
```

The *Radius* parameter specifies the distance from the center of the circle to its outer edge and it is equal to one-half of the circle's width.

As an example of how to work with the CIRCLE command, look at the following statements.

```
CIRCLE 320, 240, 200
CIRCLE 320, 240, 150
CIRCLE 320, 240, 100
CIRCLE 320, 240, 50
```

When executed, these statements draw four different-sized circles, each of which is centered about the middle of the screen, as shown in Figure 7.8.

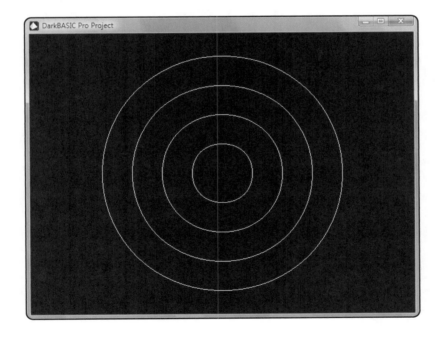

FIGURE 7.8

Using the CIRCLE command to draw a series of circles centered in the middle of the screen.

Drawing Ellipses

Using the ELLIPSE command, you can draw an elliptical shape anywhere you want on the screen or on a graphic image. By default, the elliptical is drawn using the current INK color setting. Placement of the center of the circle is based on the specification of a pair of X, Y coordinates and two radius specifications, one for the x-axis and one for the y-axis. The syntax for the ELLIPSE command is outlined here:

```
ELLIPSE X, Y, X-radius, Y-radius
```

The *X-radius* and *Y-radius* parameters specify the distance from the center of the circle to its outer edges.

As an example of how to work with the ELLIPSE command, look at the following statements.

```
ELLIPSE 320, 240, 200, 100
ELLIPSE 320, 240, 100, 200
```

When executed, these statements draw two different elliptical shapes with opposing radiuses, as shown in Figure 7.9.

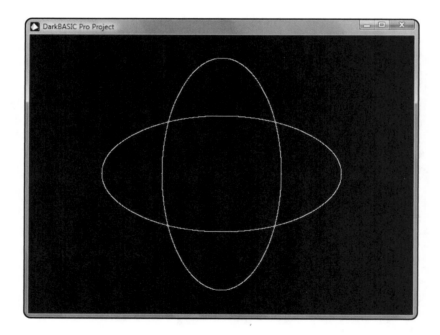

FIGURE 7.9

Using the ELLIPSE command to draw a pair of elliptical shapes in the middle of the screen.

WORKING WITH BITMAP FILES

In order to generate professional 2D computer games, you need to learn how to work with bitmap images. You need to learn how to load, display, and control the appearance of bitmap images. *Bitmap* is a term that refers to the format used to store an image. Bitmap is just one of many different popular file formats used to store images. Other graphics formats include gif, jpeg, tiff, and so on. Bitmap files are easily identified by their three character .bmp file extension. DarkBASIC Professional natively handles bitmap files and this is the format that you will want to use in all your game projects.

 Today, computer games developed by game development companies use graphics developed by professional graphic artists. Unless you are a graphic artist, this puts you at a bit of a disadvantage. However, do not fret, this can be easily overcome. As was mentioned in Chapter 1, you can purchase professionally developed graphics for your computer games directly from the Game Creators' website at http://www.thegamecreators.com. Alternatively, you may want to try your own hand at graphics design, which you can do using tools like Corel Paint Shop Pro, CorelDRAW, Adobe Photoshop, and ProMotion.

In DarkBASIC Professional, you have two ways of working with bitmaps: you can programmatically generate them or you can load externally generated bitmap files created by using graphics tools like Corel Paint Shop Pro or some other third-party graphics editor. Both of these options are explained in the sections that follow.

Loading Existing Bitmap Image Files

If you have created or purchased bitmap images for use in your computer games, you must load them into your game to work with them. To do this, you need to use the LOAD BITMAP command, which has the following syntax.

```
LOAD BITMAP FileName ReferenceNumber
```

FileName represents the name of a bitmap file that you have added to your project (either by dragging and dropping a copy of the bitmap file into the project folder or by clicking on the Media button on the Project Panel and adding it that way). *ReferenceNumber* is a number between 1 and 31 in the bitmap array where you want to store the bitmap.

To better understand how to work with the LOAD BITMAP command, create a new DarkBASIC Professional project, set it to run in a window with a 640×480 resolution, and then drag and drop a copy of the BrightEyes.bmp file into the project's folder. You'll find a copy of this bitmap file available for download on this book's companion website. Next, add the following statement to the project's code file and then compile and execute the project.

```
LOAD BITMAP "BrightEyes.bmp", 0
```

Figure 7.10 shows the window that appears when this application is executed. Once loaded, you can manipulate the bitmap file in many ways. For example, you can use any of the drawing commands that were previously discussed to further alter the appearance of the bitmap image.

FIGURE 7.10

An example of
how to load and
display a bitmap.

An interesting use of the LOAD BITMAP command might be the creation of an automated photographic book application. To set this up you could load an image and then pause the application for a few seconds to allow the picture to be viewed before loading a different picture. In this manner you could create a photographic slide show that you could then e-mail to family and friends, perhaps as a Christmas present. You could even spice things up a bit by playing a little background music. Remember, DarkBASIC can be used to build many different types of applications other than just games.

Creating Bitmap Image Files

Another way of creating bitmap images is to programmatically create them yourself. Once created, you can draw on them to customize them further. To create a new bitmap image, you need to use the CREATE BITMAP command, which has the following syntax.

```
CREATE BITMAP ReferenceNumber, Width, Height
```

ReferenceNumber is a number between 1 and 31 in the bitmap array where you want to store the bitmap. *Width* and *Height* represent the dimension of the bitmap file in pixels.

When executed, the CREATE BITMAP command creates a new bitmap image in memory, upon which drawing commands can be executed. However, the bitmap image is not automatically displayed on the screen. Once you have created a new bitmap image and finished making any needed modifications to it, you can display it using the COPY BITMAP command, which is covered a little later in this chapter.

WORKING WITH BITMAP IMAGES

DarkBASIC Professional lets you work with up to 32 bitmaps at a time. Well, actually the number of bitmaps that you can create or open at any point in time is really 31 because the screen is considered to be a bitmap. The good news is that thanks to the use of sprites, which you will learn about in Chapter 8, "Generating Animation Using Sprites," you typically will not need to work with more than a handful of bitmaps in any game.

In DarkBASIC Professional, all bitmaps that you create or load are automatically stored into an array and assigned a number from 0 to 31. DarkBASIC Professional regards the screen as a large bitmap and automatically assigns the screen an index position of 0 in the bitmaps array, leaving you index positions 1 through 31 to work with.

Displaying Bitmap Images

If you elect to create a bitmap image from scratch, DarkBASIC Professional creates a copy of the new image in memory, allowing you to manipulate further before displaying. To display your new bitmap image, you must use the COPY BITMAP command, which has the following syntax.

```
COPY BITMAP FromImage, Left, Top, Right, Bottom, ToImage, Left, Top, Right, Bottom
```

The COPY BITMAP command copies the contents of one bitmap into another bitmap. *FromImage* references the source bitmap image to be copied and *ToImage* specifies the destination bitmap into which the source bitmap image is copied.

Using just these two parameters, you can use the COPY BITMAP command to copy a new bitmap to the screen, as demonstrated here:

```
CREATE BITMAP 1, 640, 480

`SET CURRENT BITMAP 1

CIRCLE 320, 240, 200
CIRCLE 320, 240, 201
CIRCLE 320, 240, 202
CIRCLE 320, 240, 203
CIRCLE 320, 240, 204

COPY BITMAP 1, 0
```

Here a new bitmap image has been created onto which a circle whose perimeter is five pixels thick is drawn. The bitmap image is then copied onto the screen, making it visible, as demonstrated in Figure 7.11.

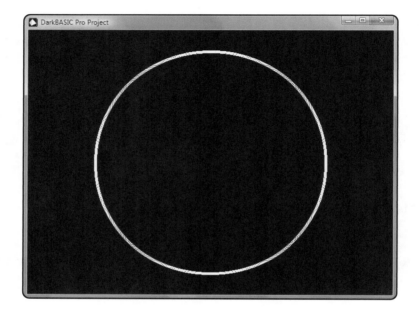

FIGURE 7.11

Creating and displaying a new bitmap file on the screen.

> **HINT**
>
> If the source and destination bitmaps differ in size, the image that is copied will be resized before displaying.

Using all of the parameters that make up the COPY BITMAP command, you can copy a portion of a bitmap onto another bitmap, as demonstrated here:

```
CREATE BITMAP 1, 640, 480

`SET CURRENT BITMAP 1

CIRCLE 320, 240, 200
CIRCLE 320, 240, 201
CIRCLE 320, 240, 202
CIRCLE 320, 240, 203
CIRCLE 320, 240, 204

COPY BITMAP 1, 0, 0, 300, 240, 0, 0, 0, 300, 240
```

In this example, a bitmap is created on which a circle is drawn. A quarter of a bitmap image is then copied onto the screen, as demonstrated in Figure 7.12.

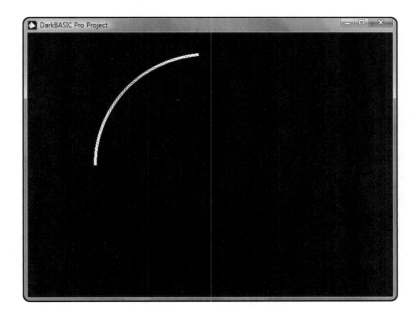

FIGURE 7.12

Copying a portion of a bitmap file to the screen.

Controlling the Display of Bitmap Images

Any drawing operations or other modifications are automatically made to the current bitmap. By default, the current bitmap number is always 0 (e.g., the screen). However, you can switch between different bitmaps using the SET CURRENT BITMAP command, which has the following syntax.

```
SET CURRENT BITMAP ReferenceNumber
```

ReferenceNumber is a number between 1 and 31 in which a bitmap has been stored in the bitmaps array.

To get a better feel for how the SET CURRENT BITMAP command works, try running the following example.

```
SET TEXT FONT "Arial"
SET TEXT SIZE 36

CREATE BITMAP 1, 640, 480
CREATE BITMAP 2, 640, 480
```

```
CREATE BITMAP 3, 640, 480

SET CURRENT BITMAP 1
CENTER TEXT 320, 150, "This is bitmap 1."

SET CURRENT BITMAP 2
CENTER TEXT 320, 150, "This is bitmap 2."

SET CURRENT BITMAP 3
CENTER TEXT 320, 150, "This is bitmap 3."

SET CURRENT BITMAP 0
CENTER TEXT 320, 150, "Keep pressing keys to view different screens."

WAIT KEY
COPY BITMAP 1, 0

WAIT KEY
COPY BITMAP 2, 0

WAIT KEY
COPY BITMAP 3, 0

WAIT KEY

END
```

Here, three bitmaps are created. Unique text messages are written to each bitmap image. The SET CURRENT BITMAP command is used repeatedly to specify on which bitmap each text string should be written. Once each screen has been created, it is displayed in sequence using the COPY BITMAP command. Once executed, the user can press any keyboard key to control the display of each of the three bitmaps.

DELETING BITMAP IMAGES

Once your application reaches a point in its execution where it no longer needs to display a given bitmap any more, it is good programming practice to delete it. By deleting the image I mean removing it from memory as opposed to removing it from the disk drive. To delete a bitmap in this manner, you must use the DELETE BITMAP command, which has the following syntax.

```
DELETE BITMAP ReferenceNumber
```

ReferenceNumber is a number between 1 and 31 in which a bitmap has been stored in the bitmaps array. Deleting a bitmap that is no longer required frees up memory, which can in turn speed up system performance. In addition, it frees up an index position in the bitmaps array where a new bitmap can then be added.

 You can delete any bitmap in the bitmap array except for bitmap 0, which represents the screen. Attempting to delete bitmap 0 will result in a runtime error.

WORKING WITH SPECIAL EFFECTS COMMANDS

As has already been demonstrated, you can load an existing bitmap image or create your own custom bitmap image. Once loaded or created, you can use various DarkBASIC Professional drawing commands to modify the image as you see fit. In addition to using drawing commands to modify the appearance of a bitmap image, you may also use any of a number of special effects commands. These commands include:

- MIRROR BITMAP
- FLIP BITMAP
- BLUR BITMAP
- FADE BITMAP

The MIRROR BITMAP Command

Using the MIRROR BITMAP command you can reverse the display of a bitmap image horizontally, in much the same way as your image is reversed when you look at yourself in an actual mirror. As such, any text printed on the image appears backward. The syntax for the MIRROR BITMAP command is outlined here:

```
MIRROR BITMAP ReferenceNumber
```

ReferenceNumber is a number between 1 and 31 to which the bitmap has been assigned in the bitmaps array.

The FLIP BITMAP Command

With the FLIP BITMAP command you can reverse the display of a bitmap image vertically. As such, any text printing on the image appears upside down. The syntax for the FLIP BITMAP command is outlined here:

```
FLIP BITMAP ReferenceNumber
```

ReferenceNumber is a number between 1 and 31 to which the bitmap has been assigned in the bitmaps array.

The BLUR BITMAP Command

As the name of the command implies, you can blur the appearance of a bitmap using the BLUR BITMAP command. The syntax for the BLUR BITMAP command is outlined here:

```
BLUR BITMAP ReferenceNumber, BlurSetting
```

ReferenceNumber is a number between 1 and 31 to which the bitmap has been assigned in the bitmaps array. *BlurSetting* is a number between 1 and 6 that specifies the intensity of the blur effect. A value of 1 produces a mild blurring of the image while a value of 6 results in a much more dramatic blurring effect.

The FADE BITMAP Command

Using the FADE BITMAP command you can fade the appearance of a bitmap image. The syntax for the FADE BITMAP command is outlined here:

```
FADE BITMAP ReferenceNumber, FadeSetting
```

ReferenceNumber is a number between 1 and 31 to which the bitmap has been assigned in the bitmaps array. *FadeSetting* is a number between 0 and 100 that specifies the effect of the fade effect. A value of 0 results in a bitmap that is faded to black. A value of 99 applies an absolute minimum amount of fading to an image and a value of 100 does not fade the bitmap at all.

A Special Effects Demonstration

As a quick demonstration of how to apply the special effects command that was just presented, look at the following example.

```
DO

  LOAD BITMAP "Kittens.bmp", 0
  WAIT 2000

  MIRROR BITMAP 0
  WAIT 2000

  FLIP BITMAP 0
  WAIT 2000

  FLIP BITMAP 0
```

```
WAIT 2000

MIRROR BITMAP 0
WAIT 2000

FADE BITMAP 0, 50
WAIT 2000

LOOP

END
```

Here, a new DarkBASIC Professional project has been created and a bitmap file named Kittens.bmp has been added to it. Within the project's code file a DO ...LOOP has been added that loads the Kittens.bmp file onto the screen. After a two-second pause, the MIRROR BITMAP command is executed, horizontally reversing the display of the image. After another two-second pause the FLIP BITMAP command is executed vertically, reversing the display of the image as shown in Figure 7.13. After another two-second pause, the FLIP BITMAP command is executed a second time followed by another two-second pause and then the MIRROR BITMAP command executes again, with the result that the bitmap now looks exactly like it did when the bitmap file was initially loaded. Next, the FADE BITMAP command is executed, resulting in a darkened view of the bitmap. After a final two-second pause, the DO...LOOP repeats showing the entire sequence over again and continues to run until the escape key is pressed.

FIGURE 7.13

Using special effect commands to manipulate the appearance of a bitmap image.

CONTROLLING GAME PLAY WITH LOOPS

All of the graphics commands that have been reviewed so far in this chapter provide the ability to display bitmap images and to create new bitmap images upon which you can draw and manipulate. Games are an interactive experience and as such, need a controlled means of collecting player input and then responding to it. For example, in a tank battle game, the game needs to collect and process a continuous stream of player input directing the game where to move the player's tank. In addition, the game must constantly be on the lookout for instruction from the player to shoot. Once collected, the game needs to integrate player input into the program and use it to continually update game status and display changes on the screen. The key to making all of this happen in a controlled and efficient manner is the game's primary loop.

Game loops are usually set up to run forever, terminating only when the player has signaled a decision to quit playing or when the player has lost. Although you can use any of the loops provided by DarkBASIC Professional, the DO...LOOP generally serves this purpose perfectly.

Managing Screen Refresh Rates

By default, DarkBASIC Professional repeats a loop as fast as the computer's processor allows it to. However, most games require some degree of timing to allow them to proceed at a smooth pace. This is especially true for games that involve the movement of objects around the screen at a predictable and fluid pace.

As things get moving around the screen during game play, DarkBASIC Professional does its best to keep the screen updated (refreshed). DarkBASIC automatically manages your game's synchronization rate or *frame rate*. By default, this rate is set equal to 40. However, using the SYNC RATE command, you can modify this setting. This command has the following syntax.

SYNC RATE *NewRate*

Here, *NewRate* is an integer value between 1 and 1000 FPS (frames per second).

To instruct DarkBASIC Professional to continually refresh the screen as fast as possible, set the frame rate to zero, as demonstrated here:

SYNC RATE 0

Turning Automatic Frame Rate Refresh Off

In a high-speed computer game, it is usually best to disable DarkBASIC Professional's automatic frame rate refresh and to handle that process yourself. This way, you can ensure that the screen is continually updated at a speed appropriate to the needs of your game, as controlled by the game's main loop.

In order to disable automatic frame rate refresh, you need to execute the SYNC ON command, which has the following syntax.

SYNC ON

When executed, this command disables DarkBASIC Professional's automatic frame rate refresh, leaving it to you to manually control when the screen is redrawn, which you can do using the SYNC command as discussed in the next section.

Manually Synchronizing Screen Refresh

Once you have disabled DarkBASIC Professional's automatic frame rate refresh by executing the SYNC ON command, you control when your game's screen is redrawn using the SYNC command. The SYNC command has the following syntax.

SYNC

When executed, this command redraws your game's screen using a programming technique known as double buffering, reflecting any changes that have been made since the last time the screen was drawn.

DarkBASIC Professional's SYNC command uses a programming technique known as *double buffering* when drawing to the screen. With double buffering, a copy of your application's screen is stored in memory and any changes that your program makes to the screen are made directly to the copy of the screen that is in memory. When you have finished making any changes to the way the screen looks, by adding, removing, and moving things around, the computer's actual screen updates by copying the contents of the screen in memory to the computer's screen.

Drawing and manipulating objects directly on the actual screen slows a game down. Drawing and manipulating objects in memory is much faster. When everything is updated the way you want it, and the SYNC command is executed, DarkBASIC Professional simply copies the screen drawn in memory to the computer's actual screen. The result is a fast, crisp, and clean update of the screen.

Typically, you will want to place the SYNC command at the end of your game's main loop to redraw the screen once any changes to the screen have been updated during the current execution of the loop. This will allow you to control all screen refreshes and will help ensure that game animation runs as smoothly as possible.

DarkBASIC Professional provides one more synchronization command that you may find helpful. This command is the FASTSYNC command, which has the following syntax.

FASTSYNC

When executed, the FASTSYNC command performs a synchronization operation but skips a mandatory window message check operation, allowing it to run a little faster than the SYNC command. Although not typically needed by most games, you may find this command useful in situations where a small performance increase results in smoother game play and animation.

Turning Automatic Frame Rate Refresh Back On

If your game pauses between different levels to display information for the player to read, or if it needs to pause and wait for the user to key in some input, you may want to turn automatic frame rate refresh back on. This will reduce the processing demands made by the game when it's idling. The command that you will need to execute to do this is the SYNC OFF command, which has the following syntax.

SYNC OFF

Pausing Game Execution

Depending on what your game is doing at any given point in time, you may need to pause its execution. You have already seen how to do this on numerous occasions using the WAIT KEY command, which halts game execution until the player presses one of the keys on the keyboard, after which game execution resumes.

Rather than depending on the player to restart game play using the WAIT KEY command, you might want to instead use the WAIT command. This command pauses application execution for a specified number of milliseconds (1000 milliseconds equals 1 second). You have already seen this command in action back in Chapter 2, when you used it to throttle the display of text statements in the development of the Fortune Teller game.

In addition to the WAIT command, you can also use the SLEEP command to temporarily pause application execution. The syntax of this command is shown here:

SLEEP *Delay*

Delay is an integer value representing the number of milliseconds for which to pause application execution. There is no difference between the WAIT and SLEEP command, so you may use whichever command you choose, but I recommend that you pick just one and use it consistently.

DETECTING COLLISIONS

In addition to knowing how to execute graphics commands, controlling the pace of game play, and the rate at which the screen is redrawn, another fundamental programming technique required by most animated computer games, like first-person shooters, space battles, and arcade-style games, is collision detection. Simply stated, a collision occurs any time two objects run into one another in a computer game. For example, a collision occurs in *Pac-Man* whenever the Pac-Man character runs into a wall or makes contact with one of the game's ghosts.

To implement collision detection, your games must track the size and location of objects on the screen and ascertain whenever they come into contact with each other. As you will learn in Chapter 8, "Generating Animation Using Sprites," DarkBASIC Professional supports a number of different ways of implementing collision detection, including bounded rectangle collision and impact collision. In bounded rectangle collision, two objects collide when any part of the rectangular image in which they are drawn make contact. With impact collision, a collision occurs only when the two actual graphics images hit one another. As you will see when you create the DB Pong game later in this chapter, collision detection can also be implemented by comparing the coordinate position of one object to another and when two objects overlap, declaring a collision.

MAKING SOME NOISE

Up to this point in the book, all of the games that you have worked on have been mute. They have not made a sound, not even a little beep. Well, things are about to change. DarkBASIC Professional provides robust support for different types of sound effects and music playback. DarkBASIC Professional provides all of the commands that you will need to load and play wave, MIDI, and MP3 files within your games. As such, you can easily play sound effects and background music to any application you create.

Loading Wave Sound Files

The first step in working with any sound file is to load it. Once loaded you can play the file and control its playback in a number of different ways. To load a wave sound file, you can use the LOAD SOUND command, which has the following syntax.

```
LOAD SOUND "FileName", Number
```

Here, *FileName* represents the name of a wave (.WAV) file that you want to load. *Number* is an integer value used to uniquely identify the sound file with your application.

As an example of how to load a wave file, look at the following example.

```
LOAD SOUND "type.wav", 1
```

Here, a wave file named type.wav is loaded, making it available for play by other commands.

> **HINT** If you want to work with MIDI or MP3 files, you must use the LOAD MUSIC command in place of the LOAD SOUND command.

Control Sound Wave File Playback

DarkBASIC Professional provides a host of commands that you can use to control the playback of wave files. For example, there are commands that let you play and loop sound files. You can also stop playback or pause it. You can also resume the playback of a paused wave file or delete a file when its playback is no longer needed. A list of commands that provide this functionality is provided next and covered in the sections that follow.

- PLAY SOUND
- LOOP SOUND
- PAUSE SOUND
- RESUME SOUND
- STOP SOUND
- DELETE SOUND

> **HINT** There are equivalent commands for playing MIDI and MP3 files for each of the commands listed above.

Playing Sound Files

Once a wave audio file has been loaded, it can be played. This is done using the PLAY SOUND command, which has the following syntax.

```
PLAY SOUND Number [, Start]
```

Number is an integer value used to uniquely identify the sound file within your application as specified when the file was loaded using the LOAD SOUND command. *Start* is an optional numeric parameter representing the number of bytes to be skipped in the sound file before beginning playback.

As an example of how to work with the PLAY SOUND command, look at the following statements.

```
LOAD SOUND "type.wav", 1
PLAY SOUND 1
```

When executed, these statements load and then play a wave file named type.wav.

The easiest way of working with external files within a DarkBASIC Professional application is to add them to the project, which you can do using the Project Panel. In the case of audio files, you will want to click on the Media button and then the Add button and then specify the name and location of the files. Once added to your project, you can refer to the audio files by name, without having to worry about their location.

The PLAY SOUND command can also be used to play part of a wave file by starting playback at a specified byte location within the file, as demonstrated in the following example.

```
LOAD SOUND "type.wav", 1
PLAY SOUND 1, 1000
```

Looping Sound Files

Another way of playing a wave file is to use the LOOP SOUND command. This command repeats the audio file's playback forever. The LOOP SOUND command has the following syntax.

```
LOOP SOUND Number [, Start, End, Initial]
```

Number is an integer value used to reference a sound file that has been previously loaded using the LOAD SOUND command. *Start* is a number representing the number of bytes to be skipped in the sound file before beginning playback. *End* is a number representing the byte location within the sound file where playback should stop before repeating again. Initial is a number representing the number of bytes to be skipped the first time the sound file is played.

The following statements demonstrate how to load and repeatedly play a wave file.

```
LOAD SOUND "type.wav", 1
LOOP SOUND 1
```

If you want, you can repeat the playback of just a portion of a wave file starting at a specified byte location within the file, as demonstrated here:

```
LOAD SOUND "type.wav", 1
LOOP SOUND 1, 1000
```

You can also repeat the playback of a portion of a wave file by specifying the byte location of the segments to be played using the starting and ending byte location points of that segment, as demonstrated here:

```
LOAD SOUND "type.wav", 1
LOOP SOUND 1, 1000, 2000
```

Lastly, you can repeat the playback of a portion of a wave file by specifying the byte location of the segments to be played using the starting and ending byte locations points of that segment, while also specifying a different starting point to be used during the first iteration of playback, as demonstrated here:

```
LOAD SOUND "type.wav", 1
LOOP SOUND 1, 1000, 2000, 1500
```

Pausing Sound Files

Using the PAUSE SOUND command, you can pause the playback of a wave file. This command has the following syntax.

```
PAUSE SOUND Number
```

Number is an integer value used to uniquely identify the sound file within your application as specified when the file was loaded using the LOAD SOUND command.

The following statement demonstrates how to use this command.

```
PAUSE SOUND 1
```

Resuming Sound Files

Using the RESUME SOUND command, you can continue the playback of a wave file that has been previously paused. This command has the following syntax.

```
RESUME SOUND Number
```

Number is an integer value used to uniquely identify the sound file within your application as specified when the file was loaded using the LOAD SOUND command.

The following statement demonstrates how to use this command.

```
RESUME SOUND 1
```

Stopping Sound Files

Using the STOP SOUND command, you can terminate the playback of a wave file. This command has the following syntax.

```
STOP SOUND Number
```

Number is an integer value used to uniquely identify the sound file within your application as specified when the file was loaded using the LOAD SOUND command.

The following statement demonstrates how to use this command.

```
STOP SOUND 1
```

Deleting Sound Files

If an application no longer needs to play a particular wave file, you can use the DELETE SOUND command to remove it. This command does not remove the file from the project. It simply unloads it from memory. This command has the following syntax.

```
DELETE SOUND Number
```

Number is an integer value used to uniquely identify the sound file within your application as specified when the file was loaded using the LOAD SOUND command.

The following statement demonstrates how to use this command.

```
DELETE SOUND 1
```

Controlling Sound Volume

By default, DarkBASIC Professional manages the sound level at which wave files are played. However, using the SET SOUND VOLUME command you can programmatically control this yourself. This command has the following syntax.

```
SET SOUND VOLUME Number, Volume
```

Number is an integer value used to uniquely identify the sound file within your application as specified when the file was loaded using the LOAD SOUND command. *Volume* is a numeric value between 1 and 100 that specifies the volume level of sound playback.

For example, the following statement demonstrates how to specify a volume setting and then play a wave file.

```
SET SOUND VOLUME 1 80
LOAD SOUND "type.wav", 1
PLAY SOUND 1
```

BACK TO THE PONG GAME

Now it is time to turn your attention back to the development of this chapter's main project, the DB Pong game. The development of this game involves the application of different drawing commands and will give you the opportunity to learn how collision detection works. This game will also give you the first taste of what is involved in developing action-based arcade-style games.

Designing the Game

The overall design of the DB Pong game is very straightforward. It makes extensive use of functions as a way of breaking down different game features into manageable units of program code. To help make things easy to understand and follow along, this game will be created by following a series of steps, as outlined here:

1. Create a new DarkBASIC project.
2. Specify game settings.
3. Document your application with comments.
4. Define the game's global variables.
5. Load sound files and set volume level.
6. Set up the game's primary loop.
7. Create the ProcessPlayerMoves() function.
8. Create the UpdateBallPosition() function.
9. Create the ManageVerticalCollisions() function.
10. Create the ProcessPlayerMisses() function.
11. Create the DisplaySplashScreen() function.
12. Create the DrawBallAndPaddles() function.
13. Create the ProcessPlayerHits() function.
14. Create the ResetBallAndPaddles() function.
15. Create the UpdateScore() function.
16. Create the EndOfGame() function.
17. Save and compile your application.

Step 1: Creating a New DarkBASIC Project

The first step in creating the DB Pong game is to create a new project. Do so by starting DarkBASIC Professional and clicking on the New Project menu item located on the File menu. The Create a New DarkBASIC Professional Project window appears.

Type in **Pong** in the Project Name file and specify where you want your new project to be saved, and then click on the OK button. In response, a new project is created for you.

Step 2: Configuring Game Settings

The next step in creating the DB Pong application is to modify a few application settings. Begin by clicking on the Project button located at the bottom of the Project Panel window. To help document this project, place the cursor in the Project Comments field and type **This is a two-player Pong game**.

Next, click on the Settings button. Type **DB Pong** in the Application Window Caption field. Select Windowed as the display setting for this game and set the resolution to 640×480.

Step 3: Documenting Your DarkBASIC Application

Now that your new project has been created and project level settings have been modified, it is time to add the program code statements needed to make your new application work. Begin by modifying the default comment statements that have been added to your application so that they match the statements shown here:

```
REM Project: Pong
REM Created: 9/24/2007 7:28:33 PM
REM Executable name: Pong.dba
REM Version: 1.0
REM Author: Jerry Lee Ford, Jr.
REM Description: This DarkBASIC Professional game is based on the original
REM                Pong game
```

As you can see, the comment statements have been modified to provide additional information about the game and its author.

Step 4: Defining Global Variables

The next step in the development of the DB Pong game is to define a number of global variables used throughout the game. In total, 10 variables must be declared and assigned initial values. The code statements that declare these variables are shown here and should be added to the end of the project's code file.

```
REM *************** Declare and Initialize Global Variables **************

GLOBAL PlayerOnePoints AS INTEGER = 0  `Keep track of player 1's score
GLOBAL PlayerTwoPoints AS INTEGER = 0  `Keep track of player 2's score

GLOBAL BallX AS INTEGER = 320  `Start the game with the ball in the middle
GLOBAL BallY AS INTEGER = 240  `Start the game with the ball in the middle

GLOBAL SpeedX AS INTEGER = 3 `Ball starts by moving to the right
GLOBAL SpeedY AS INTEGER = 1 `Ball starts by moving down at a gentle angle

`Specify coordinates for player 1's paddle
GLOBAL PaddleX2 AS INTEGER = 5    `Set horizontal location of the paddle
GLOBAL PaddleY2 AS INTEGER = 200  `Set vertical location of the paddle

`Specify coordinates for player 2's paddle
GLOBAL PaddleX1 AS INTEGER = 625  `Set horizontal location of the paddle
GLOBAL PaddleY1 AS INTEGER = 200  `Set vertical location of the paddle
```

The first two variables are used to keep track of the number of points scored by each player. The next two variables, BallX and BallY, are used to specify the location of the game's ball, which is assigned an initial starting location in the middle of the screen. Since the game's resolution is 640×480, the middle of the screen is 320, 240.

SpeedX and SpeedY are used to set the initial direction that the ball will travel. Ball movement is controlled by the game's main loop, which you will set up later in the code file. During game play, the ball will be moved three pixels in either direction along the x-axis and one pixel in either direction along the y-axis each time the loop repeats.

Whenever the ball makes contact with a paddle, the game will toggle the value assigned to SpeedX, from 3 to -3 and vice-versa, switching the ball's direction across the x-axis. Similarly, whenever the ball touches the top or bottom of the screen, the value assigned to SpeedY is toggled between 1 and -1, altering the ball's movement along the y-axis. Figure 7.14 shows how the toggling of the values assigned to SpeedX and SpeedY affect the direction in which the ball moves.

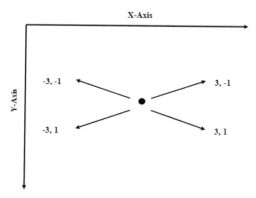

FIGURE 7.14

Controlling the direction of the ball in DB Pong.

The last two sets of variables specify the initial starting location where the game's paddles are drawn at the start of each new point in the game. Note that the coordinates for both paddles actually specify the location of each paddle's upper-left corner.

In order to understand the design and operation of the DB Pong game, it helps to see how the game's screen resolution setting as well as the size and location of the player's paddles and the location of the ball and its radius all fit together. Figure 7.15 maps each of these components, showing their dimension and their relative starting locations.

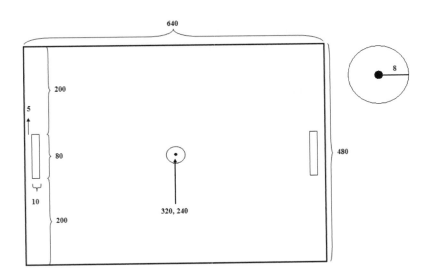

FIGURE 7.15

An overview of the
layout of the DB
Pong game and the
size and
dimensions of the
game's ball.

Step 5: Making Some Noise

The next set of code statements to be added to the DB Pong project is listed next and should be added to the end of the project's code file.

```
REM ******** Define Environment Settings and Pre-load Data Files *********


`Set the foreground color to yellow and the background color to black
INK RGB(255, 255, 0), 0


LOAD SOUND "type.wav", 1  `Load the specified audio file
LOAD SOUND "fire.wav", 2  `Load the specified audio file


SET SOUND VOLUME 1, 100 `Set the volume to be used when playing sound file
SET SOUND VOLUME 2, 85  `Set the volume to be used when playing sound file
```

As you can see, these statements clear the screen and then get the application ready for audio playback. Specifically, two sounds will be played. One sound is played when a deflection occurs and the other sound is played whenever a point is scored. In order to set up the sound playback, you must first load two wave files containing the sounds. Once loaded, the last two statements set the sound level at which the sounds are played.

You will find the sound files required to build this game on the book's companion website located at http://www.courseptr.com/downloads. Once downloaded, copy the wave files into your project's folder.

Step 6: Developing Overall Controlling Logic

Now it is time to display the game's welcome screen and then set up the game's loop. Using this loop, you will make a series of calls to functions that together manage game play. The statements responsible for making all this happen are shown next and should be added to the end of the project's code file.

```
REM ********************** Main Processing Section ************************

`Call function responsible for displaying the game's welcome screen
DisplaySplashScreen()

SYNC ON  `Disable automatic screen refresh
SYNC RATE 60  `Set the game's synchronization rate

DO  `Loop forever

  CLS  `Clear the display area

  `Call on the game's functions
  ProcessPlayerMoves()
  UpdateBallPosition()
  ManageVerticalCollisions()
  ProcessPlayerMisses()
  DrawBallAndPaddles()
  ProcessPlayerHits()
  UpdateScore()

  `Game play ends when one of the players scores 10 points
  IF (PlayerOnePoints = 10) OR (PlayerTwoPoints = 10) THEN EndOfGame()

  SYNC  `Perform a screen refresh

LOOP
```

These statements begin by executing the DisplaySplashScreen() function, which is responsible for displaying the game's welcome screen. Next, automatic screen refresh is disabled and the synchronization rate is set to 60. The game's loop is then set up using a DO…LOOP, so it runs forever. Within the loop, a series of function calls are made that together manage game play. At the end of the loop, the values assigned to PlayerOnePoints and PlayerTwoPoints are checked to see if one of the players has scored enough points to win the game, and if this is the case, then the EndOfGame() function is called on to execute. This function displays the final score and readies the game for a new round of play. The last statement in the loop executes the SYNC command to update the screen so that any changes that have occurred are reflected on the screen.

Step 7: Creating the ProcessPlayerMoves() Function

Each time the loop iterates, it checks to see if it needs to adjust the position of either of the game's paddles. It accomplishes this by monitoring the Shift and Ctrl keys for player 1 and the up and down arrow keys for player 2 and then incrementing or decrementing the values assigned to PaddleY1 and PaddleY2, which control the vertical location of player paddles. The statements responsible for making all this happen are shown next and should be added to the end of the project's code file.

```
REM ************************* Procedure Section *************************


`This function is responsible for controlling the movement of game paddles
FUNCTION ProcessPlayerMoves()

  `Player 1 uses the Shift key to move the paddle upward
  IF SHIFTKEY()
    DEC PaddleY2, 3  `Decrement vertical coordinate by 3
    `Do not allow the paddle to go past the top of the screen
    IF PaddleY2 < 0 THEN PaddleY2 = 0
  ENDIF

  `Player 1 uses the Control key to move the paddle downward
  IF CONTROLKEY()
    INC PaddleY2, 3  `Increment vertical coordinate by 3
    `Do not allow the paddle to go past the bottom of the screen
    IF PaddleY2 > 405 THEN PaddleY2 = 405
  ENDIF

  `Player 2 uses the Up Arrow key to move the paddle upward
```

```
IF UPKEY()
  DEC PaddleY1, 3  `Decrement vertical coordinate by 3
  `Do not allow the paddle to go past the top of the screen
  IF PaddleY1 < 0 THEN PaddleY1 = 0
ENDIF


`Player 2 uses the Down Arrow key to move the paddle downward
IF DOWNKEY()
  INC PaddleY1, 3  `Increment vertical coordinate by 3
  `Do not allow the paddle to go past the bottom of the screen
  IF PaddleY1 > 405 THEN PaddleY1 = 405
ENDIF


ENDFUNCTION
```

As you can see, the first IF statement code block in the function uses the SHIFTKEY() command to determine whether the Shift key is currently being pressed, and if it is, the value assigned to PaddleY2 is decremented by 3. By decrementing the value of PaddleY2, you reduce it, moving it close to its point of origin along the y-axis. The result is that when the screen is refreshed, the paddle will be drawn at a location that is three pixels higher than its previous location on the screen. To ensure that player 1's paddle does not move off of the screen, an embedded IF statement checks to see if the value of PaddleY2 is equal to 0, in which case the upper corner of the paddle is less than 0 and the paddle has moved too far upwards. To prevent the paddle from being able to go any further, the value of PaddleY2 is set to 0. The result is that the player is unable to move his paddle any further than the top of the screen.

Downward movement of player 1's paddle is controlled by an IF statement code block that uses the CONTROLKEY() command to determine whether the Ctrl key is currently being pressed. If it is, the value assigned to PaddleY2 is incremented by 3, in effect moving player 1's paddle down by three pixel positions the next time the screen is drawn. Note that an embedded IF statement prevents player 1 from moving the paddle beyond the bottom of the screen by checking the value assigned to PaddleY2 to see if it is equal to 400. Remember, the length of each paddle is 80 pixels and the value assigned to PaddleY2 is the location of the upper-left corner of the paddle. If the upper-left corner of the paddle is equal to 400 and the length of the paddle is 80 pixels, then when PaddleY2 equals 400, the bottom of the paddle is touching the bottom of the screen (e.g., the screen resolution is 640×480).

To better understand the math involved in the expressions being tested in the embedded IF statements, it may help you to refer back to Figure 7.15, which provides a visual outline showing the dimensions of the screen and paddles.

The last two IF statement code blocks in the ProcessPlayerMoves() function are nearly identical to the two code blocks just discussed, the only difference being that the UPKEY() and DOWNKEY() commands are used to control the movement of player 2's paddle.

Step 8: Creating the UpdateBallPosition() Function

The second function called in the game's main loop is the UpdateBallPosition() function, which is responsible for updating the location of the ball as it moves around the screen. The code statements that make up this function are shown next and should be added to the end of the project's code file.

```
`This function is responsible for updating the location of the ball as it
`bounces around the screen
FUNCTION UpdateBallPosition()

  INC BallX, SpeedX  `Move the ball further along its current direction
                     `on its horizontal axis
  INC BallY, SpeedY  `Move the ball further along its current direction
                     `on its vertical axis

ENDFUNCTION
```

As you can see, the values assigned to BallX and BallY, which represent the coordinate position of the ball at any moment in time, are incremented by the value assigned to SpeedX and SpeedY each time the function is called upon to execute. Remember that SpeedX is initially set to 3 at the beginning of the game and SpeedY is initially assigned a value of 1. Whenever a collision occurs with a paddle, the value assigned to SpeedX is changed by reversing its sign, thus sending the ball in the opposite direction along the x-axis. Similarly, whenever a collision occurs with the top or the bottom of the screen, the value assigned to SpeedY is changed by reversing its sign, thus sending the ball in the opposite direction along the y-axis.

To better understand the logic involved here, it may help you to refer back to Figure 7.14, which visually depicts the four possible directions that the ball can travel at any point in time.

Step 9: Creating the ManageVerticalCollisions() Function

The third function called in the game's main loop is the ManageVerticalCollisions() function, which is responsible for detecting when the ball makes contact with either the top or the bottom of the screen and for reversing the direction of the ball along its y-axis when this occurs. The code statements that make up this function are shown next and should be added to the end of the project's code file.

```
`This function is responsible for reversing the vertical direction of the
`ball when the ball touches the top or bottom edge of the screen
FUNCTION ManageVerticalCollisions()
  IF BallY < 5 OR BallY > 475
    `If the ball hits the top or bottom reverse the direction the ball
    `moves on the y-coordinate
    SpeedY = SpeedY * - 1  `Reverse the vertical direction of the ball
    PLAY SOUND 1  `Play a sound when the ball collides with the top or
                  `bottom of the screen
  ENDIF

ENDFUNCTION
```

As you can see, this function consists of a single IF statement code block that evaluates the ball's location along the y-axis to see if it is less than 5 or greater than 475. If this is the case then a collision has occurred and the statements embedded in the code block are executed. The direction that the ball is traveling along its y-axis must be reversed whenever a collision occurs with the top or bottom of the screen. This is accomplished by multiplying the current value assigned to SpeedY by -1.

> HINT   Finally, you are able to put something that you learned in high school math to use. Remember that anytime you multiply a number by -1, it changes that number's sign. In the case of the SpeedX it changes the value of 1 to -1 and -1 to 1 depending on which direction the ball is moving at the time of the collision.

The last statement embedded within the IF statement code block uses the PLAY SOUND command to play a wave file that indicates a collision has occurred.

Step 10: Creating the ProcessPlayerMisses() Function

The fourth function called in the game's main loop is the ProcessPlayerMisses() function. This function is responsible for determining when players miss the ball, allowing the other player to score a point against them. The code statements that make up this function are shown next and should be added to the end of the project's code file.

```
`This function is responsible for handling player misses
FUNCTION ProcessPlayerMisses()

  `If the ball's horizontal location is less than 9 then player 1 has
  `missed the ball
  IF BallX < 9
    PLAY SOUND 2  `Play a sound that indicates a miss
    INC PlayerTwoPoints, 1 `Increment player's score
    ResetBallAndPaddles()  `Call function responsible for resetting the
                            `ball and paddles
    `Player 1 missed the ball. Set things up so that the ball moves
    `right
    SpeedX = 3  `Reverse the horizontal direction of the ball
    SLEEP 2000  `Pause game execution for 2 seconds
  ENDIF

  `If the ball's horizontal location is greater than 631 then player 2
  `has missed the ball
  IF BallX > 631
    PLAY SOUND 2  `Play a sound that indicates a miss
    INC PlayerOnePoints, 1 `Increment player 1's score
    ResetBallAndPaddles()  `Call function responsible for resetting the
                            `ball and paddles
    `Player 2 missed the ball. Set things up so that the ball moves
    `left
    SpeedX = -3  `Reverse the horizontal direction of the ball
    SLEEP 2000   `Pause game execution for 2 seconds
  ENDIF

ENDFUNCTION
```

As you can see, this function is made up of two IF statement code blocks. The first code block determines when player 1 misses the ball and the second code block determines when player 2 misses it. To understand how the logic in this function works, it is important that you remember the following facts.

- The location of the ball on the x-axis is controlled by the value assigned to BallX.

- The radius of the game ball is 8 pixels long.

If the ball's location on the x-axis is less than 9 or greater than 631, then the ball has made contact with the side of the screen, which can only happen if a player fails to deflect the ball. Therefore, if BallX is less than 9 the ProcessPlayerMisses() function is called upon to execute. Once a miss has occurred, the PLAY SOUND command is executed and PlayerTwoPoints is incremented by 1. The ResetBallAndPaddles() function is then called to get the game ready for another point and the direction of the ball on the x-axis is set to 3 to set its direction for the start of the next point. Game play is then paused for two seconds to give both players a chance to get ready for the next point.

The second IF statement code block determines when player 2 has missed the ball, allowing player 1 to score a point. This code block is nearly identical to the first code block, the only difference being that instead of checking to see if the location of the ball on the x-axis is less than 9, it checks to see if BallX is greater than 631. The second IF statement code block also reverses the direction of the ball, setting the value of SpeedX to 3.

> To be fair, after a point has been scored, the game always sets the initial location to the opposite direction that it was traveling when the last point was scored.

Step 11: Creating the DisplaySplashScreen() Function

The fifth function called in the game's main loop is the DisplaySplashScreen() function. This function is responsible for displaying the game's welcome screen. The code statements that make up this function are shown next and should be added to the end of the project's code file.

```
`This function displays the game's welcome screen
FUNCTION DisplaySplashScreen()

  SET TEXT SIZE 48  `Set the font size to 48 points
  CENTER TEXT 320, 170, "Welcome to DB PONG!" `Display a welcome message
  SET TEXT SIZE 16  `Set the font size to 16 points
  CENTER TEXT 320, 250, "Press any key to continue"
  WAIT KEY  `Wait until the player presses a keyboard key
  CLS  `Clear the display area

ENDFUNCTION
```

As you can see, this function modifies the font size and displays two text strings before pausing game play and waiting for the player to press a keyboard key to continue.

Step 12: Creating the DrawBallAndPaddles() Function

The next function called in the game's main loop is the DrawBallAndPaddles() function. This function draws the game's ball and paddle at their current coordinates when called. The code statements that make up this function are listed next and should be added to the end of the project's code file.

```
`This function is responsible for drawing the game's ball and paddles
FUNCTION DrawBallAndPaddles()

  `Set horizontal and vertical location of the ball and its radius (size)
  CIRCLE BallX, BallY, 8

  `Set the horizontal and vertical location of the ball of game paddles
  BOX PaddleX1, PaddleY1, PaddleX1 + 10, PaddleY1 + 75
  BOX PaddleX2, PaddleY2, PaddleX2 + 10, PaddleY2 + 75

ENDFUNCTION
```

As you can see, the CIRCLE command is used to draw a circle representing the game ball. The circle is drawn at the location specified by the coordinates (BallX, BallY). The circle is assigned a radius of 8 pixels, resulting in a ball that is 16 pixels wide. The game's two paddles are drawn using the BOX command. Each paddle is 10 pixels wide and 75 pixels long.

Step 13: Creating the ProcessPlayerHits() Function

The ProcessPlayerHits() function is responsible for detecting when the ball collides with one of the game paddles and then for reversing the direction of the ball along its x-axis. The code statements that make up this function are shown next and should be added to the end of the project's code file.

```
`This function is responsible for reversing the direction that the ball is
`moving after it collides with a paddle
FUNCTION ProcessPlayerHits()

  `If the background color behind the ball is not black, then the ball has
  `made contact with a paddle
  IF POINT(BallX, BallY) > 0
    `Reverse ball direction when it collides with a paddle
    SpeedX = SpeedX * - 1
    PLAY SOUND 1  `Play a sound when the ball collides with a paddle
  ENDIF

ENDFUNCTION
```

This function consists of a single IF statement code block that when executed uses the POINT command to ascertain whether the ball has collided with a paddle, as is indicated when the background color under the center of the ball is no longer black. Once a collision with a paddle has been detected, the value assigned to SpeedX is multiplied by -1 to reverse the direction of the ball on the x-axis and the sound representing a collision is played.

The POINT command returns a value representing the background color displayed at the specified coordinate. The syntax of this command is

POINT(X, Y)

As applied in the DB Pong game, the POINT command is used to determine when the background color under the center of the ball is no longer black, indicating that the ball has come into contact with a paddle. The text that is displayed at the top of the screen, displaying player scores, is written in yellow but is regarded as a foreground color and thus does not inadvertently trigger the ProcessPlayerHits() function's collision detection logic.

Step 14: Creating the ResetBallAndPaddles() Function

Each time one of the players scores a point, the game pauses for two seconds and then the ResetBallAndPaddles() function is called. This function repositions the ball and both paddles back to their initial starting positions to ready the game for the next point. The code statements that make up this function are shown next and should be added to the end of the project's code file.

```
`This function resets the ball to the middle of the screen and repositions
`player paddles to get the game ready to play a new point
FUNCTION ResetBallAndPaddles()

  `Re-center the ball to the middle of the screen
  BallX = 320
  BallY = 240

  `Re-center player 2's paddle
  PaddleX1 = 625
  PaddleY1 = 200

  `Re-center player 1's paddle
  PaddleX2 = 5
  PaddleY2 = 200

ENDFUNCTION
```

Step 15: Creating the UpdateScore() Function

Whenever one of the players scores a point, the UpdateScore() function is executed. This function is responsible for displaying two text strings at the top of the screen showing both players' scores. The code statements that make up this function are shown next and should be added to the end of the project's code file.

```
`This function updates the display of player scores
FUNCTION UpdateScore()

  `Display player 1 and player 2's current scores
  TEXT 50, 10, "Player 1: " + STR$(PlayerOnePoints) + " Points"
  TEXT 440, 10, "Player 2: " + STR$(PlayerTwoPoints) + " Points"


ENDFUNCTION
```

Step 16: Creating the EndOfGame() Function

The last function to be added to the DB Pong game is the EndOfGame() function. As the name implies, this function is called at the end of a game, which occurs when one of the player's score reaches 10. When called, this function displays the final score for each player and prompts the players to start a new game. The code statements that make up this function are shown next and should be added to the end of the project's code file.

```
`This function ends the game when one of the players scores 10 points and
`resets player scores to zero to ready the game to be played again
FUNCTION EndOfGame()

    SYNC OFF  `Disable automatic screen refresh
    CLS  `Clear the display area
    SET TEXT SIZE 48  `Set the font size to 48 points
    CENTER TEXT 320, 120, "Game over!" `Display a welcome message
    SET TEXT SIZE 24  `Set the font size to 48 points
    CENTER TEXT 320, 210, "Player 1: " + STR$(PlayerOnePoints) + " Points"
    CENTER TEXT 320, 240, "Player 2: " + STR$(PlayerTwoPoints) + " Points"
    SET TEXT SIZE 16  `Set the font size to 16 points
    CENTER TEXT 320, 300, "Press any key to start a new game"
    WAIT KEY  `Wait until the player presses a keyboard key
    PlayerOnePoints = 0  `Reset player 1's score to its default value
    PlayerTwoPoints = 0  `Reset player 2's score to its default value
    CLS  `Clear the display area
```

```
SYNC ON   `Enable automatic screen refresh

ENDFUNCTION
```

Step 17: Saving and Compiling Your Application

At this point, your new application should be ready for testing. Before doing so, make sure that you save your work first by clicking on the Save All option located on the File menu. Once this has been done, click on the Make/EXE RUN option located on the Compile menu to try compiling and executing your application.

The Final Result

As long as you have not made any typos and followed along with each step carefully, everything should work as described at the beginning of this chapter. As you test your new game and put it through its paces, keep an eye on each player's scores to ensure that they are being updated correctly. Also, make sure that you test the operation of both paddles to ensure that they operate correctly and that they are not permitted to scroll off of the screen. In addition, make sure that the sound effects are being triggered whenever a collision occurs or one of the players misses the ball.

You will find a copy of this application's project file along with source code on this book's companion website, located at http://www.courseptr.com/downloads.

SUMMARY

This chapter has covered a lot of ground. You learned the basic steps involved in working with DarkBASIC Professional's 2D drawing commands. You learned how to create and load bitmap images and to draw on them. You also learned how to control game play with a loop, set the screen refresh rate, and detect and respond to collisions. This chapter also showed you how to incorporate sound into your applications and introduced you to a number of different commands for controlling wave file playback. With this foundation now in place, you are ready to move on to the next chapter and learn more about graphics programming, including the use of sprites.

Before you move on to Chapter 8, I suggest you set aside a few additional minutes to improve the DB Pong game by implementing the following list of challenges.

CHALLENGES

1. As currently written, the DB Pong game uses a consistent and predictable set of parameters for controlling ball movement on the x- and y-axis. Specifically, movement along the x-axis is adjusted by a value of plus or minus 3 while movement along the y-axis is always adjusted by a value of 1 or -1. Consider randomly altering these values to make ball movement less predictable.

2. As currently written, the paddles that each player uses to deflect the ball retain a consistent size. Consider making game play more challenging by shrinking the length of the paddle as time passes during the play of points, making it increasingly difficult for the players to keep the ball in play.

GENERATING ANIMATION USING SPRITES

In today's world of ultra-cool, ultra-powerful game consoles, most new computer games are being developed in 3D. However, 2D game development is still alive and strong with many new games being developed every year for the Wii, Xbox 360, and PlayStation systems. Therefore, an understanding of 2D game programming is a fundamental part of any game programmer's background and skill-set. This chapter will increase your understanding of 2D game development by introducing you to sprites and teaching you how to use them as the basis for developing animation in your computer games. In addition, this chapter will guide you through the development of the first stage of a two-stage game project called the Bricks game.

Specifically, you will learn how to:

- Use bitmaps as the basis for generating sprites
- Move sprites around the screen
- Control sprite visibility
- Use sprites as the basis for creating graphic animation
- Detect sprite collisions during game play

PROJECT PREVIEW: THE BRICKS GAME

In this chapter you will begin work on the first part of a new application called the Bricks game. The second part of this game will be completed in Chapter 9. The Bricks game is based on the *Breakout* game developed in 1976 by Atari. The goal of the game is to keep a bouncing ball in play long enough to knock out a wall of bricks located at the top of the screen.

As Figure 8.1 shows, the game begins by displaying a wall made up of three rows of bricks. In total, there are 15 bricks in each row. At the bottom of the screen is a paddle with a ball sitting on top of it. A text string displayed at the top of the game tells the player how many balls are available.

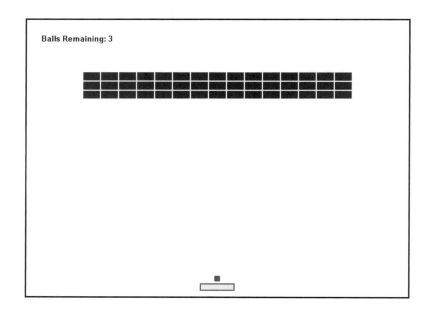

FIGURE 8.1

The goal of the game is to knock out each of the bricks in the wall by bouncing the ball into them.

Figure 8.2 shows an example of the game being played. As you can see, a total of three bricks have been knocked out so far.

The object of the game is to clear all of the bricks off of the screen without allowing the ball to drop off of the bottom of the screen, which results in a lost ball. When this occurs, a new ball is automatically placed on top of the paddle (assuming the game is not over), allowing the player to try again, as demonstrated in Figure 8.3.

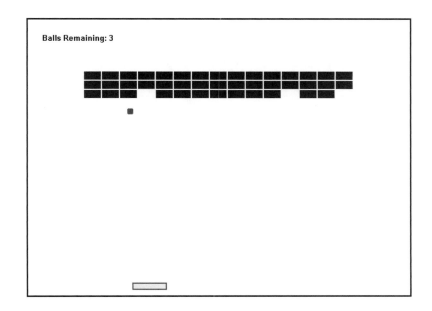

FIGURE 8.2

The ball bounces off of the paddle, walls, and bricks as it moves around the screen.

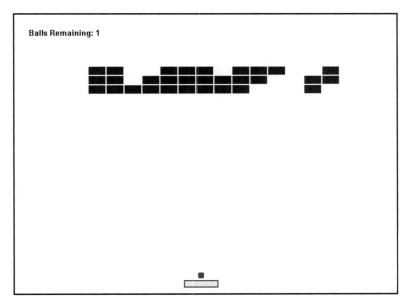

FIGURE 8.3

The player is down to her last ball.

In order to play this version of the game, the player must use the left and right arrow keys to move the paddle left and right across the bottom of the screen. In addition, the up arrow is used to launch the ball into play.

If the player manages to knock out all of the balls on the screen, a new round is automatically started and a new wall made up of three new rows of bricks is again displayed. Game play ends when the player runs out of balls, after which the screen shown in Figure 8.4 displays.

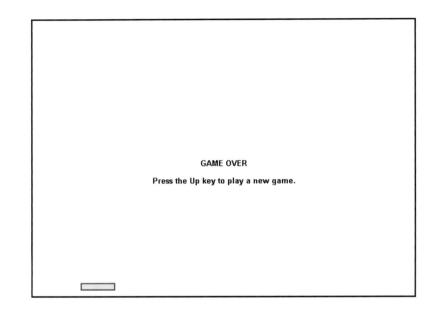

FIGURE 8.4

The Bricks game automatically ends once the player's supply of balls has been exhausted.

A FEW WORDS ABOUT 2D PROGRAMMING

Today most new computer games are being developed in 3D. However, an understanding of 2D game programming is still a fundamental part of any game programmer's background and skill-set. 2D game programming is still alive and well and is still earning a lot of companies big bucks. For example, in May 2007 Altus released *Odin Sphere*, a 2D fantasy action game for PlayStation 2. Capcom continues to develop top-notch 2D games. At the time that this book was being written, Capcom was working on *Super Street Fighter II Turbo HD Remix*, an updated remake of *Super Street Fighter Turbo*, which will run as a 2D game on Sony PlayStation 3 and Microsoft Xbox 360.

In order to create 2D computer games, you must learn how to work with sprites. *Sprites* are 2D bitmaps that represent objects like people, space ships, and tanks, that can be moved within a larger graphic image in a 2D computer game. Sprites can be moved without requiring the underlying background be redrawn and provide the basis for creating animated figures. Sprites are drawn as images on a transparent background. When drawn on the screen and moved around, only the pixels that make up the graphic image on the sprite remain visible, allowing the background to appear under any transparent parts of the sprite.

CREATING AND WORKING WITH SPRITES

Sprites are created from images stored in bitmap files. Therefore, the first step involved in creating a sprite is to load an image stored in a bitmap file into memory. Typically, bitmap files used for sprite generation are set up to hold either a single individual sprite or to store a sequence of sprites. For example, Figure 8.5 shows an example of a bitmap file that could be used as the basis for generating a sprite that would represent a basketball.

FIGURE 8.5

Using a bitmap as the basis for creating a sprite.

Today, many programming languages use the term *actor* in place of the term sprite, based on the idea that sprites do nothing more than play a role within a computer game.

Figure 8.6, on the other hand, could be used as the basis for generating an animated sprite. You can use the LOAD IMAGE command to create a sprite using images stored in bitmap files like the one shown in Figure 8.6.

FIGURE 8.6

Extracting one of a series of images from a sprite sheet.

The eight images that are drawn in the bitmap shown in Figure 8.6 can be used as the basis for generating an animated sequence that shows a bouncing basketball. To work with the bitmap images stored in the file shown in Figure 8.6, you must use two commands. For starters, you must first use the LOAD BITMAP command to load the bitmap file into memory. Once the bitmap file has been loaded, you can use the GET IMAGE command to crop out any one that you want to work with.

You can use applications like Corel Paint Shop Pro or Pro Motion to create sprite sheets like the one shown in Figure 8.6.

Generating Sprites from Bitmap Files

As was just stated, you can use the LOAD IMAGE command to generate a sprite from a bitmap file that stores an individual image. In its simplest form, this command has the following syntax.

```
LOAD IMAGE FileName ImageNumber
```

Here, *FileName* represents the name of the file that contains the image to be loaded, and *ImageNumber* represents a numeric reference to the sprite being created.

 The LOAD IMAGE command also works with other file types, including JPG, TGA, DDS, DIB, and PNG image files.

Using this command, you can copy the contents of the entire bitmap file. For example, the following statements demonstrate how to load a bitmap directly to the screen.

```
LOAD IMAGE "OneBall.bmp", 1
```

Retrieving Sprites from a Sprite Sheet

If you need to retrieve an image from a sprite sheet, then you cannot use the LOAD IMAGE command to generate a new sprite in a single command. Instead, you must first use the LOAD BITMAP command to load the bitmap file into memory. As you learned in Chapter 7, "Working with Graphics and Sound," this command has the following syntax.

```
LOAD BITMAP FileName ReferenceNumber
```

Once you have used this command to load the bitmap image into the bitmaps array, you can use the GET IMAGE command to crop out a portion of the bitmap for use as the basis for creating a sprite. In its simplest form, the GET IMAGE command has the following syntax.

```
GET IMAGE ImageNumber, Left, Top, Right, Bottom
```

Here, *ImageNumber* represents a numeric reference to the sprite being created and *Left* and *Top* specify the pixel position of the upper-left corner of the image to be extracted. *Right* and *Bottom* represent the pixel position of the lower-right corner of the image.

SETTING UP SPRITE ANIMATION

Once you have generated a sprite, you can use the SPRITE command to draw it on the screen and to move it around. This command has the following syntax.

```
SPRITE ReferenceNumber, X, Y, ImageNumber
```

ReferenceNumber represents a numeric reference to the sprite. *X* and *Y* identify the location at which the sprite is to be displayed, and *ImageNumber* represents a numeric reference to the sprite as established by a previously executed GET IMAGE command.

Once displayed, you can move a sprite to a new location on the screen by executing the SPRITE command again and supplying it with different X, Y coordinates. As an example of how to use the SPRITE command to set up and control on-screen animation, take a look at the following statements.

```
GLOBAL BackGround AS WORD = 1

SYNC ON
SYNC RATE 10

LOAD IMAGE "YellowBackground.bmp", BackGround
SET IMAGE COLORKEY 255, 255, 255
LOAD BITMAP "Basketball.bmp", 1

FOR i = 0 TO 7
  GET IMAGE 2 + i, i * 64, 0, i * 64 + 64, 64
NEXT i

SET CURRENT BITMAP 0

DO
  FOR i = 0 TO 7
    PASTE IMAGE BackGround, 0, 0
    SPRITE 1, 120, 100, 2 + i
    SYNC
  NEXT i
LOOP
```

Here, a background image that has been copied into the project's folder is loaded into memory using the LOAD IMAGE command. Next the SET IMAGE COLORKEY command is executed. This command specifies an RBG color that will be treated as transparent when displayed. As you can see, an RBG value of white has been specified. The LOAD BITMAP command is then used to load a bitmap file that has been copied into the project's folder into memory. This is the same bitmap file that was shown previously in Figure 8.6, containing eight separate pictures of a basketball in different positions. Together these eight pictures can be used to generate an animated sequence that shows a bouncing basketball. This is accomplished using a

FOR...NEXT loop to iterate through the bitmap file eight times. Each time the loop repeats, it uses the GET IMAGE command to extract a 64 pixel long by 64 pixel wide image from the file.

Once the bitmap file has been processed, the SET CURRENT BITMAP command is executed, telling DarkBASIC Professional to direct any drawing operations that follow directly to the screen. Finally, a DO...LOOP is set up to execute forever. Within this loop a second FOR...NEXT loop is set up that uses the PASTE IMAGE command to draw a copy of the background image onto the screen. The SPRITE command is then executed, drawing each of the previously extracted images one at a time to the screen. The end result is an animated sequence that shows a bouncing ball. Figure 8.7 shows a screen capture of the animation.

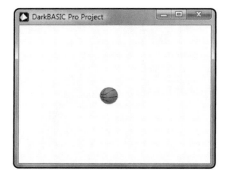

FIGURE 8.7

Generating an animated bouncing basketball.

 Note the use of the PASTE SPRITE command in the previous example. This command pastes the specified image onto the screen using the coordinates provided. In its simplest form, this command has the following syntax.

```
PASTE IMAGE ImageNumber, X, Y
```

In the previous example, the PASTE IMAGE command was used to apply the screen's background, which was nothing more than an image file made up of a yellow bitmap that was 320×200 in size.

Letting DarkBASIC Professional Do More of the Heavy Lifting

As the example demonstrated, you can draw a sprite to the screen using the LOAD BITMAP, GET IMAGE, and SPRITE commands. However, there is an easier way of managing animation, which involves the use of the CREATE ANIMATED SPRITE command. This command will load a bitmap, extract individual frames from it, and build animated sequences for you, saving you the chore of having to use the GET IMAGE command and feeding it the parameter information required to identify individual frames.

The CREATE ANIMATED SPRITE command has the following syntax.

```
CREATE ANIMATED SPRITE ReferenceNumber, FileName, Across, Down, ImageNumber
```

ReferenceNumber represents a numeric reference to the sprite. *FileName* is the name of the bitmap file from which images will be extracted. *Across* specifies the width of each image in the specified file. *Down* specifies the height of each image in the specified file. *ImageNumber* represents a numeric reference to the sprite being created.

To get a good understanding of how to work with this command, look at the following example.

```
GLOBAL BackGround AS WORD = 1

SYNC ON
SYNC RATE 60

LOAD IMAGE "YellowBackground.bmp", BackGround
SET IMAGE COLORKEY 255, 255, 255
CREATE ANIMATED SPRITE 1, "Basketball.bmp", 8, 1, 2

DO
    PASTE IMAGE BackGround, 0, 0
    PLAY SPRITE 1, 1, 8, 200
    SPRITE 1, 120, 100, 2
    SYNC
LOOP
```

Here, a background image that has been copied into the project's folder is loaded into memory using the LOAD IMAGE command. Next, the SET IMAGE COLORKEY command is executed to set up white as a transparent color. The CREATE ANIMATED SPRITE command is then executed. This command automatically generates a list of images required to generate an animated sequence. Note that the arguments passed to this command tell it to expect to find eight images in a sprite sheet that is one row long.

 By creating sprite sheets with more images showing an object at different locations, you can generate more complex and detailed animated sequences. For example, you could re-create the BasketBall.bmp file with 16 images spread out in one lone row, or in 2 rows with 8 images in each row, or in 4 rows with 4 images in each row, and then formulate the CREATE ANIMATED SPRITE command as shown here.

```
CREATE ANIMATED SPRITE 1, "Basketball.bmp", 8, 2, 2
```

A DO...LOOP is then executed to draw a background image and then execute the PLAY SPRITE and SPRITE commands. The PLAY SPRITE command automatically manages the display of each image, starting at frame 1 and ending at frame 8, with a 200 millisecond pause. The SPRITE command then draws the sprite and the SYNC command redraws the screen.

The PLAY SPRITE command automatically handles play of the animation sprite. This command has the following syntax.

```
PLAY SPRITE SpriteNumber, StartFrame, EndFrame, Delay
```

DETERMINING WHEN SPRITES COLLIDE

As was mentioned in Chapter 7, a collision occurs whenever two objects come into contact with one another. As you might expect, being able to detect sprite collisions is a key aspect of most 2D computer games. DarkBASIC Professional provides you with two different ways of detecting collisions: bounded rectangle collision detection and impact collision detection.

Bounded Collisions

A sprite is an object image displayed within a transparent rectangle, as demonstrated in Figure 8.8. Inside the rectangle, an image of a tank is drawn on a transparent background. The container rectangle is said to be *bounded*, in that it is has four distinct sides whose locations can be mapped using four sets of X, Y coordinates.

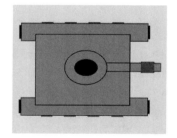

An example of a
sprite that
represents a tank.

The sprite shown in Figure 8.8 is stored within a bounded rectangle, which means that the sprite is completely enclosed within the rectangle.

A bounded collision occurs whenever two bounded sprites collide with one another. Figure 8.9 shows an example of a typical bounded collision. Here two bullet sprites have separately collided with a tank sprite.

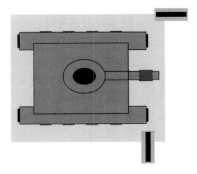

FIGURE 8.9

A tank sprite involved in two bounded collisions.

Because bounded collisions involve determining when two rectangles collide, and each rectangle consists of just four sets of coordinates, detecting a bounded collision is easy. The disadvantage of bounded collisions is that they are not precise. As a result, a bounded collision may occur in situations where two sprites might just miss one another. While not precise, bounded collision detection is useful in tracking collisions that occur in games in which large numbers of objects are in play and capable of colliding with one another. Using bounded collision detection, you can keep a look out for collisions and then when appropriate check for an impact collision.

To determine when a bounded collision occurs, you can use the SPRITE COLLISION command, which has the following syntax.

VariableName = SPRITE COLLISION(*ReferenceNumber*, *Target ReferenceNumber*)

The SPRITE COLLISION command returns a value of 1 when the specified sprite comes in contact with the target sprite. Alternatively, if you do specify a 0 in place of a *Target ReferenceNumber*, this command will return the *ReferenceNumber* of any sprite that it comes into contact with.

You will get the chance to work with this command a little later in this chapter when you begin work on the Bricks game.

Impact Collisions

Unlike a bounded collision, which occurs when the rectangles containing two sprites collide, an impact collision occurs only when the pixels that make up the actual sprites themselves come into contact with one another, as demonstrated in Figure 8.10.

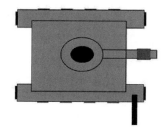

FIGURE 8.10

An example of an impact collision.

To determine when an impact collision occurs, you can use the SPRITE HIT command, which has the following syntax.

```
VariableName = SPRITE HIT(ReferenceNumber, Target ReferenceNumber)
```

The SPRITE COLLISION command returns a value of 1 when the specified sprite comes in contact with the target sprite. Alternatively, if you do specify a 0 in place of a *Target ReferenceNumber*, this command will return the *ReferenceNumber* of any sprite that it comes into contact with.

A FEW ADDITIONAL COMMANDS FOR WORKING WITH SPRITES

Later in this chapter you will begin the development of the Bricks game. Because of its size and complexity, you will continue your work on the project in Chapter 9. In order to develop the Bricks application, there are a number of additional sprite-related commands that you need to become familiar with. Two of the commands are the SPRITE WIDTH and SPRITE HEIGHT commands.

The SPRITE WIDTH command is used to retrieve the width of the specified image using the following syntax.

```
VariableName = SPRITE WIDTH(ReferenceNumber)
```

Similarly, The SPRITE HEIGHT command is used to retrieve the height of the specified image using the following syntax.

```
VariableName = SPRITE HEIGHT(ReferenceNumber)
```

Two additional commands that you need to be familiar with are the SPRITE X and SPRITE Y commands. The SPRITE X command returns the X position of the specified sprite and has the following syntax.

```
VariableName = SPRITE X(SpriteNumber)
```

Similarly, the SPRITE Y command returns the Y position of the specified sprite and has the following syntax.

VariableName = SPRITE Y(*SpriteNumber*)

BACK TO THE BRICKS GAME

Now it is time to turn your attention to the development of the first part of the Bricks game. The development of this game will provide you with first-hand experience using most of the commands and concepts that have been covered in this chapter. You will also gain valuable experience that can be applied to other game development projects.

Designing the Game

The overall design of the Bricks game is very straightforward. This game will run in full-screen mode and can be terminated at any time by pressing the Escape key. To help make things as easy as possible to understand and follow along, this game will be created by following a series of steps, as outlined here:

1. Create a new DarkBASIC Professional project.
2. Specify game settings.
3. Document your application with comments.
4. Define variables used globally throughout the game.
5. Embed data in the program.
6. Develop the game's overall controlling logic
7. Develop the ReadyGameForPlay() function.
8. Develop the LoadBricksArray() function.
9. Develop the PlayBricksGame() function.
10. Develop the DisplayBricks() function.
11. Develop the BounceTheBall() function.
12. Develop the ProcessSideOfScreenCollisions() function.
13. Develop the ProcessTopOfScreenCollisions() function.
14. Develop the ProcessMisses() function.
15. Develop the LookForCollisionWithPaddle() function.
16. Develop the ReadyBallAndPaddle() function.
17. Develop the ProcessPlayerInput() function.
18. Develop the DeflectBallOffThePaddle() function.
19. Develop the Creating the DeflectBallOffBricks() function.
20. Save and compile the application.

Step 1: Creating a New DarkBASIC Project

The first step in creating part 1 of the Bricks game is to create a new project. Do so by starting DarkBASIC Professional and clicking on the New Project menu item located on the File menu. The Create a New DarkBASIC Professional Project window appears.

Type in **Bricks** in the Project Name file and specify where you want your new project to be saved, and then click on the OK button. In response, a new project is created for you.

Step 2: Configuring Game Settings

The next step in creating the Bricks application is to modify a few application settings. Begin by clicking on the Project button located at the bottom of the Project Panel window. To help document this project, place the cursor in the Project Comments field and type **This game is based on the original Breakout game**.

Next, click on the Settings button. Type **Bricks** in the Application Window Caption field. Select Fullscreen Exclusive Mode as the display setting for this game.

Step 3: Documenting Your DarkBASIC Application

Now that you have created a new project and configured its project level settings, it is time to add the program code statements needed to make the Bricks game work like it is supposed to. Begin by modifying the default comment statements that have been automatically added to your application so that they match the statements shown here.

```
REM Project: Bricks
REM Created: 11/4/2007 10:00:44 AM
REM Executable name: Bricks.dba
REM Version: 1.0
REM Author: Jerry Lee Ford, Jr.
REM Description: This DarkBASIC Professional game is based on the original
REM              Breakout video game
```

Step 4: Defining Global Variables

The Bricks game needs to keep track of a moderate number of variables and make those variables accessible in different parts of the program. The following statements define each of the global variables used in the Bricks game. These statements should be added to the end of the program code file. Embedded comments describe each variable and identify its purpose.

```
REM **** Declare and Initialize Global Variables and Data Statements *****

Global BallX AS INTEGER = 0    `Coordinate of the ball on the x-axis
Global BallY AS INTEGER = 0    `Coordinate of the ball on the y-axis
```

```
GLOBAL SpeedX AS INTEGER = 1    `No. of pixels on x-axis the ball will move
GLOBAL SpeedY AS INTEGER = - 1 `No. of pixels on y-axis the ball will move

GLOBAL PaddleX AS word = 5      `Coordinate of the paddle on the x-axis
GLOBAL PaddleY AS word = 20     `Coordinate of the paddle on the y-axis

GLOBAL BackGroundImage AS INTEGER = 1   `The game's bitmap background image
GLOBAL BallImage AS INTEGER = 2         `The game's bitmap ball image
GLOBAL BrickImage AS INTEGER = 3        `The game's bitmap brick image
GLOBAL PaddleImage AS INTEGER = 6       `The game's bitmap paddle image

GLOBAL BallSprite AS INTEGER = 2        `Sprite representing the ball
GLOBAL BrickSprite AS INTEGER = 3       `Sprite representing a brick
global PaddleSprite as word = 5         `sprite representing the paddle

GLOBAL GameState$ AS STRING = "Initialize"   `Tracks game state
GLOBAL PlayerTurns AS INTEGER = 3            `Tracks number of turns left

DIM BricksArray(15, 15) AS INTEGER      `An array used to keep track of
                                        `bricks in memory
```

Step 5: Using DATA Statements to Embed Data

In this initial version of the Bricks game, only one level is supported. As such, each time the player clears the screen of bricks, a new set of blocks, identical to the previous set, is added to the screen. The following DATA statements, which should be added to the end of the code file, are used to define the state of each of the blocks that is displayed on the screen.

```
`Define five rows of bricks
DATA 1, 1, 1, 1, 1, 1, 1, 1, 1, 1, 1, 1, 1, 1, 1
DATA 1, 1, 1, 1, 1, 1, 1, 1, 1, 1, 1, 1, 1, 1, 1
DATA 1, 1, 1, 1, 1, 1, 1, 1, 1, 1, 1, 1, 1, 1, 1
DATA 0, 0, 0, 0, 0, 0, 0, 0, 0, 0, 0, 0, 0, 0, 0
DATA 0, 0, 0, 0, 0, 0, 0, 0, 0, 0, 0, 0, 0, 0, 0
```

Each integer value listed in each of the DATA statements represents an individual brick. A value of 1 indicates that a brick should be drawn at an exact position in a specific row on the screen. A value of zero indicates that a brick should not be drawn. As you can see, the way that these five data statements have been laid out results in three rows filled with bricks, followed by two empty rows.

This version of the Bricks game consists of a single level with three rows of bricks in it. Later, in Chapter 9, you will learn how to add additional levels to the Bricks game and additional rows of bricks to each succeeding level.

Step 6: Developing the Overall Controlling Logic

The overall controlling logic for the Bricks game is outlined in the statements that follow. Each of these statements should be added to the end of the project code file. As you can see, these statements consist of three calls to different functions defined later in the code file followed by the END command.

```
REM ********************* Main Processing Section ************************

ReadyGameForPlay()     `Call function that initializes the game
LoadBricksArray()      `Call the function that loads an array with brick data
PlayBricksGame()       `Call the function responsible for managing game play

END                    `Terminate the execution of this application
```

Step 7: Creating the ReadyGameForPlay() Function

From this point on, the code statements that make up the Bricks project's code file are organized into different functions, each of which is designed to perform a particular task. The code statements that make up the ReadyGameForPlay() function are shown next and should be added to the end of the code file.

```
REM ************************* Procedure Section *************************

FUNCTION ReadyGameForPlay()

  SYNC ON            `Disable automatic screen refresh
  SYNC RATE 60       `Set the game's synchronization rate
  HIDE MOUSE         `Prevent the display of the mouse
  RANDOMIZE TIMER()  `Use the Timer command to seed random number generation

  SET TEXT FONT "Arial"    `Set font to Arial
  SET TEXT SIZE 16         `Set point size to 24
  SET TEXT TO BOLD         `Display text in bold
  INK 0, 0                 `Set color to black

  LOAD IMAGE "Background.bmp", BackGroundImage    `Load background image
```

```
LOAD IMAGE "Paddle.bmp", PaddleImage        `Load paddle image
LOAD IMAGE "GameBall.bmp", BallImage        `Load ball image
LOAD IMAGE "Brick.bmp", BrickImage          `Load brick image

SPRITE PaddleSprite, 999, 999, PaddleImage  `Create sprite paddle
SPRITE BallSprite, 999, 999, BallImage      `Create sprite ball
SPRITE BrickSprite, 999, 999, BrickImage    `Create sprite brick

`Determine width and length of the paddle
PaddleX = (SCREEN WIDTH() / 2) - (SPRITE WIDTH(PaddleSprite) / 2)
PaddleY = SCREEN HEIGHT() - 25
```

```
ENDFUNCTION
```

This function is responsible for performing a number of initialization activities, including disabling automatic screen refresh, hiding the mouse, and seeding random number generation. In addition, bitmap files representing the game's background, paddle, ball, and brick are loaded and then sprites are created for the paddle, ball, and brick. Finally, the width and length of the game's paddle are calculated.

Step 8: Creating the LoadBricksArray() Function

The code statements that make up the LoadBricksArray() function are shown next and should be added to the end of the code file.

```
`This function loads an array with data on the current level's brick layout
FUNCTION LoadBricksArray()

  FOR j = 1 TO 5      `It takes 5 DATA statements to create 1 level
    FOR i = 1 TO 15   `Each DATA statement contains 15 bricks
      READ BricksArray(i, j)  `Load the current data item into the array
    NEXT i
  NEXT j
```

```
ENDFUNCTION
```

This function is responsible for loading the data stored in the game's DATA statements into an array. This data represents the bricks that are displayed on the screen during game play.

Step 9: Creating the PlayBricksGame() Function

The code statements that make up the PlayBricksGame() function are shown next and should be added to the end of the code file.

```
`This function manages the overall game play
FUNCTION PlayBricksGame()

  DO    `Loop forever

    PASTE IMAGE BackGroundImage, 0, 0    `Display the background image

    `There are three distinct stages in this game each of which must be
    `handled differently
    SELECT GameState$      `Retrieve current game state

      CASE "Play":        `If current state is play the game is in progress
        DisplayBricks()   `Call function responsible for displaying bricks
        BounceTheBall()   `Call function responsible for moving the ball
        LookForCollisionWithPaddle()  `Call function that handles
                                      `collision with the paddle
      ENDCASE

      CASE "Initialize":  `It is time to begin a new point
        ReadyBallAndPaddle()  `Call function that gets the ball and paddle
                              `ready for a new point
        DisplayBricks()   `Call function responsible for displaying bricks
        RESTORE                 `Restore all DATA statements
        IF UPKEY() = 1 `THEN GameState$ = "Play"  `Start point when the player
                                                  `presses the up key
          GameState$ = "Play"  `Adjust game state
        ENDIF
      ENDCASE

      CASE "Over":              `The current game has ended
        `Notify the player that the game has ended
        CENTER TEXT SCREEN WIDTH() / 2, SCREEN HEIGHT() / 2, "GAME OVER"
        CENTER TEXT SCREEN WIDTH() / 2, SCREEN HEIGHT() / 2 + 30, "Press the Up key to
        ↳ play a new game."
```

```
    IF UPKEY() = 1          `Press the Up key to start a new game
       PlayerTurns = 3         `Reset variable to prepare for a new game
       RESTORE                 `Restore all DATA statements
       GameState$ = "Initialize"  `Reset the game state
       LoadBricksArray()          `Call the function that loads
                                  `the brick data into the game's array

    ENDIF
  ENDCASE

ENDSELECT

IF GameState$ <> "Over"

  ProcessPlayerInput()    `See if the player is moving the paddle

  `Keep the player informed of the number of balls left to play
  TEXT 25, 25, "Balls Remaining: " + STR$(PlayerTurns)

ENDIF

SYNC    `Redraw the screen

LOOP

ENDFUNCTION
```

This function is responsible for controlling the play of individual points. It does so using a DO…LOOP that continually draws the game's background image and then executes various function calls, depending on the current state of the game.

If the current state of the game, as indicated by the value assigned to the GameState$ variable, is Play, functions that draw the bricks, move the ball, and respond to collisions are called. If the current state of the game is Initialize, functions that place the ball on top of the paddle and draw the bricks are called. In addition, the UPKEY command is executed to determine if the player is pressing the up arrow key, signaling the start of a new point, at which time the value assigned to the GameState$ variable is set equal to Play.

If the current state of the game is Over, instructions on how to start a new game are displayed. The UPKEY command is executed to determine if the player is pressing the up arrow key, signaling the start of a new game, at which time the variable used to track the number of remaining player turns is reset back to its starting value. The RESTORE command is then executed, readying the game to re-process the DATA statements used to specify the layout of the bricks. The value assigned to GameState$ is then set to Initialize, and the function that draws the game's bricks is called.

The last few statements in the loop call on the function responsible for moving the paddle and display a message on the screen showing the player how many balls remain to be played.

Step 10: Creating the DisplayBricks() Function

The code statements that make up the DisplayBricks() function are shown next and should be added to the end of the code file.

```
`This function is responsible for displaying rows of bricks
FUNCTION DisplayBricks()


  Width = SPRITE WIDTH(BrickSprite) + 2    `Determine brick width
  Height = SPRITE HEIGHT(BrickSprite) + 2  `Determine brick height

  BlockCount = 0          `Keep a count of bricks that should not be drawn

  FOR i = 1 TO 15         `Loop through every brick in a row
    FOR j = 1 TO 5        `Loop through all five rows
      if BricksArray(i, j) = 1  `An array item with a value of 1 indicates
                                `that a brick should be drawn and a value
                                `of 0 indicates no brick should be drawn
        INC BlockCount  `Keep track of the number of bricks drawn

        `Draw the brick
        SPRITE BrickSprite, 65 + Width * i, 75 + Height * j, BrickImage
        `Past the brick on the screen
        PASTE SPRITE BrickSprite, 65 + Width * i, 75 + Height * j

        `Determine if a collision has occurred with the brick and the ball
        IF SPRITE COLLISION(BrickSprite, BallSprite) = 1
          BricksArray(i, j) = 0   `Assign 0 to the array item representing
                                  `the brick in order to hide it when the
                                  `screen is redrawn
          DeflectBallOffBricks()  `Call function that redirects the ball
```

```
      ENDIF
    ENDIF
  NEXT j
NEXT i

`All blocks have been cleared
IF BlockCount = 0              `If no bricks were drawn the level is over
    GameState$ = "Initialize"    `Update game state
    LoadBricksArray()            `Call function that reloads the bricks
ENDIF

ENDFUNCTION
```

This function is responsible for keeping track of and drawing the game's bricks. In addition, it uses the SPRITE COLLISION command to perform a bounded rectangle collision check for each brick and the ball, calling the DeflectBallOffBricks() function when collisions occur. Take note of the last set of statements in the function. It is responsible for changing the value assigned to GameState$ to Initialize once all of the bricks have been knocked off of the screen.

Step 11: Creating the BounceTheBall() Function

The code statements that make up the BounceTheBall() function are shown next and should be added to the end of the code file.

```
`This function is responsible for moving the ball around the screen
FUNCTION BounceTheBall()

  BallX = BallX + SpeedX   `Move the ball along the x-axis
  BallY = BallY + SpeedY   `Move the ball along the y-axis

  `Check for a collision with the side of the screen
  ProcessSideOfScreenCollisions()

  `Check for a collision with the top of the screen
  ProcessTopOfScreenCollisions()

  `Check to see if the player missed the ball
  ProcessMisses()
```

```
`Draw the ball at the specified coordinates
SPRITE BallSprite, BallX, BallY, BallImage

ENDFUNCTION
```

When called, this function moves the ball around the screen by modifying the values assigned to BallX and BallY by adding the values assigned to SpeedX and SpeedY to them. In addition, calls are made to three functions that are responsible for managing collisions with the top and side of the screen and for dealing with misses. Note that the SPRITE command is executed at the end of the function to draw the ball at its new location.

Step 12: Creating the ProcessSideOfScreenCollisions() Function

The code statements that make up the ProcessSideOfScreenCollisions() function are shown next and should be added to the end of the code file. This function reverses the direction of the ball when it collides with the side of the screen.

```
`This function redirects the ball when it collides with either side of
`the screen
FUNCTION ProcessSideOfScreenCollisions()

  `If the ball has made contact with the left side of the screen then
  `reverse its direction
  IF BallX < 1
    BallX = 1        `Do not let the ball go past the side of the screen
    SpeedX = SpeedX * -1   `Reverse the ball's direction
  ENDIF

  `If the ball has made contact with the right side of the screen then
  `reverse its direction
  IF BallX > SCREEN WIDTH()  - 14
    BallX = SCREEN WIDTH() - 14    `Do not let the ball go past the side
                                   `of the screen
    SpeedX = SpeedX * -1           `Reverse the ball's direction
  ENDIF

ENDFUNCTION
```

Step 13: Creating the ProcessTopOfScreenCollisions() Function

The code statements that make up the `ProcessTopOfScreenCollisions()` function are shown next and should be added to the end of the code file. This function reverses the direction of the ball when it collides with the top of the screen.

```
`This function redirects the ball when it collides with the top of the
`screen
FUNCTION ProcessTopOfScreenCollisions()

  `If the ball has made contact with the top of the screen then reverse
  `its direction
  IF BallY < 0
    BallY = 0      `Do not let the ball go past the top of the screen
    SpeedY = SpeedY * -1    `Reverse the ball's direction
  ENDIF

ENDFUNCTION
```

Step 14: Creating the ProcessMisses() Function

The code statements that make up the `ProcessMisses()` function are shown next and should be added to the end of the code file.

```
`This function is responsible for dealing with misses
FUNCTION ProcessMisses()

  `The point is lost because the ball has gotten past the player's paddle
  IF BallY > SCREEN HEIGHT() - 6
    PlayerTurns = PlayerTurns - 1 `Decrement the number of turns remaining
    IF PlayerTurns < 1         `If no turns are left then the game is over
      GameState$ = "Over"      `Update game state
    ELSE
      GameState$ = "Initialize"  `Update game state
    ENDIF
  ENDIF

ENDFUNCTION
```

This function is responsible for determining when the player misses the ball, ending the current point. Note that if the value of `PlayerTurns` is less than one, the game ends, as reflected by the change of the value assigned to GameState$. Otherwise, the value of GameState$ is updated to reflect the end of the current point.

Step 15: Creating the LookForCollisionWithPaddle() Function

The code statements that make up the LookForCollisionWithPaddle() function are shown next and should be added to the end of the code file.

```
`This function handles collisions between the ball and the paddle
FUNCTION LookForCollisionWithPaddle()

  IF SPRITE COLLISION(PaddleSprite, BallSprite) = 1  `Check for collision
    DeflectBallOffThePaddle()  `Call on the function that deflects the ball
  ENDIF

ENDFUNCTION
```

When called, this function determines whether the ball and the paddle have collided. In the event of a collision, the DeflectBallOffThePaddle() function is called.

Step 16: Creating the ReadyBallAndPaddle() Function

The code statements that make up the ReadyBallAndPaddle() function are shown next and should be added to the end of the code file.

```
`This function attaches the ball to the paddle at the start of each point
FUNCTION ReadyBallAndPaddle()

  `Set coordinates representing the center of the paddle
  BallX = PaddleX + (SPRITE WIDTH(PaddleSprite) / 2) - (SPRITE WIDTH(BallSprite) / 2)
  BallY = PaddleY - 14  `Set coordinate on the y-axis just above the top
                        `of the paddle

  `Set a random speed and direction for the ball
  SpeedX = rnd(2) + 1
  SpeedY = rnd(2) - 6

  `Draw the ball at the specified coordinates
  SPRITE BallSprite, BallX, BallY, BallImage

ENDFUNCTION
```

When called this function places the ball just above the center of the paddle to ready the game to play a new point. In addition, the speed and direction at which the ball will travel when released from the paddle is calculated using a randomly generated number. The end result is an unpredictable direction and pace that makes the game a lot more challenging.

Step 17: Creating the ProcessPlayerInput() Function

The code statements that make up the ProcessPlayerInput() function are shown next and should be added to the end of the code file.

```
`This function processes player input for controlling paddle movement
FUNCTION ProcessPlayerInput()

  `Do not let the paddle go past the left edge of the screen
  IF PaddleX < 6 THEN PaddleX = 6

  `Determine the location of the right side of the paddle
  RightSideOfPaddle = PaddleX + SPRITE WIDTH(PaddleSprite)

  `Do not let the paddle go past the right edge of the screen
  IF RightSideOfPaddle > SCREEN WIDTH()
    PaddleX = SCREEN WIDTH() - SPRITE WIDTH(PaddleSprite)
  ENDIF

  `When the player presses the Left arrow, move the paddle to the left
  `by 6 pixels
  IF LEFTKEY()
    DEC PaddleX, 6
  ENDIF

  `When the player presses the Right arrow, move the paddle to the right
  `by 6 pixels
  IF RIGHTKEY()
    INC PaddleX, 6
  ENDIF

  `Draw the ball at the specified coordinates
  SPRITE PaddleSprite, PaddleX, PaddleY, PaddleImage

ENDFUNCTION
```

This function is responsible for moving the paddle to the left and right when the player presses on the left and right arrow keys. In addition, it is also responsible for preventing the player from moving the paddle off of either side of the screen.

Step 18: Creating the DeflectBallOffThePaddle() Function

The code statements that make up the DeflectBallOffThePaddle() function are shown next and should be added to the end of the code file.

```
`This function deflects the ball when it collides with the paddle
FUNCTION DeflectBallOffThePaddle()

  `Determine where the center of the ball is
  CenterOfBall = sprite x(BallSprite) + sprite width(BallSprite) / 2

  `Determine where the left edge of the paddle is
  LeftSideOfPaddle = sprite x(PaddleSprite)

  `Determine where the right edge of the paddle is
  RightSideOfPaddle = sprite x(PaddleSprite) + sprite width(PaddleSprite)

  `Randomly alter the speed of the ball when it collides with the
  `left-hand side of the paddle
  IF CenterOfBall < LeftSideOfPaddle + 15
    SpeedX = -rnd(4) - 1
  ENDIF

  `Randomly alter the speed of the ball when it collides with the
  `right-hand side of the paddle
  IF CenterOfBall > RightSideOfPaddle - 15
    SpeedX = rnd(4) - 1
  ENDIF

  `Change the direction of the ball and randomly change its speed as well
  SpeedY = -rnd(2) - 3

ENDFUNCTION
```

This function begins by identifying the center location of the ball as well as the left and right hand side of the paddle. If the center of the ball makes contact with either side of the paddle (e.g., the last 15 pixels of it), the angle at which the ball is traveling is randomly changed. Otherwise, a collision with the middle of the paddle simply results in the deflection of the ball with no change in angle.

Step 19: Creating the DeflectBallOffBricks() Function

The code statements that make up the last function in the project file are shown next and should be added to the end of the code file.

```
`This function manages ball movement when the ball collides with a brick
FUNCTION DeflectBallOffBricks()

  `Determine where the center of the ball is
  CenterOfBall = SPRITE X(BallSprite) + SPRITE WIDTH(BallSprite) / 2

  `Determine where the left-hand side of the ball is
  LeftSideOfBlock = SPRITE X(BallSprite)

  `Determine where the right-hand side of the ball is
  RightSideOfBlock = SPRITE X(BallSprite) + SPRITE WIDTH(BallSprite)

  IF CenterOfBall < LeftSideOfBlock or CenterOfBall > RightSideOfBlock
    SpeedX = SpeedX * - 1  `Change ball's direction on the x-axis when
                           `it hits the side of a block
  ELSE
    SpeedY = SpeedY * - 1 `Change ball's direction on the y-axis when it
                          `hits the top or bottom of a block
  ENDIF

ENDFUNCTION
```

The DeflectBallOffBricks() function is responsible for managing the deflection of the ball when it comes in contact with a brick. The ball can make contact with the brick from either side as well as from the top and from below. When the ball makes contact with the left or right side of a block, its direction is reversed along the x-axis. Similarly, when the ball makes contact with the top or bottom of a block, its direction is reversed along the y-axis.

Step 20: Saving and Compiling Your Application

If you have not already done so, now is a good time to pause and save your work by clicking on the Save All option located on the File menu. Once your project has been saved, click on the Make/EXE RUN option located on the Compile menu to compile and test the execution of your new game.

The Final Result

Okay, assuming that you have not made any typographical errors and that you have carefully followed along with each step required to develop the Bricks game, everything should work as described at the beginning of this chapter. Of course, there is still more work to do, but you will get to that in Chapter 9, "Working with Input Devices." Still, even at this point in the development of the game, all of the basic elements are in place.

You will also find a copy of this application's project file along with copies of the graphic files for the background, ball, paddle, and brick bitmaps on this book's companion website, located at http://www.courseptr.com/downloads.

SUMMARY

This chapter has provided you with a good introduction to 2D programming using sprites. You learned how to use bitmaps as the basis for creating sprites. You learned how to use the SPRITE command to draw and move sprites around the screen. You also learned how to use sprites as the basis for graphic animation. This chapter also provided you with more detailed information regarding collision detection. Lastly, you began work on the development of the Bricks game.

You will get the opportunity to work further on the development of the Bricks game in Chapter 9. Specifically, you will add sound to the game, an opening welcome screen, along with directions for playing the game. In addition, you will add more levels to the game and modify the game so that it can be played using the mouse in place of the keyboard. However, before moving on to Chapter 9, you may want to go ahead and set aside a few additional minutes to improve the appearance of the Bricks game by implementing the following challenges.

CHALLENGES

1. The graphics used to represent the Bricks game's ball, paddle, and bricks are quite rudimentary, consisting of plain, solid-color shapes. Consider replacing them with custom artwork of your own. Alternatively, you might want to spend a few minutes searching on the Internet for free game graphics developed by enthusiastic game and graphic developers who like to share their work.

WORKING WITH INPUT DEVICES

I n this chapter, you will learn new ways of interacting with the user input devices like the keyboard, mouse, and joystick. This includes learning how to capture keyboard input in a number of different ways, including non-blocking input collection that permits a game's main loop to contine running while input collection is underway. You will learn how to interact with the mouse and joystick and to detect mouse location. You will also learn how to track mouse and joystick movement. In addition to learning how to interact with and control the keyboard, mouse, and joystick, this chapter will guide you through the development of the second part of the Bricks game.

Specifically, you will learn how to:

- Collect keyboard input without blocking execution of the game's main loop
- Track mouse location and movement
- Identify and react to mouse clicks
- Track joystick movement and direction
- Identify and react to joystick button clicks

Project Preview: Part Two of the Bricks Game

In this chapter, you will work on part two of the Bricks game. You are going to learn how to apply a number of enhancements to the game. For starters, you will modify the game so that its paddle is controlled using the mouse instead of the left and right arrows on the keyboard. In addition, you will modify the game so that the left mouse button is used in place of the up arrow key when launching the ball in order to begin a new point. You will also add a welcome screen that is displayed at the beginning of the game that greets the player and provides instructions for playing the game, as shown in Figure 9.1.

Welcome to the

Bricks game

Use the left mouse button to begin play. Use the mouse to control

the movement of the paddle. Press any key to continue.

Figure 9.1

A new welcome screen will be added to the Bricks game.

Once game play beings, a screen displaying three rows of bricks will be displayed, as shown in Figure 9.2.

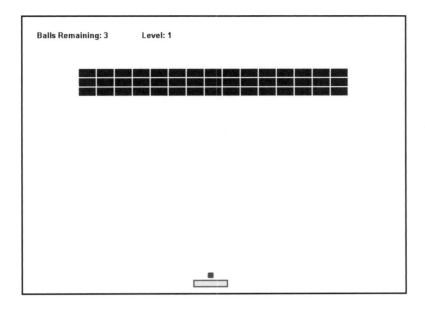

Figure 9.2 represents the first level of the game. In addition to this level, you will modify the game to include two additional levels, each of which will contain an increasing number of bricks. Figure 9.3 shows the number of bricks that makes up the second level.

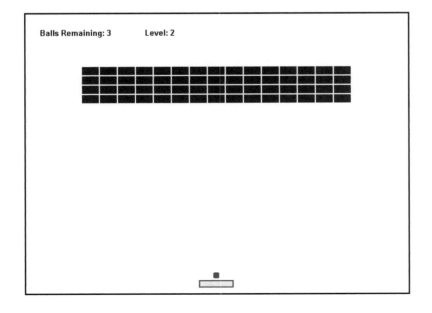

As Figure 9.4 shows, the third level of the Bricks game contains even more bricks.

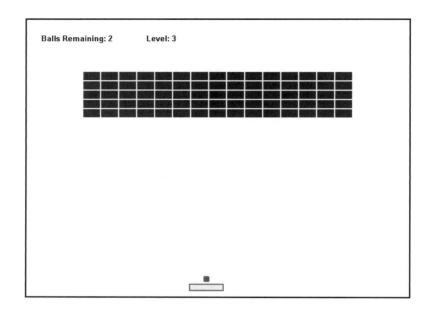

If the player manages to successfully clear out all of the bricks on each of the game's three levels, the game starts over again at the first level, allowing the player to replay each level for as long as she can keep her three balls in play.

COLLECTING PLAYER INPUT

In order to play any type of game, players require a means of providing input. The type of input required will vary based on the type of game being played. A word game may be played using only the keyboard as an input source. A strategy game may require the use of a mouse to position resources and select objects to be controlled or targeted. Action and arcade-style games may be designed to work with either the keyboard or mouse, or with a joystick if one is attached to the computer.

DarkBASIC Professional provides strong support for the keyboard, mouse, and joystick, providing access to dozens of commands that let you exploit the unique capabilities of each of these devices.

COLLECTING KEYBOARD INPUT

Most computer keyboards have at least 104 keys, though many have even more keys. Each keyboard key operates in precisely the same manner, and from DarkBASIC Professional's perspective exists in one of the three following states.

- **Up.** A key that has not been pressed.
- **Down.** A key that is currently being pressed.
- **Pressed.** A key whose state has just changed from down to up.

Four of the most commonly used keyboard keys in computer games are the up, down, left, and right arrow keys. These keys are typically used to control movement and directions within a game. In other games, like first-person shooters, the w, a, s, and d keys are used in place of the arrow keys to free up the player's right hand to work with the mouse.

Collecting Data and Controlling Program Execution Using Blocking Controls

As you have already seen, DarkBASIC Professional includes commands that provide the ability to halt game play to collect a player's input using the keyboard. Specifically, you have used the INPUT$ command on a number of occasions to display a text prompt and then to collect and assign player input to a variable, which can then be analyzed and used in any number of ways. You have also learned how to use the WAIT KEY command as a means of pausing program execution, allowing execution to resume only after one of the keys on the computer's keyboard is pressed. INPUT$ and WAIT KEY are blocking commands, meaning that they halt the execution of a computer program until the player presses a key on the computer's keyboard.

Collecting Data Using Non-Blocking Controls

DarkBASIC Professional provides access to commands that you can use to collect keyboard input without halting program execution. As such, these commands can be used within loops to collect keyboard input. An effective demonstration of this capability was provided through the development of the DB Pong game in Chapter 7 "Working with Graphics and Sound," where the Shift, Ctrl, up arrow, and down arrow keys were used to control both game paddles.

Capturing Individual Keystrokes

Instead of pausing application execution to capture user input with the INPUT$ command, you can use the INKEY$ command to capture individual keystrokes. The INKEY$ command has the following syntax.

VariableName = INKEY$()

Here, *VariableName* represents the name of a variable that will be used to store a character representing the currently pressed key (if there is one).

To get a better feel for the capabilities of the INKEY$() command, take a look at the following example.

```
PRINT "Press the q key to quit."

DO

  IF (INKEY$() = "Q" OR INKEY$() = "q")
    PRINT
    PRINT "OK. I am out of here!"
    SLEEP 1000
    EXIT
  ENDIF

LOOP

END
```

This example begins by displaying a message that instructs the user to press the q key to terminate program execution. A loop is then set up that runs forever. Within the loop, an IF statement code block is set up to determine whether the user has pressed the q key (upper- or lowercase). As you can see, the IF statement uses the INKEY$ command to capture the user's input. Once the user finally enters the q key, a message is displayed for one second, after which the program terminates its execution.

 TRAP In this example, the INKEY$ command is case-sensitive, so an uppercase letter is viewed as being different from its lowercase equivalent.

In addition to returning a character representing a letter pressed on the keyboard, the INKEY$ command can also be used to determine when other types of keys are pressed. To use this command in this manner, you need to specify the ASCII value of whatever keyboard character you want to check on. Table 9.1 provides a partial listing of keyboard keys that you are most likely to use.

Code	Key
	TABLE 9.1 ASCII KEYBOARD KEY CODES
8	Backspace
12	Carriage Return (Enter)
27	Escape
32	Spacebar

The following example demonstrates how to use the INKEY$ command to keep an eye out for the spacebar key.

```
PRINT "Press the spacebar to quit."

DO

  IF INKEY$() = CHR$(32)
    PRINT
    PRINT "OK. I am out of here!"
    SLEEP 1000
    EXIT
  ENDIF

LOOP

END
```

Here, a DO...LOOP has been set up that executes until the user presses the spacebar key.

Capturing Special Keystrokes

When it comes to computer games, some keyboard keys have more significance than others do. In recognition of this fact, a collection of nine special DarkBASIC Professional commands have been set up to detect the up and down state of some of the more commonly used keyboard keys. The commands are listed here along with a brief explanation of their purpose.

- CONTROLKEY. Returns a value of 0 if the Control key is in an up state and a value of 1 if it is in a down state.

- DOWNKEY. Returns a value of 0 if the Down key is in an up state and a value of 1 if it is in a down state.

- ESCAPEKEY. Returns a value of 0 if the Escape key is in an up state and a value of 1 if it is in a down state.
- LEFTKEY. Returns a value of 0 if the Left key is in an up state and a value of 1 if it is in a down state.
- RETURNKEY. Returns a value of 0 if the Enter key above the Shift key is in an up state and a value of 1 if it is in a down state. This command does not work with the Enter key on the keyboard's numeric keypad.
- RIGHTKEY. Returns a value of 0 if the Right key is in an up state and a value of 1 if it is in a down state.
- SHIFTKEY. Returns a value of 0 if either of the Shift keys is in an up state and a value of 1 if both of the Shift keys are in a down state.
- SPACEKEY. Returns a value of 0 if the Spacebar is in an up state and a value of 1 if it is in a down state.
- UPKEY. Returns a value of 0 if the Up key is in an up state and a value of 1 if it is in a down state.

As an example of how to work with these special keystroke commands, consider the following example.

```
PRINT "Press the spacebar to quit."

DO

  IF SPACEKEY() = 1
     PRINT
     PRINT "OK. I am out of here!"
     SLEEP 1000
     EXIT
  ENDIF

LOOP

END
```

Here, a DO...LOOP has been set up that executes until the user presses the spacebar, as signified when the value returned by the SPACEKEY command is equal to 1.

Capturing Keystrokes Stored in the Windows Keyboard Buffer

In addition to the INKEY$ command and the nine special keyboard commands, DarkBASIC Professional also allows you to capture more than one character at a time without having to halt application execution to do it. Specifically, DarkBASIC Professional provides access to a pair of commands that you can use to retrieve a string representing all of the input keyed in by the user from the Windows keyboard buffer. These commands are named ENTRY$ and CLEAR ENTRY BUFFER.

The Windows keyboard buffer is a section of computer memory that Windows uses to keep track of keyboard keystrokes until the computer is ready to respond to them.

Using the ENTRY$ command, you can retrieve a string containing all of the keystrokes currently stored in the keyboard buffer. Once you have retrieved the user's keyboard input, you can execute the CLEAR ENTRY BUFFER command to delete the contents of the keyboard buffer, readying it for a new string. To get a better understanding of how to work with these commands, take a look at the following example.

```
CLEAR ENTRY BUFFER

PRINT "Type a few words and then press the Enter key."

DO

  IF RETURNKEY() = 1
    EXIT
  ENDIF

LOOP

SET TEXT FONT "Arial"
SET TEXT SIZE 26
TEXT 1, 100, "You typed: " + ENTRY$()

WAIT KEY

END
```

Here, the CLEAR ENTRY BUFFER command is executed to clear out anything already stored in the keyboard buffer. The user is then instructed to type in a few words and then to press the Enter key. A DO...LOOP has been set up to run until the Enter key is pressed, at which time it stops executing and the text that the user typed is retrieved from the keyboard buffer using the ENTRY$ command and then displayed. Figure 9.5 demonstrates the execution of this example and shows how output is displayed.

FIGURE 9.5

Capturing keyboard input without blocking application execution.

INTERACTING WITH THE MOUSE

Like keyboards, there are many different types of mouse devices. The traditional mouse has two buttons. Newer mice often support a wheel located in between the primary mouse buttons and may also come equipped with more than two buttons. Touch pad and track ball devices can also be regarded as variations of mice, performing the exact same function and producing the same output as a traditional mouse. Regardless of the exact type of device that is used, they all provide input that specifies X and Y location information. These devices also provide input that indicates when their buttons are clicked, which, depending on the type of game being played, might trigger the firing of a laser cannon, display of an inventory of items collected during the game, or serve any number of other purposes.

Similar to keyboard keys, mouse buttons are viewed by DarkBASIC Professional as having a number of different states, as outlined here:

- Up. A button that has not been pressed.
- Down. A button that is currently being pressed.
- Clicked. A button whose state has just changed from down to up.
- Double Clicked. A button that has just been clicked twice in rapid succession.

Putting the Pointer Where You Want It

One of the most basic mouse commands that you want to be familiar with is the POSITION MOUSE command, which gives you the ability to place the pointer anywhere you want on the screen. This command is typically used at the beginning of a game to control the initial location of the pointer. This command has the following syntax.

```
POSITION MOUSE X, Y
```

X, *Y* specify the pointer's starting location along the x-axis and the y-axis. The following statement demonstrates how to use the POSITION MOUSE command to place the pointer in the middle of a screen set to 640×480 resolution.

```
POSITION MOUSE 320, 240
```

Tracking Mouse Position and Movement

A primary use of the mouse is to control the movement of the pointer or cursor around the screen. DarkBASIC Professional provides access to a number of commands that you can use to track mouse movement. The MOUSEX command is used to retrieve the location of the pointer on the x-axis. The MOUSEY command is used to retrieve the location of the pointer on the y-axis. The MOUSEZ command is used to retrieve the location of the pointer on the z-axis, which if present represents the movement of the mouse wheel. Each of these commands shares a common syntax, as outlined here:

```
VariableName = MOUSEX()
VariableName = MOUSEY()
VariableName = MOUSEZ()
```

As an example of how to work with these three commands, take a look at the following.

```
SET TEXT FONT "Arial"  `Set the font type to Arial
SET TEXT SIZE 26  `Set the font size to 26 points

SYNC ON

POSITION MOUSE (SCREEN WIDTH() / 2), (SCREEN HEIGHT() / 2)

DO

  TEXT 50, 30, "X Coordinate: " + STR$(MOUSEX())
  TEXT 50, 50, "Y Coordinate: " + STR$(MOUSEY())
```

```
TEXT 350, 30, "Z Coordinate: " + STR$(MOUSEZ())

IF SPACEKEY() = 1
  EXIT
ENDIF

SYNC
CLS

LOOP
```

Here, the POSITION MOUSE command is used to place the pointer in the middle of the screen. Next, a loop is set up that continuously displays the current location of the mouse along the X, Y, and Z axes. The loop repeatedly executes until the user hits the spacebar, signaling that it is time to terminate execution. Figure 9.6 demonstrates the execution of this example and shows how output is displayed.

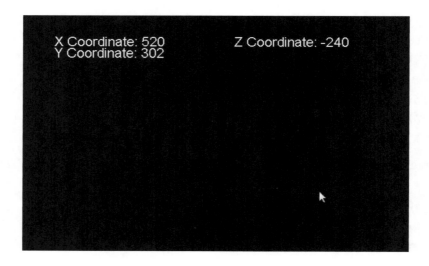

FIGURE 9.6

Tracking the pointer location on the screen.

Take note of the execution of the POSITION MOUSE command in this example. In order to avoid having to hardcode the center location of the screen based upon a specific resolution, the SCREEN WIDTH and SCREEN HEIGHT commands were used to retrieve values representing the screen's width and height. The values were then divided in half to determine the screen's center coordinates.

In addition to locating the current position of the pointer on the screen, DarkBASIC Professional also provides commands that you can use to determine the distance between the current and previous mouse position. These commands include the MOUSEMOVEX command, which identifies the distance that the pointer has moved on the x-axis, the MOUSEMOVEY command, which identifies the distance that the pointer has moved on the y-axis, and the MOUSEMOVEZ command, which identifies the distance that the wheel has moved on the z-axis. Each of these commands shares a common syntax, as outlined here:

```
VariableName = MOUSEMOVEX()
VariableName = MOUSEMOVEY()
VariableName = MOUSEMOVEZ()
```

Detecting Mouse Button Clicks

In addition to tracking the location of the pointer, you also need to know how to determine when the user clicks on one of the mouse's buttons. This will allow your game to use mouse button clicks as a means of controlling when game objects jump, shoot, and so on. To determine when a mouse button is clicked, you need to use the MOUSECLICK command, which retrieves the value of all currently pressed mouse button(s). This command uses the following syntax:

```
VariableName = MOUSECLICK()
```

DarkBASIC Professional supports up to four buttons on a mouse. Each button is assigned a specific value, as listed in Table 9.3.

TABLE 9.3 MOUSE CLICK VALUES	
Button	**Value**
Left	1
Right	2
Third	4
Fourth	8

Using the MOUSECLICK command, you retrieve an integer value representing the total number of mouse buttons that are being pressed when the command executes. For example, if the MOUSECLICK command returns a value of 1, then you know that the left mouse button is being clicked, and if it returns a value of 2, you know that the right mouse button is being clicked. If, on the other hand, a value of 3 is returned, then both the left and right mouse buttons are being clicked. Similarly, a value of 7 would indicate that the left, right, and third buttons are all being clicked. And a value of 15 would indicate that left, right, third, and fourth buttons are all being clicked. To get a better understanding of how to work with the MOUSECLICK command, take a look at the following example.

```
SET TEXT FONT "Arial"  `Set the font type to Arial
SET TEXT SIZE 26  `Set the font size to 26 points

SYNC ON

POSITION MOUSE (SCREEN WIDTH() / 2), (SCREEN HEIGHT() / 2)

DO

  TEXT 50, 30, "X Coordinate: " + STR$(MOUSEX())
  TEXT 50, 50, "Y Coordinate: " + STR$(MOUSEY())
  TEXT 350, 30, "Z Coordinate: " + STR$(MOUSEZ())
  TEXT 350, 50, "Mouse Button: " + STR$(MOUSECLICK())

  IF SPACEKEY() = 1
    EXIT
  ENDIF

  SYNC
  CLS

LOOP
```

This example is very similar to the last example that you were shown when learning about the MOUSEX, MOUSEY, and MOUSEZ commands. Only now the example has been modified to use the MOUSECLICK command to display a value representing any currently pressed mouse buttons. Figure 9.7 demonstrates the execution of this example and shows how output is displayed.

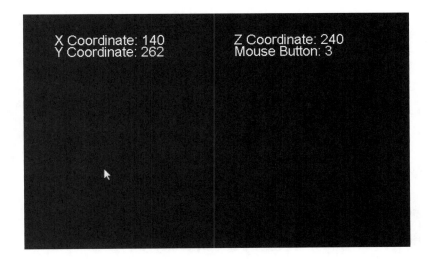

```
X Coordinate: 140        Z Coordinate: 240
Y Coordinate: 262        Mouse Button: 3
```

FIGURE 9.7

Tracking pointer
location and
mouse clicks.

Hiding and Displaying the Mouse

Depending on the nature of your DarkBASIC Professional games, there may be times when you do not want to see the mouse cursor. For example, you might create a game in which the player scores points by shooting at enemy tanks. In order to aim at enemy tanks, you might want to set up a custom cursor that looks like the crosshairs in a gun scope.

To suppress the display of the cursor, you must use the HIDE MOUSE command, which has the following syntax.

```
HIDE MOUSE
```

When executed, the HIDE MOUSE command prevents the cursor from displaying on any part of the screen. If you need to, you can re-enable the display of the cursor at any time during the execution of your application using the SHOW MOUSE command, which has the following syntax.

```
SHOW MOUSE
```

TRICK By eliminating the display of the mouse pointer, you can substitute a sprite in its place. For example, the following statements suppress the display of the course and then load a bmp image that is then used as a sprite to simulate the crosshairs of a gun target.

```
HIDE MOUSE

LOAD IMAGE "CrossHair.bmp", 1
```

```
DO
  CLS
  SPRITE 1, MOUSEX(), MOUSEY(), 1
LOOP

WAIT KEY
END
```

Figure 9.8 demonstrates the execution of this example and shows how output is displayed.

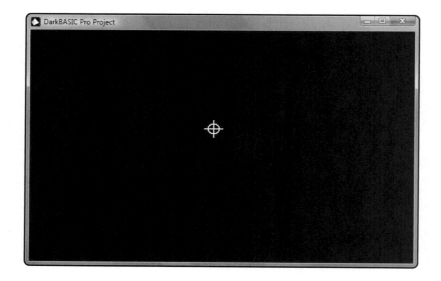

FIGURE 9.8

Replacing the cursor with a sprite.

DarkBASIC Professional also lets you replace the default cursor with a cursor of your own using the CHANGE MOUSE command, which you can learn more about using DarkBASIC Professional's help files.

USING JOYSTICK INPUT

Joysticks are an absolute requirement of modern gaming consoles like the Wii, Xbox 360, and PlayStation 3. However, they are far less commonly found on personal computers. Still, you will be pleased to know that DarkBASIC Professional provides a full range of commands for working with joysticks.

Although traditional joysticks have been connected to the computer via a game port located on the back of many audio cards, more and more joysticks are following the same trend being set by keyboards and mice, connecting to the computer via a USB connection. Since USB connections represent a faster connection, the player is given greater control during game play. Regardless of how they are connected to the computer, DarkBASIC Professional should be able to work with most joysticks.

Much like a mouse, a joystick returns a continuous stream of input reflecting X, Y information and usually has one or more buttons that also provides input. Joysticks with a wheel in between the two mouse buttons also provide information regarding the Z position.

Tracking Joystick Position

Joysticks can be used to control the movement of objects during games. DarkBASIC Professional provides access to a number of commands that can be used to detect joystick input. The JOYSTICK X command is used to retrieve the location of the pointer on the x-axis. The JOYSTICK Y command is used to retrieve the location of the pointer on the y-axis. The JOYSTICK Z command is used to retrieve the location of the pointer on the z-axis, which if present represents the movement of the joystick's wheel. Each of these commands shares a common syntax, as outlined here:

```
VariableName = JOYSTICK X()
VariableName = JOYSTICK Y()
VariableName = JOYSTICK Z()
```

Each of these commands returns a value in the range of –1000 to 1000.

Tracking Joystick Movement

DarkBASIC Professional also provides access to commands that can determine the movement direction of joysticks. Unlike mouse movement commands, DarkBASIC's joystick movement commands do not return information regarding the distance that a joystick has moved. Instead, these commands return a value that indicates the direction in which the joystick is currently moving.

The JOYSTICK UP command is used to determine if the joystick is moving in an upward direction, returning a value of 1 if this is the case and a value of 0 if this is not the case. Similarly, the JOYSTICK DOWN command is used to determine if the joystick is moving in a downward direction, and the JOYSTICK LEFT and JOYSTICK RIGHT commands determine if the joystick is moving left or right. Each of these commands shares a common syntax, as outlined here:

```
VariableName = JOYSTICK UP()
VariableName = JOYSTICK DOWN()
VariableName = JOYSTICK LEFT()
VariableName = JOYSTICK RIGHT()
```

Detecting Joystick Button Clicks

As is the case with the mouse, DarkBASIC Professional can also detect when joystick buttons are pressed. For starters, you can track the usage of the first four joystick buttons using the `JOYSTICK FIRE A`, `JOYSTICK FIRE B`, `JOYSTICK FIRE C`, and `JOYSTICK FIRE D` commands. Each of these commands returns a value of 1 if its associated button is being pressed and a value of 0 if it is not. Each of these commands shares a common syntax, as outlined here:

```
VariableName = JOYSTICK FIRE A()
VariableName = JOYSTICK FIRE B()
VariableName = JOYSTICK FIRE C()
VariableName = JOYSTICK FIRE D()
```

If you need to support joysticks with more than four buttons, you can do so using the `JOYSTICK FIRE X` command. This command allows you to specify and check on the use of up to 32 joystick buttons, using the following syntax.

```
VariableName = JOYSTICK FIRE X(ButtonReference)
```

ButtonReference is an integer value used to specify a value in the range of 1 to 32.

Other Joystick Commands

In addition to providing all of the basic joystick commands discussed in the previous sections, DarkBASIC Professional also provides commands that you can use to work with features found on many high-end joysticks, including joystick sliders, twists, and hats. A *slider* is a joystick button or control that can be moved up and back. For example, a game might make use of a slider control to instruct a flight simulation game to accelerate the speed of a plane. The term *twist* refers to the ability of a joystick to twist or rotate in place, giving the player additional control over joystick movements. A *hat* is a multi-directional button on a joystick and is very much like a miniature joystick on a joystick.

DarkBASIC Professional also provides support for *force feedback*, which is a joystick feature that allows a game to send back instructions to a joystick to provide the player with physical feedback. Using force feedback, a joystick can be made to simulate the feel of a machine gun when firing or the impact incurred when an object being controlled by the player takes a hit. To learn more about these advanced joystick commands that support slider, twist, hat, and force feedback features, consult DarkBASIC Professional's Input Commands Help file.

BACK TO THE BRICKS GAME

Okay, it is time to turn your attention to the development of this chapter's main project, the Bricks game. You already developed part one of this game back in Chapter 8. The rest of this chapter is devoted to adding a number of enhancements to that version. Specifically, you will add a welcome screen that is displayed at the beginning of the game to provide the player with instructions on how to play the game. You will add sound effects for when the ball collides with the paddle and bricks. You will also modify the game so that it presents the player with three different levels, each with more bricks than the previous level. Finally, you will modify the game to allow the player to play it using the mouse, resulting in better control over the movement of the paddle.

Designing the Game

Since you already worked on developing the first part of this game in Chapter 8, I am not going to spend time going over its initial creation again. Instead, I am going to re-list the program, showing any additions and modifications to the code statements in bold to make them stand out.

The overall organization of the game has not changed much from its design in the preceding chapter, except for the addition of a new function. In addition, a number of changes must be made to different program functions. The project's overall organization is outlined next. Note that entries shown in bold represent areas within the program code file where additions and modifications will occur.

1. **Initial comment statements used to provide high-level documentation.**
2. **The declaration of global variables and** DATA **statements.**
3. **The main processing section containing the program's overall controlling logic.**
4. **The** DisplayWelcomeScreen() **function.**
5. **The** ReadyGameForPlay() **function.**
6. The LoadBricksArray() function.
7. **The** PlayBricksGame() **function.**
8. **The** DisplayBricks() **function.**
9. The BounceTheBall() function.
10. The ProcessSideOfScreenCollisions() function.
11. The ProcessTopOfScreenCollisions() function.
12. The ProcessMisses() function.
13. **The** LookForCollisionWithPaddle() **function.**
14. The ReadyBallAndPaddle() function.
15. **The** ProcessPlayerInput() **function.**
16. The DeflectBallOffThePaddle() function.
17. The Creating the DeflectBallOffBricks() function.

Initial Comments Statements

As pointed out next in bold print, there is only one change that you need to make to the comment statements located at the beginning of the project code file. This change reflects updates made in creating this new version of the Bricks game.

```
REM Project: Bricks
REM Created: 11/4/2007 10:00:44 AM
REM Executable name: Bricks.dba
REM Version: 1.1
REM Author: Jerry Lee Ford, Jr.
REM Description: This DarkBASIC Professional game is based on the original
REM                 Breakout video game
```

Before you make any changes to the Bricks project, I suggest creating a copy of the project and applying all changes to the new copy. This way, if something goes wrong, you can always start over with the with the Version 1.0 copy of your application.

The Declaration of Global Variables and DATA Statements

There are a number of changes that need to be made to the declaration section of your program code. The first changes create two new global variables. The first variable will be used to store a wave file in memory, so that it can be played back whenever a collision occurs between the ball and the paddle or the ball and the bricks. The second global variable will be used to keep track of which of three levels is being played so that the game will be able to determine what level to load the next time the screen is clear of all bricks.

The remainder of the changes made in this part of the program reflect the addition of two more levels to the game. Each level consists of a new set of bricks, which are defined using a set of five DATA statements.

```
REM **** Declare and Initialize Global Variables and Data Statements *****

Global BallX AS INTEGER = 0     `Coordinate of the ball on the x-axis
Global BallY AS INTEGER = 0     `Coordinate of the ball on the y-axis

GLOBAL SpeedX AS INTEGER = 1    `No. of pixels on x-axis the ball will move
GLOBAL SpeedY AS INTEGER = - 1  `No. of pixels on y-axis the ball will move

GLOBAL PaddleX AS INTEGER = 5   `Coordinate of the paddle on the x-axis
GLOBAL PaddleY AS INTEGER = 25  `Coordinate of the paddle on the y-axis
```

```
GLOBAL BackGroundImage AS INTEGER = 1    `The game's bitmap background image
GLOBAL BallImage AS INTEGER = 2          `The game's bitmap ball image
GLOBAL BrickImage AS INTEGER = 3         `The game's bitmap brick image
GLOBAL PaddleImage AS INTEGER = 6        `The game's bitmap paddle image

GLOBAL BallSprite AS INTEGER = 2         `Sprite representing the ball
GLOBAL BrickSprite AS INTEGER = 3        `Sprite representing a brick
GLOBAL PaddleSprite AS INTEGER = 5       `Sprite representing the paddle
GLOBAL CollisionSound AS INTEGER = 4 `Sound played when the ball hits a
                                         `brick or the paddle

GLOBAL GameState$ AS STRING = "Initialize"  `Tracks game state
GLOBAL PlayerTurns AS INTEGER = 3           `Track number of turns left
GLOBAL CurrentLevel AS Integer = 1          `Keep track of the current level

DIM BricksArray(15, 15) AS INTEGER       `An array used to keep track of
                                         `bricks in memory


`There are three rows of bricks in level 1
DATA 1, 1, 1, 1, 1, 1, 1, 1, 1, 1, 1, 1, 1, 1, 1
DATA 1, 1, 1, 1, 1, 1, 1, 1, 1, 1, 1, 1, 1, 1, 1
DATA 1, 1, 1, 1, 1, 1, 1, 1, 1, 1, 1, 1, 1, 1, 1
DATA 0, 0, 0, 0, 0, 0, 0, 0, 0, 0, 0, 0, 0, 0, 0
DATA 0, 0, 0, 0, 0, 0, 0, 0, 0, 0, 0, 0, 0, 0, 0

`There are four rows of bricks in level 2
DATA 1, 1, 1, 1, 1, 1, 1, 1, 1, 1, 1, 1, 1, 1, 1
DATA 1, 1, 1, 1, 1, 1, 1, 1, 1, 1, 1, 1, 1, 1, 1
DATA 1, 1, 1, 1, 1, 1, 1, 1, 1, 1, 1, 1, 1, 1, 1
DATA 1, 1, 1, 1, 1, 1, 1, 1, 1, 1, 1, 1, 1, 1, 1
DATA 0, 0, 0, 0, 0, 0, 0, 0, 0, 0, 0, 0, 0, 0, 0

`There are five rows of bricks in level 3
DATA 1, 1, 1, 1, 1, 1, 1, 1, 1, 1, 1, 1, 1, 1, 1
DATA 1, 1, 1, 1, 1, 1, 1, 1, 1, 1, 1, 1, 1, 1, 1
DATA 1, 1, 1, 1, 1, 1, 1, 1, 1, 1, 1, 1, 1, 1, 1
DATA 1, 1, 1, 1, 1, 1, 1, 1, 1, 1, 1, 1, 1, 1, 1
DATA 1, 1, 1, 1, 1, 1, 1, 1, 1, 1, 1, 1, 1, 1, 1
```

The Main Processing Section

A new function named `DisplayWelcomeScreen()` is going to be added that when called will welcome the player and display instructions for playing the game. The function is called just once, at the beginning of the game from the main processing section where the program's high-level controlling logic is defined. To accommodate this addition to the game, the new statement shown next in bold must be added to the program's code file.

```
REM ********************* Main Processing Section ***********************

DisplayWelcomeScreen() `Call function that displays the welcome screen
ReadyGameForPlay()      `Call function that initializes the game
LoadBricksArray()      `Call the function that loads an array with brick data
PlayBricksGame()       `Call the function responsible for managing game play

END                    `Terminate the execution of this application
```

The DisplayWelcomeScreen() Function

The code statements required to generate the game's welcome screen are shown next and should be inserted into the project's code file immediately after the main processing section and before any other functions.

```
REM ************************* Procedure Section **************************

FUNCTION DisplayWelcomeScreen()

  CLS RGB(255, 255, 255)  `Set background color to white

  SET TEXT FONT "ARIAL"  `Set the font type to Arial
  SET TEXT SIZE 48  `Set the font size to 48 points

  ForegroundColor = RGB(0, 0, 160)       `Set foreground color to blue
  BackgroundColor = RGB(255, 255, 255)   `Set background color to white
  INK ForegroundColor, BackgroundColor   `Apply color settings

  CENTER TEXT SCREEN WIDTH() / 2, 100, "Welcome to the"  `Display a welcome message
  CENTER TEXT SCREEN WIDTH() / 2, 170, "Bricks game"
  SET TEXT SIZE 16  `Set the font size to 24 points
  SET TEXT TO BOLD  `Display text in bold
```

```
`Display instructions for playing the game
TEXT 130, 350, "Use the left mouse button to begin play. Use the mouse to control"
TEXT 160, 380, "the movement of the paddle. Press any key to continue."

WAIT KEY    `Pause game play until the player presses a keyboard key

ENDFUNCTION
```

The ReadyGameForPlay() Function

Before the wave file associated with the CollisionSound global variable can be played, it must first be loaded into memory. This is accomplished by adding the statement shown in bold to the ReadyGameForPlay() function.

```
FUNCTION ReadyGameForPlay()

  SYNC ON          `Disable automatic screen refresh
  SYNC RATE 60     `Set the game's synchronization rate
  HIDE MOUSE       `Prevent the display of the mouse
  RANDOMIZE TIMER() `Use the Timer command to seed random number generation

  SET TEXT FONT "Arial"    `Set font to Arial
  SET TEXT SIZE 16         `Set point size to 16
  SET TEXT TO BOLD         `Display text in bold
  INK 0, 0                 `Set color to black

  LOAD SOUND "Type.wav", CollisionSound         `Load wave file

  LOAD IMAGE "Background.bmp", BackGroundImage  `Load background image
  LOAD IMAGE "Paddle.bmp", PaddleImage          `Load paddle image
  LOAD IMAGE "GameBall.bmp", BallImage          `Load ball image
  LOAD IMAGE "Brick.bmp", BrickImage            `Load brick image

  SPRITE PaddleSprite, 999, 999, PaddleImage    `Create sprite paddle
  SPRITE BallSprite, 999, 999, BallImage        `Create sprite ball
  SPRITE BrickSprite, 999, 999, BrickImage      `Create sprite brick

  `Determine width and length of the paddle
  PaddleX = (SCREEN WIDTH() / 2) - (SPRITE WIDTH(PaddleSprite) / 2)
  PaddleY = SCREEN HEIGHT() - 25

ENDFUNCTION
```

The LoadBricksArray() Function

No changes are required to the LoadBricksArray() function, which is responsible for filling an array with information stored in DATA statements that define the layout of bricks for each of the game's three levels.

```
`This function loads an array with data on the current level's brick layout
FUNCTION LoadBricksArray()

  FOR j = 1 TO 5       `It takes 5 DATA statements to create 1 level
    FOR i = 1 TO 15    `Each DATA statement contains 15 bricks
      READ BricksArray(i, j)  `Load the current data item into the array
    NEXT i
  NEXT j


ENDFUNCTION
```

The PlayBricksGame() Function

A number of changes need to be made to the PlayBricksGame() function, as the statements shown next in bold indicate. To accommodate the addition of two new levels in the game, program logic must be added to determine when level 3 has been completed so that the game can reset itself to level 1 again and execute the RESTORE command reusing the brick information stored in the project's DATA statements.

The other changes made to this function replace the use of the UPKEY command with the MOUSECLICK command, allowing the game to use the mouse's left button as the trigger for initiating the beginning of a new point instead of requiring that the player press the keyboard's up key.

The last two statements that are highlighted in bold show a pair of new statements that are used to display information about the current level on the screen so that the player can easily keep track of game progress.

```
`This function manages the overall game play
FUNCTION PlayBricksGame()

  DO   `Loop forever

    PASTE IMAGE BackGroundImage, 0, 0   `Display the background image

    `There are three distinct stages in this game, each of which must be
    `handled differently
```

```
SELECT GameState$      `Retrieve current game state

  CASE "Play":         `If current state is play the game is in progress
    DisplayBricks()    `Call function responsible for displaying bricks
    BounceTheBall()    `Call function responsible for moving the ball
    LookForCollisionWithPaddle()  `Call function that handles
                                  `collision with the paddle
  ENDCASE

  CASE "Initialize":   `It is time to begin a new point
    ReadyBallAndPaddle()  `Call function that gets the ball and paddle
                          `ready for a new point
    DisplayBricks()    `Call function responsible for displaying bricks
    IF CurrentLevel > 3  `After the third level things start over
      CurrentLevel = 0   `Reset current level back to zero
      RESTORE            `Restore all DATA statements
    ENDIF
    IF MOUSECLICK() = 1  `Start point when the player clicks the
                         `mouse button
      GameState$ = "Play"  `Adjust game state
    ENDIF
  ENDCASE

  CASE "Over":                    `The current game has ended
    `Notify the player that the game has ended
    CENTER TEXT SCREEN WIDTH() / 2, SCREEN HEIGHT() / 2, "GAME OVER"
    CENTER TEXT SCREEN WIDTH() / 2, SCREEN HEIGHT() / 2 + 30, "Press the left mouse
    ↳ button to play a new game."
    IF MOUSECLICK() = 1   `Press the mouse button to start a new game
      PlayerTurns = 3     `Reset variable to prepare for a new game
      CurrentLevel = 1    `Reset current level back to zero
      RESTORE             `Restore all DATA statements
      GameState$ = "Initialize"  `Reset the game state
      LoadBricksArray()            `Call the function that loads
                                   `brick data into the game's array
    ENDIF
  ENDCASE
```

```
ENDSELECT

IF GameState$ <> "Over"

  ProcessPlayerInput()    `See if the player is moving the paddle

  `Keep the player informed of the number of balls left to play
  TEXT 25, 25, "Balls Remaining: " + STR$(PlayerTurns)

  `Display the current level
  TEXT 200, 25, "Level: " + STR$(CurrentLevel)

ENDIF

SYNC    `Redraw the screen

LOOP

ENDFUNCTION
```

The DisplayBricks() Function

As shown in bold, two new statements need to be added to the DisplayBricks() function. The first statement uses the PLAY SOUND command to play the wave file that indicates when a collision has occurred between the ball and paddle or the ball and the bricks. The second statement increments the value assigned to the CurrentLevel variable to identify that the current level has been completed and a new level is being started.

```
`This function is responsible for displaying rows of bricks
FUNCTION DisplayBricks()


  Width = SPRITE WIDTH(BrickSprite) + 2     `Determine brick width
  Height = SPRITE HEIGHT(BrickSprite) + 2   `Determine brick height

  BlockCount = 0          `Keep a count of bricks that should not be drawn

  FOR i = 1 TO 15        `Loop through every brick in a row
    FOR j = 1 TO 5       `Loop through all five rows
      if BricksArray(i, j) = 1 `An array item with a value of 1 indicates
```

```
                              `that a brick should be drawn and a value
                              `of 0 indicates no brick should be drawn
        INC BlockCount   `Keep track of the number of bricks drawn


        `Draw the brick
        SPRITE BrickSprite, 65 + Width * i, 75 + Height * j, BrickImage
        `Paste the brick on the screen
        PASTE SPRITE BrickSprite, 65 + Width * i, 75 + Height * j


        `Determine if a collision has occurred with the brick and the ball
        IF SPRITE COLLISION(BrickSprite, BallSprite) = 1
            PLAY SOUND CollisionSound    `Play sound indicating a collision
            BricksArray(i, j) = 0    `Assign 0 to the array item representing
                                     `the brick in order to hide it when the
                                     `screen is redrawn
            DeflectBallOffBricks()   `Call function that redirects the ball
        ENDIF
      ENDIF
    NEXT j
  NEXT i


  `All blocks have been cleared
  IF BlockCount = 0                `If no bricks were drawn the level is over
      GameState$ = "Initialize"    `Update game state
      LoadBricksArray()            `Call function that reloads the bricks
      CurrentLevel = CurrentLevel + 1 `Keep track of the current level
  ENDIF


ENDFUNCTION
```

The BounceTheBall() Function

There are no changes or modifications to the BounceTheBall() function, which is responsible for moving the ball around the screen.

```
`This function is responsible for moving the ball around the screen
FUNCTION BounceTheBall()


  BallX = BallX + SpeedX `Move the ball along the x-axis
  BallY = BallY + SpeedY `Move the ball along the y-axis
```

```
`Check for a collision with the side of the screen
ProcessSideOfScreenCollisions()

`Check for a collision with the top of the screen
ProcessTopOfScreenCollisions()

`Check to see if the player missed the ball
ProcessMisses()

`Draw the ball at the specified coordinates
SPRITE BallSprite, BallX, BallY, BallImage

ENDFUNCTION
```

The ProcessSideOfScreenCollisions() Function

There are no changes or modifications to the ProcessSideOfScreenCollisions() function, which is responsible for redirecting the ball whenever it collides with the left or right side of the screen.

```
`This function redirects the ball when it collides with either side of
`the screen
FUNCTION ProcessSideOfScreenCollisions()

  `If the ball has made contact with the left side of the screen then
  `reverse its direction
  IF BallX < 1
    BallX = 1        `Do not let the ball go past the side of the screen
    SpeedX = SpeedX * -1   `Reverse the ball's direction
  ENDIF

  `If the ball has made contact with the right side of the screen then
  `reverse its direction
  IF BallX > SCREEN WIDTH()  - 14
    BallX = SCREEN WIDTH() - 14   `Do not let the ball go past the side
                                  `of the screen
    SpeedX = SpeedX * -1          `Reverse the ball's direction
  ENDIF

ENDFUNCTION
```

The ProcessTopOfScreenCollisions() Function

There are no changes or modifications to the ProcessTopOfScreenCollisions() function, which is responsible for redirecting the ball whenever it collides with the top of the screen.

```
`This function redirects the ball when it collides with the top of the
`screen
FUNCTION ProcessTopOfScreenCollisions()

  `If the ball has made contact with the top of the screen then reverse
  `its direction
  IF BallY < 0
    BallY = 0      `Do not let the ball go past the top of the screen
    SpeedY = SpeedY * -1    `Reverse the ball's direction
  ENDIF

ENDFUNCTION
```

The ProcessMisses() Function

There are no changes or modifications to the ProcessMisses() function, which is responsible for dealing with player misses.

```
`This function is responsible for dealing with misses
FUNCTION ProcessMisses()

  `The point is lost because the ball has gotten past the player's paddle
  IF BallY > SCREEN HEIGHT() - 6
    PlayerTurns = PlayerTurns - 1 `Decrement the number of turns remaining
    IF PlayerTurns < 1          `If no turns are left then the game is over
      GameState$ = "Over"        `Update game state
    ELSE
      GameState$ = "Initialize"  `Update game state
    ENDIF
  ENDIF

ENDFUNCTION
```

The LookForCollisionWithPaddle() Function

You need to add one statement to the LookForCollisionWithPaddle() function. This statement plays the game's wave file signaling that a collision has occurred.

```
`This function handles collisions between the ball and the paddle
FUNCTION LookForCollisionWithPaddle()

  IF SPRITE COLLISION(PaddleSprite, BallSprite) = 1  `Check for collision
    PLAY SOUND CollisionSound                        `Play collision sound
    DeflectBallOffThePaddle()  `Call on the function that deflects the ball
  ENDIF

ENDFUNCTION
```

The ReadyBallAndPaddle() Function

There are no changes or modifications to the ReadyBallAndPaddle() function, which is responsible for placing the ball on top of the paddle at the beginning of each new point.

```
`This function attaches the ball to the paddle at the start of each point
FUNCTION ReadyBallAndPaddle()

  `Set coordinate representing the center of the paddle
  BallX = PaddleX + (SPRITE WIDTH(PaddleSprite) / 2) - (SPRITE WIDTH(BallSprite) / 2)
  BallY = PaddleY - 14  `Set coordinate on the y-axis just above the top
                        `of the paddle

  `Set a random speed and direction for the ball
  SpeedX = rnd(2) + 1
  SpeedY = rnd(2) - 6

  `Draw the ball at the specified coordinates
  SPRITE BallSprite, BallX, BallY, BallImage

ENDFUNCTION
```

The ProcessPlayerInput() Function

As the bold statements indicate, a number of modifications are required for the Process-PlayerInput() function. These changes include the elimination of statements that the previous version of the game used to allow the player to move the game's paddle with the left and right arrow keys. Now this functionality is provided via the computer's mouse.

```
`This function processes player input for controlling paddle movement
FUNCTION ProcessPlayerInput()
```

```
`Determine the location of the right side of the paddle
RightSideOfPaddle = PaddleX + SPRITE WIDTH(PaddleSprite)

`Do not let the paddle go past the right edge of the screen
IF RightSideOfPaddle > SCREEN WIDTH()
  POSITION MOUSE SCREEN WIDTH() - SPRITE WIDTH(PaddleSprite), 1
ENDIF

`Move the paddle along the x-axis in accordance with the movement of
`the mouse
PaddleX = MOUSEX()

`Draw the ball at the specified coordinates
SPRITE PaddleSprite, PaddleX, PaddleY, PaddleImage
```

```
ENDFUNCTION
```

As you can see, the POSITION MOUSE command is used to reposition the mouse, and the MOUSEX command is used to retrieve the mouse's location on the x-axis so that this information can be used to assign the location to which the paddle should be moved.

The DeflectBallOffThePaddle() Function

There are no changes or modifications to the DeflectBallOffThePaddle() function, which is responsible for deflecting the ball whenever it comes into contact with the paddle.

```
`This function deflects the ball when it collides with the paddle
FUNCTION DeflectBallOffThePaddle()

  `Determine where the center of the ball is
  CenterOfBall = sprite x(BallSprite) + sprite width(BallSprite) / 2

  `Determine where the left edge of the paddle is
  LeftSideOfPaddle = sprite x(PaddleSprite)

  `Determine where the right edge of the paddle is
  RightSideOfPaddle = sprite x(PaddleSprite) + sprite width(PaddleSprite)

  `Randomly alter the speed of the ball when it collides with the
  `left-hand side of the paddle
```

```
IF CenterOfBall < LeftSideOfPaddle + 15
  SpeedX = -rnd(4) - 1
ENDIF

`Randomly alter the speed of the ball when it collides with the
`right-hand side of the paddle
IF CenterOfBall > RightSideOfPaddle - 15
  SpeedX = rnd(4) - 1
ENDIF

`Change the direction of the ball and randomly change its speed as well
SpeedY = -rnd(2) - 3

ENDFUNCTION
```

The DeflectBallOffBricks() Function

There are no changes or modifications to the project file's final function, which is responsible for deflecting the ball whenever it comes into contact with the game's bricks.

```
`This function manages ball movement when the ball collides with a brick
FUNCTION DeflectBallOffBricks()

  `Determine where the center of the ball is
  CenterOfBall = SPRITE X(BallSprite) + SPRITE WIDTH(BallSprite) / 2
  `Determine where the left-hand side of the ball is
  LeftSideOfBrick = SPRITE X(BallSprite)

  `Determine where the right-hand side of the ball is
  RightSideOfBrick = SPRITE X(BallSprite) + SPRITE WIDTH(BallSprite)

  IF CenterOfBall < LeftSideOfBrick or CenterOfBall > RightSideOfBrick
    SpeedX = SpeedX * - 1  `Change ball's direction on the x-axis when
                           `it hits the side of a block
  ELSE
    SpeedY = SpeedY * - 1 `Change ball direction on the y-axis when it
                          `hits the top or bottom of a block
  ENDIF

ENDFUNCTION
```

The Final Result

All right, assuming that you did not have any problems creating the first part of the Bricks game in Chapter 8 or make any typos or skip any of the required additions and modifications to the Bricks game as you followed along in this chapter, everything should work as described at the beginning of this chapter.

 You will also find a copy of this application's project file along with source code on this book's companion website, located at http://www.courseptr.com/ downloads.

SUMMARY

This chapter has covered a lot of ground. You learned how to work with the keyboard, mouse, and joystick as input controls and to capture and track their input. You learned how to collect keyboard input without blocking program execution, how to identify the mouse's location and track its movement, how to identify mouse clicks, how to track joystick movement and direction, and how to identify and react to joystick clicks. On top of all this, you learned how to modify the Bricks game, including converting it to use mouse input in place of keyboard input.

Before you move on to Chapter 10, I suggest you set aside a few additional minutes to try and improve the Bricks game by implementing the following list of challenges.

CHALLENGES

1. As currently designed, the Bricks game limits the player to just three balls. Consider rewarding the player every time all three of the game's levels are cleared by awarding an additional ball.

2. At present, the game's sound effects are limited to a single sound played when a collision occurs between the ball and the paddle or the ball and the bricks. Consider adding a different sound for whenever the player misses the ball. Also, if you have access to an appropriate tune, consider adding music playback during game play.

3. Consider expanding the number of levels in the game and experimenting with different configurations of bricks.

4. As currently written, the Bricks game utilizes bounded rectangle collision to detect collisions. Consider incorporating impact collision testing for more precise results.

5. Consider assigning a point value to bricks and keeping a running tabulation of the number of points scored by the player. This will provide the player with a clear way of evaluating her performance at the end of each game.

CHAPTER

FINDING AND FIXING APPLICATION ERRORS

I n this book's final chapter, you will learn how to deal with the different types of errors that all DarkBASIC Professional programs are subject to. This includes learning how to fix syntax errors, track down and identify logical errors, and deal with run-time errors. For errors that prove difficult to track down, you will learn how to work with DarkBASIC Professional's built-in debugger. This chapter will also provide a brief overview of 3D programming and will demonstrate how to generate and display 3D objects. In addition, you will be guided through the development of the book's final game project, the 3D Fortune Teller game.

Specifically, you will learn:

- How to identify and deal with syntax, logical, and run-time errors
- How to work with DarkBASIC Professional's built-in debugger
- How to set breakpoints and to execute detailed control over statement execution
- About the coordinate system used in 3D programming
- How to create and draw 3D primitive objects

PROJECT PREVIEW: THE 3D FORTUNE TELLER GAME

This chapter's game project is the 3D Fortune Teller game, which is an updated version of the Fortune Teller game that you worked on in Chapter 2, "Getting Comfortable with the DarkBASIC Integrated Development Environment." This updated 3D version of the game will make a number of improvements to the original game, making it easier to understand and manage while at the same time helping to make it easier to update and debug. In addition, this game will serve as a sneak peak, providing a small glimpse of DarkBASIC Professional's 3D programming capabilities.

As shown in Figure 10.1, the 3D Fortune Teller game begins by displaying a welcome screen that instructs the player to press any key to continue.

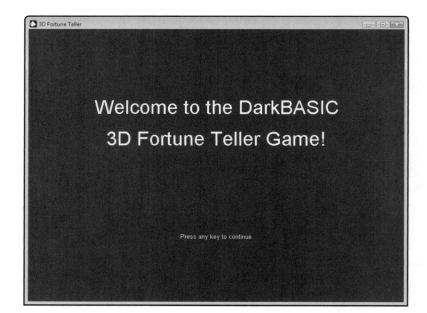

FIGURE 10.1

The 3D Fortune Teller game's welcome screen.

As shown in Figure 10.2, the game then displays instructions, which includes informing the player what kinds of questions can be answered and how to end game play.

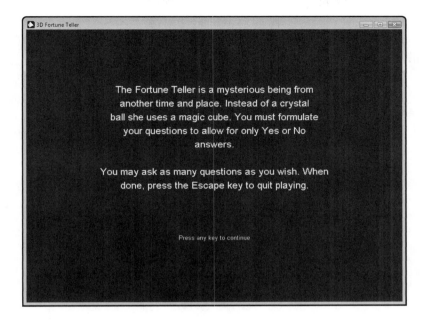

FIGURE 10.2

The 3D Fortune
Teller game's
instructions.

As Figure 10.3 shows, the player is then prompted to think of a question and to press a keyboard key to see the Fortune Teller's answer.

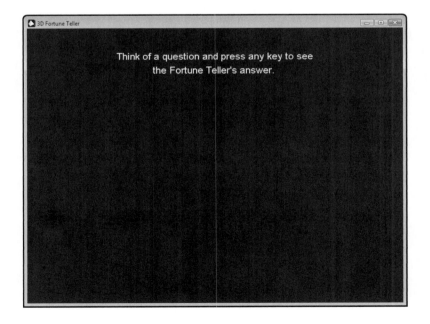

FIGURE 10.3

The player is
prompted to think
of a question.

Once the player presses a keyboard key, the screen is cleared and a three-dimensional cube displays. The cube then starts rotating on all three of its axes. Figure 10.4 shows how the cube looks early in its rotation cycle.

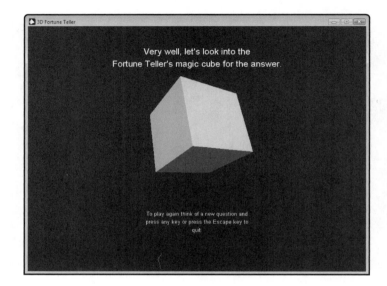

Figure 10.5 shows how the cube looks towards the end of its 360-degree rotation cycle.

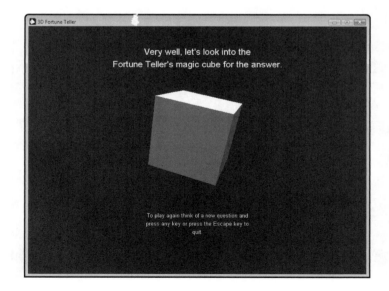

FIGURE 10.5

The 3D Fortune Teller game's magic cube continues its rotation.

Once the cube has completed a full 360-degree rotation cycle, its stops and displays the Fortune Teller's answer, as demonstrated in Figure 10.6.

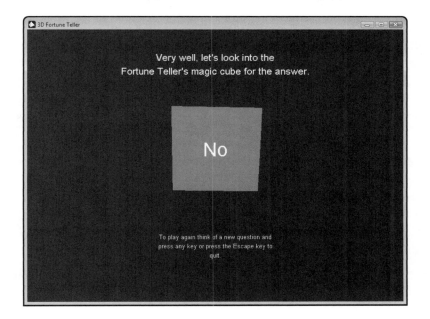

FIGURE 10.6

The 3D Fortune Teller has answered the player's question.

Compared to the original version of the Fortune Teller game, the 3D Fortune Teller game has even more responses from which to draw when answering player questions.

Understanding and Dealing with Errors

If there is one inevitable truth in programming, it is that errors are going to happen. No programmer, no matter how experienced or how talented, can escape this fact. Naturally, the opportunities for errors increase as your programming projects grow longer and more complex. Since errors are a fact of every programmer's life, it is important that you learn how to deal with them. The purpose of this chapter is to provide a basic understanding of the different types of errors that DarkBASIC Professional programs are subject to and to provide tips for writing program code that is less subject to errors. In addition, you will receive guidance on how to track down and fix errors when they do happen.

Regardless of the programming language involved, all computer applications are susceptible to errors. When they occur, errors result in unpredictable results. Certain types of errors may cause your applications to perform in an unpredictable manner while other types of errors may generate difficult to understand error messages and then unexpectantly terminate the application's execution. Errors are often referred to as bugs and your job as a programmer is to seek out and eliminate all of the bugs in your applications.

There are many different steps that you can follow to reduce the number of errors in your DarkBASIC Professional applications. For starters, don't just sit down and start writing program code when beginning a new programming project. Instead, spend a little time thinking about your new project and what you want it to do. It may help to develop a flowchart or to use pseudo code to outline the overall logic involved. Once you are ready to begin writing your program code, do so a piece at a time, testing frequently along the way. The best way to do this is to make liberal use of functions and to separate related program statements into manageable groups.

Application testing is another key step in the development of any computer program. When testing, don't just make sure that your program works the way you expect it to. In addition, try supplying invalid input to see if your application handles it properly, and if it does not, then you may want to modify your application by adding program logic to deal with the invalid input. In additional to following these programming practices, there are a number of other steps that you should follow for every application that you develop, including:

- Commenting your program code to ensure that it is well documented and easy to understand
- Indenting your program code so that it is visually easy to read and understand
- Adding program code that validates any input passed to the program
- Providing users with clear instruction on the proper use of the application
- Adopting a consistent naming scheme for variables, arrays, and functions and giving them names that are as descriptive as possible
- Not forgetting to place an `END` statement in your program code between the main programming code and the program's functions

 Unlike many programming languages, DarkBASIC Professional does not provide any error handling commands. There are no `ON ERORR` or `TRY...CATCH` statements that allow you to trap and deal with errors like you typically find in other BASIC programming languages. Therefore, it is up to you to do your best to anticipate the places within your program code where errors are most likely to occur and include additional programming logic to either prevent or deal with these errors.

UNDERSTANDING DIFFERENT TYPES OF ERRORS

Like every other major programming language, DarkBASIC Professional is subject to three basic types of errors, as listed here:

- Syntax errors
- Logical errors
- Run-time errors

Dissecting Syntax Errors

The most common type of error that you will have to deal with is syntax errors. A *syntax error* is an error that occurs as a result of not carefully following DarkBASIC Professional's syntax requirements. One of the most common causes of a syntax error is typos. For example, suppose you want to display the string Hello World! on the screen using the following statement.

```
PRONT "Hello World!"
```

Instead of getting the result you want, DarkBASIC Professional will display an error message when you attempt to compile the program that contains this statement. The PRINT command was mistyped as PRONT. Syntax errors can occur for a host of additional reasons. For example, you might forget to supply a required argument when executing a statement or you might forget to add an opening or closing parenthesis or quotation mark when keying in a statement.

To see an example of the type of error messages that DarkBASIC Professional displays when it finds a syntax error, take a look at the following statement.

```
INPUT "Enter your name: " Name$
```

Here, a required comma is missing between the string argument and the variable name argument that is passed to the INPUT command for processing. When the program containing this statement is executed, the popup dialog window shown in Figure 10.7 is displayed and program compilation is halted.

FIGURE 10.7

A syntax error generated as the result of an incorrectly formatted statement.

To correct this error you must add the required comma between the text string and the Name$ variable, as shown here:

```
INPUT "Enter your name: ", Name$
```

As Figure 10.7 demonstrated, DarkBASIC Professional syntax error messages provide a brief explanation of the error that has been found as well as the line number of the statement where the error resides. Once you have identified and fixed the reported syntax error, you can attempt to recompile your project. If no other syntax errors are found, DarkBASIC Professional will compile your new program. However, if another syntax error is discovered, another popup dialog window will display identifying the error and the compilation process will be halted again.

As another example of a syntax error, consider the following statements.

```
`Call on the function that displays the player's age
DisplayAge(10)

WAIT KEY

END

FUNCTION DisplayAge(Age)

  PRINT "Alexander is " + Age + " years old."

ENDFUNCTION
```

Here, a syntax error is generated because string and numeric data are not compatible and therefore cannot be concatenated. When executed, this example results in the popup dialog window shown in Figure 10.8.

Errors like the one demonstrated in this example are easily corrected. In order to correct this error all you have to do is use the STR$ command to convert the value stored in the Age variable to a string, as shown here:

```
Age = 10
PRINT "Alexander is " + STR$(Age) + " years old."
```

In addition to displaying an error message that notifies you that a syntax error has been found, DarkBASIC Professional also highlights in red the line in your program code where the syntax error was found, as demonstrated in Figure 10.9.

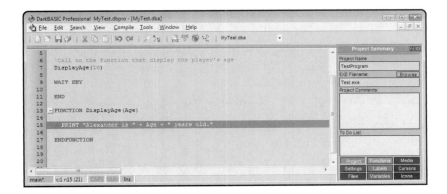

FIGURE 10.9

Syntax errors are highlighted to make them stand out.

Most of the time all that you will need to identify and fix a syntax error is a description of the error and to know the location of the offending statement. Fortunately, DarkBASIC Professional puts both of these pieces of information at your fingertips. However, if after examining the statement you are unable to determine where the problem is, you can turn to DarkBASIC Professional's help file and look up the syntax of the command in question.

Finding the Fault Behind Logical Errors

Another type of error that you need to be on the lookout for is logical errors. A *logical error* is one that occurs when you mistakenly apply faulty logic when attempting to perform a task. As an example of a simple logical error, consider a situation in which you are keeping track of the number of points that a player earns while a game is being played. Each time player 1 scores a point, you might increment her total score as shown here:

```
PlayerScore = PlayerScore + 1
```

However, it is very easy to accidentally mess things up in a number of ways. For example, you might accidentally mistype the name of the second instance of the variable, as demonstrated here:

```
PlayerScore = PlayerScorr + 1
```

Here, instead of incrementing the value of *PlayerScore* like you wanted, DarkBASIC Professional instead creates *PlayerScorr* as a new integer variable and assigns it a default value of 0. As a result, the player's score is not incremented when points are won.

Another way to logically mess things up would be to accidentally subtract 1 instead of add 1 to the player's score each time a point is won, as demonstrated here:

```
PlayerScore = PlayerScore - 1
```

Yet another way to introduce a logical error would be to accidentally mistype the value that you want to use when incrementing the player's score, as demonstrated here:

```
PlayerScore = PlayerScore + 2
```

Here, the player is awarded 2 points each time 1 point is earned.

The difficulty with logical errors is that your application will usually compile and execute just fine; it just will not run as you expect it to.

The best way of dealing with logical errors is to prevent them from ever happening in the first place. This can be done through careful planning and testing. For example, when thinking about how best to increment and keep track of a player's total score, you should consider using the INC command in place of manually calculating the value. When used without any arguments, it automatically increments a variable's assigned value by 1, as demonstrated here:

```
INC PlayerOneScore
```

Using the INC command allows you to avoid the possibility of accidentally typing a minus sign in place of a plus sign or a 2 in place of a 1, or to mistype the second instance of a variable name.

Of course, from time to time all programmers make logical errors. Fortunately, careful testing provides an opportunity to detect and then correct logical errors. Once you realize during testing that things are not working like they are supposed to, you can review your program code and look for the problem. If you are unable to find the problem this way, you might try embedding a few PRINT commands at strategic points in your program to identify when things are occurring and display the values assigned to certain variables, so that you can keep an eye on their values. For example, in tracking down the problem with the score assigned to a player, you might add a PRINT command to the program that prints a message in the corner of the screen indicating when a point is scored followed by a message that displays the value assigned as the player's score. This would allow you to determine if the variable is being incremented after points are scored.

As long as your program code file is not too large, using PRINT commands to display messages and variables might be all you need to track down and find logic problems. However, as your applications grow in terms of both size and complexity, this method of tracking and monitoring program execution and variable values begins to become difficult to implement. Fortunately, DarkBASIC Professional has a solution in the form of a built-in debugger that you can use to execute your applications and track both logical execution flow as well as variable values. Instructions regarding the operation of the debugger and how to use it to monitor application execution and track down errors is provided later in this chapter.

Chasing Down Run-time Errors

In order to execute, a DarkBASIC Professional application must be free of syntax errors. Otherwise, it cannot even be compiled. However, just because you have an application that compiles with no syntax errors and have taken extra care to ensure that it also contains no logical errors, that does not mean you are home free. There is a third category of error that all programmers have to deal with—a run-time error. A *run-time* error is an error that occurs when an application attempts to perform an illegal action.

For example, a run-time error may occur if your application tries to perform a DarkBASIC Professional graphics command that is not supported by the graphic card installed on a player's computer. In this situation, your game might generate an error message, which the player most likely will not understand and won't be able to do anything about anyway, or the game may simply stop running without explanation or warning. Obviously, this is a situation that you will want to avoid. One way of preventing this type of problem from occurring is to avoid making use of cutting-edge commands that require the player's computer to have the latest high-end video cards installed and instead develop games that can be played using features that are generally available on most computers. Another way of approaching this type of problem is to clearly identify your game's hardware and software requirements so that the player can determine whether her PC meets minimum requirements.

One of the big problems with run-time errors is that the compiler cannot detect them. Extensive testing can often root them out, especially if the testing involves running the application on different computers, each of which has different hardware configurations. For example, you might test a new game on three computers, one equipped with cutting-edge hardware and software, another with hardware and software that are one to two years old, and a third with hardware and software that are two to three years old. If your game works on all of these computers then you can feel more confident about it being ready for prime time.

Another way of testing your application is to pass it along to a number of your friends and ask them to try it out. The more people you get to put your game through its paces, the better.

Run-time errors can sometimes hide deep inside seldom used functions. Unless you extensively test the execution of each function in your application, you'll never catch it, leaving it to your friends or customers to find it for you. Clearly, this is not a desirable way to learn that your application has a run-time error.

As a quick example of how easy it is to cause a run-time error, take a look at the following statement.

```
x = 5 / 0
```

This statement generates a run-time error because it is illegal to divide a number by zero. To verify this, create a new DarkBASIC Professional program containing this statement and run it. If you do, you see the error reported in Figure 10.10, after which your program will terminate.

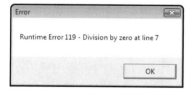

FIGURE 10.10

A run-time error is generated if you attempt to divide a number by zero.

Run-time errors can occur for many different reasons and can be difficult to anticipate. For example, suppose you used DarkBASIC Professional to create a simple calculator program that worked perfectly every time you tested it, but the first person with whom you shared it ran into a problem because they tried to divide a number by 0. To try to head off this type of problem, you would need to analyze the user's input and check for and reject any attempt to use a 0 as the denominator in a division calculation.

As the previous example demonstrated, one source of run-time errors may be faulty user input. Another may result from attempting to run an application on a computer with inadequate hardware. If your program was a network computer game and the network crashed, so would your program unless you had thought to build in the extra logic required to verify network access before allowing the application to attempt to switch from single-player to network mode.

As you have probably learned from personal experience, no application is perfect. As a result, no matter how hard you try, you may never be able to make all of your applications bullet proof. However, to be successful, you want to do everything possible to minimize your game's susceptibility to run-times errors.

KEEPING A WATCHFUL EYE ON PROGRAM EXECUTION

If you are creating a new game that is not working the way it should or is occasionally experiencing run-time errors, and you are unable to track it down using information provided in error messages or by reviewing its program code, do not despair; all hope is not lost. DarkBASIC Professional comes equipped with a powerful built-in debugger that you can use to track down and fix even the most difficult to find errors.

A *debugger* is a program that executes an application in a special mode that provides programmers with the ability to execute detailed control over statement execution while at the same time monitoring program variables to keep an eye on their values. Using DarkBASIC Professional's debugger, you can step through the execution of every statement in an application and observe the effects of their execution and ultimately to identify the source of the error you are trying to track down and fix.

Executing a Program Using the Debugger

In order to run a program using DarkBASIC Professional's built-in debugger, open the default editor and then click on either the Run in Debug Mode toolbar button or the Run in Step-Through Mode button. If you choose to run your program using the Run in Debug Mode option, your program will load and run normally until one of the following things occurs.

- The program finishes its normal execution and ends.
- The program reaches a breakpoint and then pauses allowing you to view variable values and then decide how to continue program execution.
- You press the Escape key, pausing program execution and allowing you to view variable values and then decide how to continue program execution.

 You can also run the debugger by executing the Run in Debug Mode or Run in Step-Through Mode commands located on the Compile menu.

If you choose to run your program using the Run in Step-Through Mode option, your program will load but pause execution before executing the first program statement, allowing you to view variable values and then decide how to continue program execution.

Working with the Command Line Interface

Once you have loaded and paused the execution of your DarkBASIC Professional program in the debugger, you can begin debugging it using any of several tools. Each of these tools is displayed as a menu bar button at the top of the debugger window.

The first of the three tools provided by the debugger is the Command Line Interface, which allows you to execute any valid DarkBASIC Professional command. For example, you could use the command line to change the value assigned to a variable to see how your program will handle it. As another example, suppose you were working on a 2D game and you noticed that the pace of the animation appeared to be a bit clunky, leading you to suspect that screen refresh might not be occurring at an optimal speed. To test this theory, you could change it on the fly when debugging your program by executing the following steps.

1. Start your program by loading it into the IDE and then clicking on the Debugger window's Run in Debug Mode toolbar button.
2. At an appropriate moment press the Escape key to pause the game's execution and enter into Debug mode.
3. Execute the SYNC RATE command, assigning it a different value, as shown in Figure 10.11.

FIGURE 10.11

The Debugger window provides access to three different debugging tools.

4. Click on the Debugger window's Step Through Mode toolbar button and then click on the Play Program button, allowing your game to resume its execution so that you can observe any changes that may occur and determine whether you found a solution to the problem.

HINT

The Command Line Interface can also be used to test command execution in real-time, providing you with the ability to experiment with commands and see how they work.

Analyzing Variable Values Using Variable Watcher

If you suspect that something may be going wrong with the assignment of one or more variable values in a program, and you are having a problem tracking down just where things are going wrong, you can use the debugger's Variable Watcher view to keep a close eye on the program's variables and their values. Further, when used in conjunction with Step Through Mode view, discussed in the next section, you can identify when specific program statements execute and thus observe the effects that they have on the value of variables.

The debugger's Variable Watcher view displays a listing of every program variable along with each variable's current value, as demonstrated in Figure 10.12.

FIGURE 10.12

The debugger lets you keep a watchful eye on variables and their assigned values.

Variables and their associated values are displayed on the left-hand side of the window. In the event that there are more variables that can be viewed at one time, you can scroll down to view the status of the other variables. Alternatively, you can add specific variables to either of two watch lists, displayed in tabs on the left-hand side of the window, to make them easier to monitor. To add a variable to a watch list, all you have to do is click on the Watch List tab to which you want to assign a variable and then click on that variable. For example, in Figure 10.12 two variables have been added to the watch list on tab Watch A. To remove a variable from a watch list, all you have to do is locate and click on it.

Exercising Line By Line Control over Statement Execution

If you start a debug session by clicking on the Run in Debug Mode toolbar button, the debugger will load and begin executing your program. The program will continue to run until it either finishes its execution or until you press the Escape key. If you start a debug session by clicking on the Run in Step Through Mode button, the debugger will load and compile your program but will pause before executing its first statement.

Once in Debug mode, you exercise line by line control over the execution of your DarkBASIC Professional program by clicking on the Step Through Mode button. When you do so, a set of four additional buttons are displayed on the right-hand side of the window, as shown in Figure 10.13.

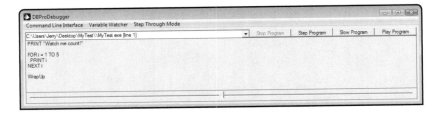

FIGURE 10.13

The Step Through Mode option lets you exercise control over statement execution.

These four new buttons provide the ability to control how program code statements are executed. The purpose of each button is outlined here:

- **Stop Program.** Pauses a running program's execution and highlights the line where execution has been paused.
- **Step Program.** Executes the next statement in the program and then pauses the program again. If the next statement in the program is a function, execution pauses at the first statement in the function.
- **Slow Program.** Resumes program execution at a slow pace, allowing program statements to run at a pace that can be easily monitored so that you can track the program's logical execution flow.
- **Play Program.** Allows a program halted during a Run in Debug Mode session to resume regular execution.

Setting Breakpoints

Another way of halting program execution when debugging an application is to add breakpoints to your program file. A *breakpoint* is a marker that instructs the debugger to halt program execution at a specified location in a program. By letting you set breakpoints at different points within a program, DarkBASIC Professional makes it easy for you to specify in advance where you want program execution to be halted in a debug session.

 Breakpoints have no effect on program execution when you compile and execute your application normally. Breakpoints only take effect when your program runs in Debug mode.

To set a breakpoint, right-click on the code statement where you want execution to halt and then select Toggle Breakpoint from the context menu that appears. A red circle is displayed in the gutter to identify that a breakpoint has been set, as demonstrated in Figure 10.14.

You can add as many breakpoints as you feel are necessary to your program file. Once you have finished debugging your program, you can remove any breakpoints by right-clicking on the code line where they have been set and selecting Toggle Breakpoint from the context menu that appears.

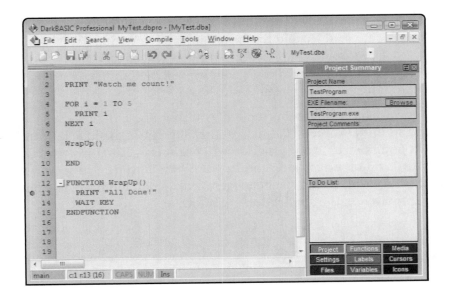

A Debugging Demonstration

To get a better understanding of how to work with the DarkBASIC Professional debugger, let's use it to demonstrate how to debug and fix the program logic associated with a small program that is supposed to count from 1 to 5. The first step is, of course, to write the program that is to be executed. Begin by keying in the following statements as the example program.

```
PRINT "Watch me count!"

DO
  PRINT i
  IF i = 5 THEN EXIT
LOOP

PRINT "Now the counting is done!"

WAIT KEY

END
```

Now, let's run this program normally by clicking on the Make EXE/Run button. Instead of counting from 1 to 5 and then ending, the program displays an endless series of zeros on the screen. This is a clear indication that not only has something gone wrong but that the program is stuck in a loop. Press the Escape key to terminate the program execution.

Okay, so we now know that the example program has at least one problem that needs to be fixed. Let's use the debugger to track down and fix the program's errors. Start by clicking on the Run in Step Through Mode button. Your application window will be displayed as will the DBProDebugger window. However, the application's window will be completely blank since none of the program's code statements have been executed yet.

Go ahead and click on the Variable Watcher button and you should see the i variable listed and that this variable has an initial value of 0. Click on the Step Through Mode button and then click on the Slow Program button. Your program will begin executing in slow motion. Let it run for a few moments and then click on the Stop Program button. You should have witnessed each statement executing within the debugger. You also should have seen output similar to the following displayed in the application's window.

```
Watch me count!
0
0
0
0
0
```

As you can see things are not working correctly. Now, click on the Variable Watcher button and let's check on the value assigned to i. As you will see, i is still set to 0. Obviously, the value assigned to i is not being incremented like you want it to. So, let's take a look at the program statements that make up this program's loop. If you look closely, you will see that there is no statement in the loop to increment the value of i. Let's fix this by inserting an INC command, as shown here:

```
PRINT "Watch me count!"

DO
  PRINT i
  INC i
  IF i = 5 THEN EXIT
LOOP

PRINT "Now the counting is done!"

WAIT KEY

END
```

Now, let's run the program again by clicking on the Run in Step Through Mode button. Click on the Variable Watcher button and you should see the i variable listed and that this variable has an initial value of 0. Click on the Step Through Mode button and then click on the Slow Program button. Allow the program to run to completion while toggling between the Variable Watch and Step Through Mode view and watching as the value of i changes during the execution of the program.

Things are definitely looking better. However, one problem remains. The program is displaying the numbers 0 through 5 instead of the numbers 1 through 5. Although in a program of this size it is probably pretty obvious where the problem lies, let's pretend that we cannot see it and continue our debug session. To do so, run the program again by clicking on the Run in Step Through Mode button. Now, click on the Step Through Mode button and click on the Step Program button two times. At this point, the words Watch me count! should be visible on the application's window and the statement initializing the starting value of i to 0 should have been executed. A quick check of the value of i by clicking on the Variable Watch button will confirm this. Click on the Step Through Mode button again and observe that the following statement is currently highlighted.

```
PRINT i
```

Knowing that this statement is about to display the value of i, and that i is currently set to 0, it should now be obvious that the problem is that the value of i is not being incremented prior to being displayed. This can easily be fixed by moving the following statement ahead of the PRINT statement.

```
INC i
```

To test this out while still in the debugger, click on the Command Line Interface button and enter the previous statement. Click on the Variable Watch button and verify that the value of i is not equal to 1. Click on the Step Through Mode button and then click on the Step Program button. This executes the currently highlighted statement and then halts program execution again. Now, look at the application window and you should see that the number1 has been correctly displayed.

Go ahead and close your application window, which will also close the debugger session, and then modify the program's source code as shown here:

```
PRINT "Watch me count!"

DO
  INC i
  PRINT i
  IF i = 5 THEN EXIT
LOOP
```

```
PRINT "Now the counting is done!"

WAIT KEY

END
```

Now run the program normally and it should run correctly, as demonstrated in Figure 10.15.

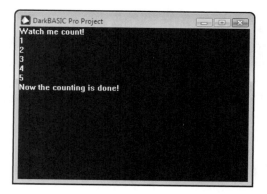

FIGURE 10.15

The debugged program now runs like it is supposed to.

Although the sample program used in the previous example was very simple, it served its purpose well, providing the opportunity to work with all of the major functionality provided by DarkBASIC Professional's built-in debugger.

BACK TO THE 3D FORTUNE TELLER GAME

This book's final game project is the 3D Fortune Teller game. This project will take the Fortune Teller game that you developed back in Chapter 2 and update it, using all of the major programming concepts that you have learned in this book since Chapter 2. This includes the use of conditional and looping logic as well as local and global loops. This game will also use functions to organize programming logic and to facilitate argument passing. In addition, this new version of the Fortune Teller game also provides a working demonstration of DarkBASIC Professional's ability to support 3D application development.

> HINT
>
> Entire books have been written just for the purpose of addressing 3D application development. Although DarkBASIC Professional goes a long way in simplifying it, 3D programming is an incredibly complex endeavor and there simply is not room in this chapter to do it justice. Instead, I suggest you look at the development of the 3D Fortune Teller game as a sneak peek at what lies ahead, should you choose to dive into the world of 3D game programming.

A Quick DarkBASIC Professional 3D Programming Overview

Before starting the development of the 3D Fortune Teller game, you need to learn a few fundamental 3D programming concepts. In addition, you need to know how to work with a few DarkBASIC Professional 3D commands. The commands reviewed will show you how to create 3D primitive objects, how to control the location at which the objects are drawn and how to control the movement of the object by rotating on their axes.

Understanding Location in a 3D World

In 2D programs, objects are placed on a two-dimensional plane that consists of an x-axis and a y-axis. Objects are moved by changing their location on one or both of these axes. 3D programs work in very much the same way, except that in addition to horizontal and vertical dimensions, a third dimension is added, which represents depth along the z-axis. Figure 10.16 shows a representation of how these three dimensions relate to one another.

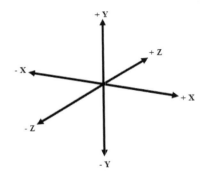

HINT

In order to make it easier to visualize the relationship between all three axes, Figure 10.16 has been rotated just a bit to make the z-axis easier to visualize. Normally, the z-axis runs straight back and forth making it difficult to see.

To determine the position of an object in a 3D game, you must specify its location along all three coordinates. All objects exist in a common world axis. In addition, each object has its own local axis, as demonstrated in Figure 10.17.

Working with 3D Objects

Just like you can draw simple objects like lines, rectangles, and ellipses in a 2D game, DarkBASIC Professional provides commands for generating an assortment of objects in 3D games. These objects are known as *primitives* and represent 3D shapes like cubes, spheres, cones, and cylinders. Each of these shapes is made up of polygons. A *polygon* is a many-sided

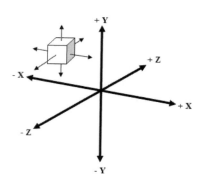

FIGURE 10.17

Each object in a 3D world has its own local axis.

enclosed shape. The most basic type of polygon is a triangle, although many other types of polygons exist (octagons, pentagons, etc.). The point of interception of any two sides on a polygon is known as a *vertex*.

Every 3D shape that is generated in a 3D game is made up of polygons, as demonstrated in Figure 10.18. The more polygons that are used, the more realistic the object will appear.

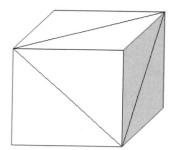

FIGURE 10.18

All objects are made up of polygons.

HINT

DarkBASIC Professional's support for 3D programming includes a host of advanced capabilities, such as support for cameras and lights. Virtual cameras provide a view into a 3D world and DarkBASIC Professional lets you view games from different angles using different cameras. In addition, like a real camera, you can zoom in and out when viewing different parts of the 3D world. With lighting you can illuminate different parts of a 3D world as necessary to set up different moods and scenery.

Drawing Primitive 3D Objects

In this chapter's 3D Fortune Teller game, a 3D cube will be displayed. This cube will be created using the MAKE OBJECT CUBE command, which has the following syntax.

```
MAKE OBJECT CUBE ObjectNumber, ObjectSize
```

Here, a cube object is created and assigned a unique object number, which will be needed by other commands to refer back to and interact with the object. *ObjectSize* sets the size of the object in pixels.

In addition to cubes, DarkBASIC Professional provides a number of other commands for generating various primitive shapes. These commands include:

- `MAKE OBJECT BOX`
- `MAKE OBJECT CONE`
- `MAKE OBJECT CYLINDER`
- `MAKE OBJECT SPHERE`
- `MAKE OBJECT TRIANGLE`

Controlling 3D Object Placement

Once created you can move a 3D object to any location within the 3D world using the `POSITION OBJECT` command, which has the following syntax.

```
POSITION OBJECT ObjectNumber, X, Y, Z
```

ObjectNumber refers to the object number assigned when the object was created and *X*, *Y*, and *Z* specify the object's coordinate position. For example, to create a sphere and display it in the center of the 3D world, use the following commands:

```
MAKE OBJECT CUBE 1, 40
POSITION OBJECT 1, 0, 0, 0
```

Rotating a 3D Object on Its Axes

The last 3D topic that needs to be covered before starting to work on the 3D Fortune Teller game involves the use of commands that allow you to rotate 3D objects on their local axes. To provide this capability, DarkBASIC Professional provides three commands, `XROTATE OBJECT`, `YROTATE OBJECT`, and `ZROTATE OBJECT`. Each of the commands can be used to rotate an object on one of its three axes. The commands share a common syntax, as outlined here:

```
XROTATE OBJECT ObjectNumber, XAngle
YROTATE OBJECT ObjectNumber, YAngle
ZROTATE OBJECT ObjectNumber, ZAngle
```

ObjectNumber refers to the object number assigned when the object was created and *XAngle*, *YAngle*, and *ZAngle* specify the degree to which the object should rotate on a particular axis.

Designing the Game

Now that you have had a brief overview of the DarkBASIC Professional 3D commands needed to create the 3D Fortune Teller game, it is time to begin work on developing the game. The game will run within a window with a resolution of 800×600 and will have minimize, maximize, and close buttons in its upper-right corner, just like any other typical application window.

To help make things as easy as possible to understand and follow along, this game will be created by following a series of steps, as outlined here:

1. Create a new DarkBASIC project.
2. Configure game settings.
3. Document the application.
4. Declare and initialize global variables.
5. Develop the game's overall controlling logic.
6. Create the `DisplayWelcomeScreen()` function.
7. Create the `DisplayInstructions()` function.
8. Create the `PromptPlayer()` function.
9. Create the `PlayAnimation()` function.
10. Create the `GenerateAnswer()` function.
11. Save and compile your application.

Step 1: Creating a New DarkBASIC Project

The first step in creating the 3D Fortune Teller game is to create a new DarkBASIC Professional project. Since this project is based on the Fortune Teller project that you created back in Chapter 2, the easiest way to accomplish this step is to make a copy of the original Fortune Teller project, renaming it 3DFortuneTeller.

Step 2: Configuring Game Settings

The next step in creating the 3D Fortune Teller application is to change a number of application settings. Begin by clicking on the Project button located at the bottom of the Project Panel window and changing the value stored in the Project Name field to **3DFortunerTeller.** Then change the value stored in the EXE Filename file to **3DFortuneTeller.exe**.

Next, click on the Settings button. Change the value stored in the Application Windows Caption field to **3D Fortune Teller** and then select Windowed as the display setting for this game and set the resolution to 800×400.

Step 3: Documenting Your DarkBASIC Application

The next step in updating the Fortune Teller game to the 3D Fortune Teller game is to modify the command statements located at the beginning of the project's code file, as shown here:

```
REM Project: 3DFortuneTeller
REM Created: 9/29/2007 9:43:02 PM
REM Executable name: 3DFortuneTeller.dba
REM Version: 1.0
REM Author: Jerry Lee Ford, Jr.
REM Description: This DarkBASIC application simulates a session with
REM                a Fortune Teller while displaying a rotating 3D cube.
```

As you can see, the name of the project should be changed as should its executable name. Also, take note of the change to the description statement.

 Depending on how you like to work, you may want to delete the rest of the code statements in the project file and key them from scratch as you follow along with the development of the 3D Fortune Teller game. Alternatively, you may want to save yourself a little time by copying, pasting, and modifying existing code when possible.

Step 4: Declaring and Initializing Global Variables

To help make the 3D Fortune Teller game less prone to errors, it makes use of local variables when working with all data. There is one exception to this rule. Specifically, a global variable will be set up to store the location of the center of the screen on the x-axis. Once calculated, this value will be referenced over and over again throughout the application when displaying centered text strings. This value is calculated one time at the beginning of the code file to make the application run more efficiently. The statements that generate this global variable are shown next and should be inserted into the project's code file immediately after the opening comment statements.

```
REM ************* Declare and Initialize Global Variables   ***************

CenterOfScreen = Screen Width() / 2       `Retrieve the screen width
GLOBAL Width AS Integer = CenterOfScreen   `Set global variable representing
                                           `the screen width
```

Step 5: Laying Out the Main Controlling Logic

Unlike the original version of the Fortune Teller game, the 3D Fortune Teller game makes extensive use of functions as a means of grouping related programming statements, each of which is designed to perform a specific task. This change in overall design will make the application's source code easier to read and maintain and will result in program code that is easier to update and thus less prone to error.

The overall controlling logic of the 3D Fortune Teller game is managed by calling on the application's functions, which are managed from statements placed in the program file's new main processing section, as outlined here:

```
REM ********************** Main Processing Section ***********************

`Call the function that displays the game's welcome screen
DisplayWelcomeScreen()

`Call the function that displays the game's instructions
DisplayInstructions()

`Call the function that prompts the player to think of a question
PromptPlayer()

DO   `This loop allows the player to ask an unlimited number of questions

  PlayAnimation()  `Call function that displays the rotating cube
  WAIT KEY          `Pause to allow the player time to read the Fortune
                    `Teller's answer
LOOP `Repeat the loop

END `Terminate game play
```

As you can see, the first function that is called is responsible for displaying the game's welcome screen. The next function displays the game's instructions, and a third function prompts the player to think of a question for the fortune teller to answer. The rest of the statements execute under the control of a DO...LOOP, which repeatedly calls upon the PlayAnimation() function, which allows the player to ask as many questions as she wants.

Step 6: Developing the DisplayWelcomeScreen() Function
The code statements that make up the game's welcome screen are now contained in a function named DisplayWelcomeScreen(). This function should be placed in the code file just after the statements that make up the program's overall controlling logic.

```
REM ************************** Procedure Section **************************

`This function displays the game welcome screen
FUNCTION DisplayWelcomeScreen()

  CLS RGB(0, 0, 128) `Clear the display area

  SET TEXT FONT "Arial"  `Set the font type to Arial
  SET TEXT SIZE 48  `Set the font size to 48 points

  CENTER TEXT Width, 150, "Welcome to the DarkBASIC" `Display welcome message
  CENTER TEXT Width, 220, "3D Fortune Teller Game!"

  SET TEXT SIZE 16  `Set the font size to 16 points
  CENTER TEXT Width, 450, "Press any key to continue"  `Display instructions

  WAIT KEY  `Wait until the player presses a keyboard key

ENDFUNCTION
```

Step 7: Developing the DisplayInstructions() Function

The code statements that display the game's instructions have been modified and are now contained in a function named DisplayInstructions(). This function should be placed in the code file immediately following the DisplayWelcomeScreen() function.

```
`This function displays instructions for playing the game
FUNCTION DisplayInstructions()

  CLS RGB(0, 0, 128) `Clear the display area

  SET TEXT SIZE 24  `Set the font size to 24 points

  `Display game instructions
  CENTER TEXT Width, 120, "The Fortune Teller is a mysterious being from"
  CENTER TEXT Width, 150, "another time and place. Instead of a crystal"
  CENTER TEXT Width, 180, "ball she uses a magic cube. You must formulate"
  CENTER TEXT Width, 210, "your questions to allow for only Yes or No"
  CENTER TEXT Width, 240, "answers."
```

```
CENTER TEXT Width, 300, "You may ask as many questions as you wish. When"
CENTER TEXT Width, 330, "done, press the Escape key to quit playing."

SET TEXT SIZE 16  `Set the font size to 16 points
CENTER TEXT Width, 450, "Press any key to continue"

WAIT KEY  `Wait until the player presses a keyboard key

ENDFUNCTION
```

Step 8: Developing the PromptPlayer() Function

The next function to be added to the code file is the PromptPlayer() function, which when called instructs the player to think of a question to be posed to the Fortune Teller. These statements are shown next and should be placed in the code file immediately following the DisplayInstructions() function.

```
`This function prompts the player to think of an initial question
FUNCTION PromptPlayer()

  CLS RGB(0, 0, 128) `Clear the display area

  SET TEXT SIZE 24   `Set the font size to 24 points

  `Prompt the player to think of a question
  CENTER TEXT Width, 50, "Think of a question and press any key to see"
  CENTER TEXT Width, 80, "the Fortune Teller's answer. "

  WAIT KEY  `Wait until the player presses a keyboard key

ENDFUNCTION
```

Step 9: Developing the PlayAnimation() Function

The next function to be added to the code file is the PlayAnimation() function, which when called generates the 3D rotating cube and displays answers to the player's questions. These statements are shown next and should be placed in the code file immediately following the PromptPlayer() function.

```
`This function generates the 3D rotating cube and displays answers to
`player's questions
FUNCTION PlayAnimation()

  SYNC ON        `Disable automatic screen refresh
  SYNC RATE 40   `Set the game's synchronization rate

  MAKE OBJECT CUBE 1, 120    `Create a cube object
  POSITION OBJECT 1, 0, 0, 200  `Set the cube's location

  `Set up a loop to rotate the block one degree at a time for a total
  `of 360 degrees
  FOR Degree = 1 TO 360

    SET TEXT SIZE 24     `Set the font size to 24 points

    `Tell the player where to look to find the answer
    CENTER TEXT Width, 50, "Very well, let's look into the"
    CENTER TEXT Width, 80, "Fortune Teller's magic cube for the answer."

    SET TEXT SIZE 16     `Set the font size to 16 points

    `Tell player how to ask a new question and how to quit the game
    CENTER TEXT Width, 450, "To play again think of a new question and"
    CENTER TEXT Width, 470, "press any key or press the Escape key to"
    CENTER TEXT Width, 490, "quit."

    XROTATE OBJECT 1, Degree     `Rotate the cube by 1 degree on its x-axis
    YROTATE OBJECT 1, Degree     `Rotate the cube by 1 degree on its y-axis
    ZROTATE OBJECT 1, Degree     `Rotate the cube by 1 degree on its z-axis

    WAIT 10    `Add a brief pause to slow down the spinning of the cube

    IF Degree = 360              `On the final rotation
      Answer$ = GenerateAnswer() `Call the function that generates answers

      SET TEXT SIZE 48             `Set the font size to 48 points
      `Display the answer in the center of the cube now that it has
```

```
   `stopped spinning
   CENTER TEXT SCREEN WIDTH() / 2, SCREEN HEIGHT() / 2 - 60, Answer$

 ENDIF

 SYNC   `Redraw the screen

NEXT Degree

DELETE OBJECT 1

ENDFUNCTION
```

When called, the `PlayAnimation()` function begins by disabling automatic screen refresh and setting a sync rate of 40. Next, the `MAKE OBJECT CUBE` command is used to define a 3D cube, which is then placed in the center of the screen using the `POSITION OBJECT`. Next, a `FOR ...NEXT` loop is set up for the purpose of rotating the cube object a full 360 degrees along all three of its axes.

Upon each iteration of the loop, text strings are displayed at the top and bottom of the screen. The `XROTATE OBJECT`, `YROTATE OBJECT`, and `ZROTATE OBJECT` commands are then executed, each of which rotates the cube by 1 degree, as specified by the value assigned to the `Degree` variable. The `WAIT` command is used to briefly pause the execution of the loop to slow its execution so that the cube does not rotate too quickly. An `IF` statement code block is then set up that executes upon the last execution of the loop, at which time the `GenerateAnswer()` function is called. The value returned by the `GenerateAnswer()` function is then displayed in the middle of the screen, directly in the center of the cube.

Finally, the last statement executed in the loop is the `SYNC` command, which redraws the screen. Finally, once the loop has finished executing, the `DELETE OBJECT` command is executed, deleting the cube object.

Step 10: Developing the GenerateAnswer() Function

The next function to be added to the code file is the `GenerateAnswer()` function, which when called, randomly generates answers on behalf of the fortune teller. These statements are shown next and should be placed in the code file immediately following the `PlayAnimation()` function.

```
`This function is responsible for generating random answers to player
`questions
FUNCTION GenerateAnswer()

  Reply$ AS STRING = ""  `Define a local variable

  Seed = TIMER()  `Use the TIMER() function to retrieve a seed

  RANDOMIZE Seed   `Seed the random number generator

  Answer = RND(4) + 1  `Generate a random number between 1 and 5

  `Use the randomly generated number to select an answer
  SELECT Answer
    CASE 1
      Reply$ = "Yes"
    ENDCASE
    CASE 2
      Reply$ = "No"
    ENDCASE
    CASE 3
      Reply$ = "Maybe"
    ENDCASE
    CASE 4
      Reply$ = "Doubtful"
    ENDCASE
    CASE 5
      Reply$ = "Go away!"
    ENDCASE
  ENDSELECT

ENDFUNCTION Reply$ `Return the answer to the calling statement
```

The GenerateAnswer() function begins by using the TIMER command to create a seed, which is then used to randomize DarkBASIC Professional's random number generator. Next, a random number between 1 and 5 is created and then assigned to a variable named Answer. A SELECT statement code block is then set up that assigns an answer based on the matching of Answer to a series of embedded CASE statements. Finally, the randomly selected answer, which is stored in a variable named Reply$, is passed back to the statement that called upon the GenerateAnswer() function to execute.

Step 11: Saving and Compiling Your Application

All right, your new version of the 3D Fortune Teller game should be ready to test. Before you begin testing, do not forget to you save your work by clicking on the Save All option located on the File menu. Once this has been done, click on the Make/EXE RUN option located on the Compile menu to compile and execute your application.

The Final Result

As long as you have not made any typos and followed along with each step carefully, everything should work as described at the beginning of this chapter.

You will also find a copy of this application's project file, along with the source code on this book's companion website, located at http://www.courseptr.com/downloads.

SUMMARY

Congratulations on making it through this book's final chapter. In this chapter you learned about the different types of errors that DarkBASIC Professional applications are susceptible to and how to deal with them. This included learning how to track down and fix errors using DarkBASIC Professional's built-in debugger. You learned how to set breakpoints, how to keep an eye on variable values, and how to exercise step-by-step control over statement execution. You also learned a little about DarkBASIC Professional's support for 3D programming, including how to create and draw primitive objects like a cube and how to specify the placement of 3D objects using X, Y, and Z coordinates.

Before you finish the book, I suggest you set aside a little extra time to improve the 3D Fortune Teller game by implementing the following list of challenges.

CHALLENGES

1. Consider increasing the number of responses that the game has to choose from to make its responses less predictable.
2. Try experimenting with other 3D primitive objects to see how they work in place of the cube.
3. Consider modifying the game so that it can be controlled using the mouse's left button in place of the keyboard.
4. As currently designed, the 3D Fortune Teller game runs without making a sound. If you have access to any appropriate sound files, consider playing them in the background while the application executes to help set an appropriate atmosphere for the game.

Part

IV

What's on the Companion Website?

To learn how to become a game programmer you must dedicate yourself to the task of learning as much about the art and science of computer programming and game development as possible. As you continue your journey and move on to larger and more complex programming challenges, it helps to have access to a reliable collection of source code upon which you can draw for examples.

If you have been creating all of the DarkBASIC game projects that have been covered in each of the chapters in this book, then you already have access to a good collection of source code. By drawing upon this source code, you can find examples of how to accomplish may different types of tasks. As a result, you can save yourself a lot of time and avoid having to reinvent solutions to challenges that you have already faced and dealt with before. Once you have located a series of statements that accomplish a particular type of task, you can copy and paste them into other DarkBASIC applications, modifying them as necessary to adapt to and solve new challenges.

If, however, you jumped around a bit as you worked your way through this book, you may have skipped the review of one or more game applications. Just in case this is your situation, no worries, copies of all the source code for every game application developed in this book have been added to this book's companion website, allowing you to download them.

DarkBASIC Application Source Code

You can visit this book's companion website, located at http://www.courseptr.com/downloads to download all of the DarkBASIC source code for the computer games developed in this book. Table A.1 provides an overview of all the DarkBASIC game projects that you will find on the companion website.

TABLE A.1	DarkBASIC Project Files Located on the Companion Website	
Chapter	**Application/Solution File**	**Description**
Chapter 1	DarkJokes.dba	This DarkBASIC game displays a series of humorous jokes, demonstrating how to control the display of text within application windows.
Chapter 2	FortuneTeller.dba	This DarkBASIC game simulates a session with a virtualized fortune teller, providing random answers to questions posed by the player.
Chapter 3	NumberGuess.dba	This DarkBASIC game demonstrates how to use variables to collect, process, and analyze data collected from the player during game play.
Chapter 4	RockPaperScissors.dba	This DarkBASIC game is a computerized implementation of the Rock, Paper, Scissors game.
Chapter 5	SlotMachine.dba	This DarkBASIC game simulates the operation of a casino slot machine.
Chapter 6	TicTacToe.dba	This DarkBASIC game is a two-player implementation of the Tic-Tac-Toe game.
Chapter 7	DarkPong.dba	This DarkBASIC game is an updated version of the original *Pong* game in which two players compete by keeping a bouncing ball in play.
Chapter 8	Bricks.dba	This chapter begins the process of developing a 2D game reminiscent of the classic Atari *Breakout* game in which the player is challenged to keep a ball in play long enough to knock down all the bricks in a wall.
Chapter 9	Bricks.dba	This chapter completes the development of the Bricks game, adding new levels, sound effects, and mouse control.
Chapter 10	3DFortuneTeller.dba	This DarkBASIC game is an updated version of the Fortune Teller game developed in Chapter 2 that now incorporates 3D graphic effects.

WHAT NEXT?

ongratulations on making it all the way through this book. In doing so, you have built a strong understanding of the art and science involved in the development of computer programs and computer games in particular. As a result of making it this far, you have established a strong foundation as a DarkBASIC Professional programmer. However, while you have certainly learned a lot, there is plenty left to learn.

This book only scratched the surface of 2D and 3D programming. If you are going to become a world-class game developer, then you need to continue your programming education. It also means that you need to move on and tackle more advanced challenges. To help you get off to the best possible start, this appendix provides a list of resources that you can explore to learn more about DarkBASIC Professional, DirectX, and game programming in general. This information includes websites where you can go to learn more about DarkBASIC and Direct X.

Also provided in this appendix is information about alternative DarkBASIC integrated development environments (project editors) that you may want to investigate. Lastly, you'll find information about a number of excellent books, each of which provides more advanced discussion of the different game programming topics covered in this book.

LOCATING DARKBASIC RESOURCES ONLINE

There is an incredible amount of information available on the web that you can use to learn more about DarkBASIC, DirectX, and game programming. To get you started, this appendix provides an essential list of websites that you'll want to visit and explore.

The Game Creators Website

For starters, you will want to spend time visiting the Game Creators website located at http://thegamecreators.com, as shown in Figure B.1.

FIGURE B.1

The home page of the Game Creators website.

Here you will learn more about DarkBASIC Professional and stay on top of the latest developments. You'll also be able to find updates so that you can download and install them to keep your copy of DarkBASIC Professional up to date.

Wikipedia's DarkBASIC Professional Page

Another excellent website to visit is Wikipedia's DarkBASIC Professional page located at http://en.wikipedia.org/wiki/DarkBASIC_Professional, as shown in Figure B.2.

Here you will find ever expanding encyclopedic information on DarkBASIC Professional and related products developed by the Game Creators.

FIGURE B.2

Wikipedia's DarkBASIC Professional page.

Codebase

If you are interested in getting your hands on free DarkBASIC code samples, check out the Codebase website located at http://codebase.dbp-site.com/, and shown in Figure B.3.

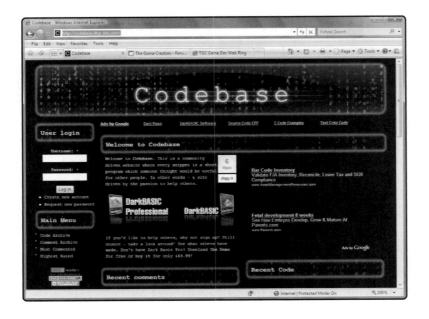

FIGURE B.3

The Codebase website is a repository of DarkBASIC and DarkBASIC Professional code.

Codebase is a DarkBASIC community website where many DarkBASIC Professional programmers go to share code that they have developed. This site is an excellent resource when trying to find a solution to a coding challenge that you are struggling with.

DBP-Site.com

Another site worth checking out is DBP-Site.com, located at http://www.dbp-site.com, as shown in Figure B.4. This site catalogs the results of various DarkBASIC programming challenges, providing easy access to the source for each project.

FIGURE B.4

DBP-Site.com provides easy access to the source code for different DarkBASIC projects.

Dark BASIC Games

Another good website to keep tabs on is Dark BASIC Games, located at http://www.darkbasicgames.com, as shown in Figure B.5. Here you can view information about dozens of games created using DarkBASIC. These games are distributed as either freeware or shareware, allowing you to download and play them.

The TGC Game Dev Web Ring

One final site that is certainly worth mentioning is the TGC Game Dev Web Ring, located at http://tgcwebring.codersturf.com/index.php?view=cat&cat_name=dark-basic, as shown in Figure B.6. Here, you will find links to many other websites that focus on DarkBASIC game development.

FIGURE B.5

The Dark BASIC Games website is an excellent place to visit to see examples of what other people are creating using DarkBASIC Professional.

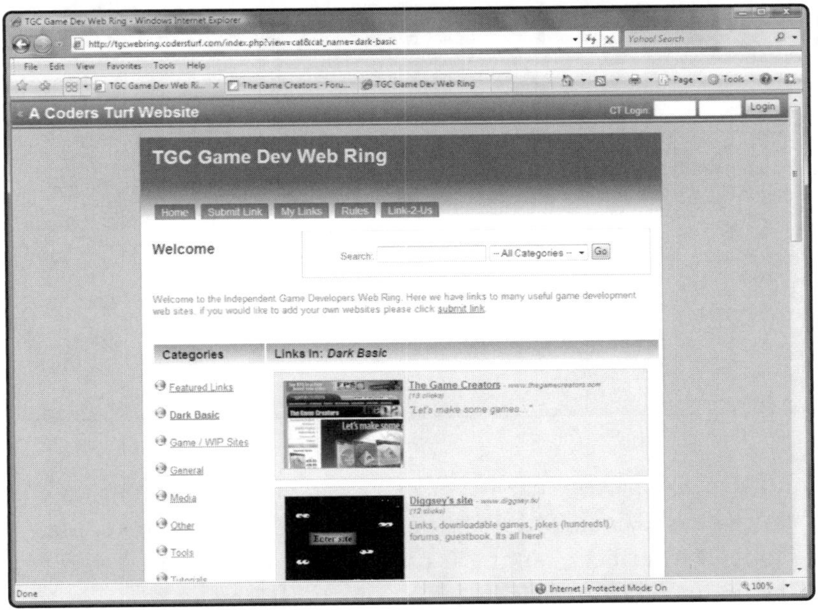

FIGURE B.6

If you want to show off your DarkBASIC programming skills, you can submit your website to the TGC Game Dev Web Ring.

ALTERNATIVE DARKBASIC IDES

As was stated in Chapter 2, "Getting Comfortable with the DarkBASIC Development Environment," DarkBASIC Professional's default integrated development environment, or IDE, can sometimes act a little buggy and is no longer actively supported. Fortunately, numerous third-party IDEs have been developed to address the situation. These IDEs provide DarkBASIC with a shiny new appearance and a much improved development environment.

CodeSurge

The DarkBASIC IDE replacement that seems to have the most support within the DarkBASIC community is CodeSurge. CodeSurge can be downloaded from the Game Creators' website at http://darkbasicpro.thegamecreators.com/?f=codesurge, as shown in Figure B.7.

FIGURE B.7

CodeSurge is a free DarkBASIC IDE editor that provides numerous advanced features.

Unlike DarkBASIC's default IDE, CodeSurge has never been known to lose program code or crash unexpectedly. CodeSurge has a Visual Studio-like appearance and features syntax statement color coding and a tabbed interface, making it easy to switch between different code files. Perhaps the best thing about CodeSurge is its price, which is free.

Synergy IDE

Another candidate replacement IDE for DarkBASIC Professional is Synergy IDE (http://www.digitalzenith.net/). Synergy IDE provides syntax color coding of DarkBASIC keywords and function folding, which allows you to hide fully tested functions from view to make the rest of your program code easier to work with.

Synergy IDE is not free. As of the writing of this book, Synergy IDE cost $19.99 and could be purchased directly from the Game Creators' website at http://synergyide.thegamecreators.com/?f=order, as shown in Figure B.8.

FIGURE B.8

Synergy IDE is a multi-purpose IDE, supporting multiple programming languages that include DarkBASIC Professional.

Other key features of Synergy IDE include tabbed windows, which make switching between different code files a snap, and a snippet database that can be used to store and access commonly used pieces of code.

> **HINT**
>
> There is also a lite version of Synergy IDE that you can download and work with to see if this is the right IDE for you. Although not all of the Synergy IDE's features are available in the trial version, enough functionality is available to help you decide if this is the right IDE for you.

BlueIDE

Another possible replacement for the default DarkBASIC Professional IDE is BlueIDE. BlueIDE, available at http://blueide.sourceforge.net, as shown in Figure B.9, is a full-featured IDE replacement. It features a tabbed interface that makes it easy to navigate between different code files and a code library that programmers can use to manage commonly used code snippets.

BlueIDE includes Intellisense, which assists programmers in completing code statements and a four-way split code view, which allows you to view and edit as many as four separate code files at the same time.

DIRECTX RESOURCES

DarkBASIC depends on Microsoft DirectX for much of its capabilities. As such, a good understanding of DirectX is very helpful to any Windows game developer. The next several sections will provide you with suggestions of good websites where you can go to get more information about DirectX.

The DirectX Home Page

Of course, there is no better place to learn about DirectX than the DirectX home page located at http://www.gamesforwindows.com/en-US/AboutGFW/Pages/DirectX10.aspx, as shown in Figure B.10.

FIGURE B.10

The DirectX home page is your best source for staying up to date on DirectX.

From this site you can learn about games that support DirectX. You can also learn about DirectX-compatible computer hardware.

The Wikipedia DirectX Page

A quick and easy way to learn more about Microsoft DirectX is to visit the DirectX page at Wikipedia (http://en.wikipedia.org/wiki/DirectX), as shown in Figure B.11.

The Wikipedia DirectX page provides a solid overview of DirectX and the subset of technologies that make it up. In addition, you will find links to numerous other DirectX websites.

The DirectX Resource Center

Another web page well worth your time is the DirectX Resource Center located at http://msdn2.microsoft.com/en-us/xna/aa937781.aspx, as shown in Figure B.12.

FIGURE B.11

The Wikipedia
DirectX web page.

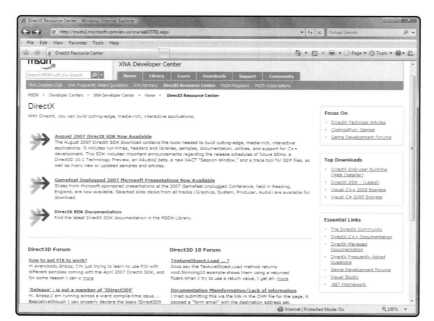

FIGURE B.12

The DirectX
Resource Center
website.

If you really want to get into the nitty-gritty of what makes DirectX work, there is no better place to visit than the DirectX Resource Center website. Here you will get access to technical articles, game development forums, and find links to lots of other DirectX sites where more information can be found.

OTHER DARK**BASIC** RESOURCES

In addition to all of the DarkBASIC Professional and DirectX resources provided on the previously discussed websites, the folks at the Game Creators also provide you with access to a collection of resources to which you can turn for additional information.

These resources include:

- The Game Creators' Newsletter
- The Game Creators' Forums
- Codebase

The Game Creators' Newsletter

The Game Creators publish and distribute a free newsletter packed with information on DarkBASIC Professional and game development. To sign up for the Game Creators' DarkBASIC newsletter, visit http://www.thegamecreators.com/?gf=newsletter, as shown in Figure B.13.

FIGURE B.13

Signing up for the Game Creators' monthly newsletter.

This letter is sent out monthly and provides information on all sorts of game development topics. To sign up all you have to do is provide your e-mail address. Then each month you will receive the latest information on DarkBASIC. In addition to signing up for the newsletter, you can browse and read previous editions of the newsletter, going back several years.

The Game Creators' Forums

Another useful resource provided by the Game Creators website is a collection of forums located at http://forum.thegamecreators.com/?m=forum, as shown in Figure B.14.

FIGURE B.14

Interacting with other DarkBASIC programmers through Game Creators sponsored forums.

There are dozens of different forums to choose from, covering a range of topics from Dark-BASIC Professional to 2D and 3D game development. As the partial list below shows, there is even a forum for reporting bugs.

- **DarkBASIC Professional Discussion.** This board is dedicated to all things related to the DarkBASIC Professional programming.

- **DarkBASIC Discussion.** This board is dedicated to all things related to the original DarkBASIC programming language.

- **Newcomers DBPro Corner.** This board provides a place for programmers new to DarkBASIC to meet and share their experiences and questions.

- **Code Snippets.** This board provides a place where you can post sample code that you created and get access to code posted by other programmers.
- **Bug Reports.** This board provides DarkBASIC programmers with a place to report bugs and to view entries posted by other programmers.

Codebase

The Game Creators' Codebase page, located at http://developer.thegamecreators.com/?m=codebase_list, as shown in Figure B.15, provides DarkBASIC programmers with access to over a thousand code samples. These code samples include everything from small code snippets to full-blown games and applications.

FIGURE B.15

The Game Creators' Codebase page.

RECOMMENDED READING

In addition to all of the websites listed in this appendix, you'll find a lot of information on DarkBASIC and game programming in the following books.

- **Beginner's Guide to DarkBASIC Game Programming.** ISBN 1592000096; Course Technology PTR, 2003. This book provides coverage of both DarkBASIC and DarkBASIC Professional and is also a good source for learning more about 2D and 3D game development.

- **Game Programming for Teens.** ISBN 1592000681; Course Technology PTR, 2003. This book provides beginner-level instructions of computer game development using Blitz Basic as a teaching and development platform.
- **Game Design for Teens.** ISBN 1592004966; Course Technology PTR, 2004. This book provides a good overview of game design process and game design theory.
- **DarkBASIC Pro Game Programming, Second Edition.** ISBN 1598632873; Course Technology PTR, 2006. This book provides game development instruction using DarkBASIC Professional and is a great source for advanced instruction on 2D and 3D game development.

GLOSSARY

.dba. The file extension associated with DarkBASIC Professional code files.

.dbpro. The file extension associated with DarkBASIC Professional project files.

2D programming. The development of computer games and applications that are played on a two-dimensional world where objects can move up, down, left, and right.

3D Canvas Pro. A software tool designed to facilitate the development of 3D models and animation.

3D Gamemaker. A software program that guides you through the creation of several different types of games, such as a *Doom*-styled first-person shooter and car racing games, without requiring any programming.

3D programming. The development of computer games and applications that are played on a three-dimensional world where objects can move up, down, left, and right as well as forward and backwards.

Ac3d. A 3D modeling program designed to facilitate the development of 3D game objects and characters.

Actor. Another term used to refer to a sprite.

API (application programming interface). An interface between application software and computer hardware that allows the communication and exchange of information.

Argument. A value, literal, or variable passed to a subroutine or function for processing.

Array. An index list of values stored and processed as a unit.

ASCII (American Standard Code for Information Interchange). A standardized set of codes that define characters used by computers and computer software.

Assistant view. An optional view within the default DarkBASIC IDE that divides the screen into two parts in which the left-hand side displays the code editing area and the right-hand side displays the DarkBASIC Pro Assistant panel.

BASIC (Beginner's All-Purpose Symbolic Instruction Code). A programming language initially created to teach people how to program.

Bitmap. A term that refers to the format used to store an image.

Blue IDE. An alternative replacement for DarkBASIC Professional's default IDE that provides an enhanced user-friendly interface and a number of advanced editor features.

Bounded collision. A collision that occurs when two bounded sprites collide with one another.

Bounded rectangle. A sprite is completely enclosed within the rectangle.

Break point. A point within a program's source code where the debugger will pause in order to facilitate debugging and the analysis of variable values.

C++. A programming language known for its power, speed, and high learning curve.

Code Editor. A specialized text editor used to create and save program source code.

CodeSurge. An alternative replacement for DarkBASIC Professional's default IDE that provides an enhanced user-friendly interface and a number of advanced editor features.

Collision. Occurs any time two objects run into one another in a computer game.

Comment. Statements embedded inside a computer program for the purpose of documenting the program.

Compiler. A computer program that translates program language statements into machine code, resulting in the creation of a computer application that can be executed by the computer operating system.

Concatenation. The process of joining two or more strings together to create a new string.

Constant. A descriptive name assigned to a known value that does not change during program execution.

DarkBASIC. A programming language specializing in the development of computer games.

DarkBASIC Professional. An advanced programming language specializing in the development of computer games.

Dark Game SDK. A special version of the DarkBASIC Professional game engine that can be used as a separate, standalone C++ library, simplifying the development of games developed using C++.

DarkMATTER. A collection of animated 3D objects, equipped with pre-designed animated sequences that include running, jumping, driving, flying, and so on.

Data. The information that your applications collect, store, process, and modify during execution.

Debugger. A software utility used to locate and analyze errors that occur during the application development process, allowing programmers to monitor and pause program execution to check the status of program flow and variable value assignments.

Direct3D. The most commonly referenced DirectX API, which is responsible for rendering 3D graphics and animation on Microsoft Windows, Microsoft Xbox, and Microsoft Xbox 360.

DirectX. A Microsoft Windows technology designed to facilitate the execution of high-end graphics and audio in multimedia applications and games.

DO...LOOP. A loop that executes forever.

Double buffering. A programming technique in which a copy of an application's screen is stored and managed in memory and then copied to the screen, allowing for faster and smoother graphic effects.

Endless loop. A loop that is set up to run forever, without any means of terminating its own execution.

Enhancement pack. An add-on software package for DarkBASIC that provides it with some of the advanced capabilities provided by DarkBASIC Professional.

ExGen. A software program specializing in the development of computer effects such as explosions and smoke.

Expression. A statement that is evaluated and produces a result.

Flow chart. A tool used by programmers to graphically depict the logical flow of all or part of a program.

Force feedback. An advanced joystick feature that allows a game to send back instructions to a joystick that allows it to provide the player with physical feedback.

FOR...NEXT. A loop that repeats a specified number of times.

FPS Creator. A specialized first-person shooter creation tool that allows you to create computer games using a 3D editor so that you can design different levels, placing walls, obstacles, lights, enemies, ammo, and weapons where you want them.

Frame rate. A term that refers to the frequency at which the screen is redrawn during application execution.

Function. A collection of statements that is called and executed as a unit and which has the ability to return a value back to the statement that called upon it.

Function library. An external collection of functions that can be added to a DarkBASIC Professional project and called upon for execution just as if they were part of the main code file.

Game engine. A collection of over 1,000 commands specifically designed to support game development, providing everything required to display graphic images, collect player input, and play various types of sounds and music.

Global variable. A variable that is accessible throughout the program.

Gutter. A vertical strip located on the left-hand side of the default DarkBASIC Professional editor that displays line numbers.

Hat. A multi-directional button on a joystick that is very much like a miniature joystick on a joystick.

IDE (Integrated Development Environment). An application or group of applications designed to facilitate application development, which usually includes a code editor, compiler, and debugger.

IF. A programming statement that tests a condition and then alters the execution flow of an application based on the result of its analysis.

Impact collision. Occurs only when the pixels that make up the actual sprites themselves come into contact with one another.

Integer. A whole number.

Intellisense. An editor feature that assists programmers in writing code by monitoring the status of the function or statement that is currently being keyed and then, when prompted, displaying suggestions on how to complete the function or statement.

Local variable. A variable that is accessible only within the scope in which it is created.

Logical error. An error created by a programmer mistake when developing the logic used to perform a given task.

Loop. A set of programming statements that are repeatedly executed.

Midi (Musical Instrument Digital Interface). A communications protocol that provides the ability to allow electronic musical instruments and computers to communicate.

Non-blocking commands. Commands used to collect keyboard input that does not halt program execution.

Object-oriented. A type of programming that views resources as objects, which contain methods and properties that can be used to manipulate and configure their behavior.

Order of precedence. A set of rules that dictate the order in which the different parts of a numeric expression are evaluated.

Parameter. A variable defined within a function that maps to an argument that the function is passed when executed.

Pixel (Picture Element). The smallest addressable area that can be written to or drawn on the screen or window.

Point. 1/72 of an inch.

Polygon. A term used to describe a multi-sided enclosed area, such as a triangle, that is used as the basis for generating 3D graphics.

Primitive. A basic shape, such as a cone, cube, sphere, or cylinder that can be drawn in 3D.

Program. A file, often referred to as a computer application, that contains code statements that when executed tell the computer to do something.

Project. A container used to store and manage the files that make up a DarkBASIC Professional application.

Project Manager panel. A panel displayed on the right-hand side of the default DarkBASIC Professional IDE that can be used to configure project settings.

Pro Motion. A graphic program that facilitates the development of graphics and animated objects.

Pseudo code. An English-like outline of all or part of the programming logic that makes up a computer program.

Real. A number that includes a decimal point.

REPEAT...UNTIL. A loop that repeats until a specified condition becomes true.

Run-time error. An error that occurs when an application performs an illegal action.

SELECT. A programming statement used to set up a series of conditional tests, each of which is compared to a single value.

SkyMATTER. A collection of high-resolution textures that you can purchase and use in your DarkBASIC Professional games to provide realistic backgrounds.

Slider. A joystick button or control that can be moved forward and backward.

SoundMATTER. A collection of thirteen professional-quality sound effects that you can purchase and add to your DarkBASIC Professional games.

Source code. The list of statements that make up a computer program.

Sprite. A 2D bitmap that represents an object such as a tank or game character, which can be moved within a larger graphic image in a 2D computer game.

Statements. Instructions that make up a computer program.

String. A set of characters enclosed within matching double quotation marks.

Subroutine. A collection of programming statements called upon to execute as a unit.

Synergy IDE. An alternative replacement for DarkBASIC Professional's default IDE that provides an enhanced user-friendly interface and a number of advanced editor features.

Syntax error. An error that occurs when a programmer fails to write a program statement in accordance with the rules of the programming language.

Texture Maker 3. A graphics tool specializing in the creation of textures for computer games.

Transparent. The display of a sprite object on a background, which is not visible during game play.

Twist. A joystick feature in which the joystick twists or rotates in place, giving the player additional control over joystick movements.

Variable. A pointer to a location in memory where an individual piece of data is stored.

Wave. A digital audio file used to store uncompressed raw audio data.

Vertex. A point where two lines on a polygon intersect.

WHILE...WEND. A loop that repeats for as long as a specified condition remains true.

Windows keyboard buffer. A portion of computer memory used by the operating systems to keep track of keyboard keystrokes until the computer is ready to respond to them.

Index